The Astrolog

The astrology of intimacy has long been a popular subject among professional astrologers and psychologists. Many have sought the answer to what makes some people have successful relationships with one another, while others struggle. *Web of Relationships* examines this topic not only in intimate affiliations, but also in families and friendships.

Editor Joan McEvers has brought together the wisdom and experience of eight astrology experts. Listen to what one author says about the mythological background of planets as they pertain to relationships. Discover how past life regression is illustrated in the chart. Consider the relationship of astrology and transactional analysis.

- Examine the charts of Johnny Carson and Ed McMahon and see why they were destined to become the famous late-night duo.

- Find out why Richard and Karen Carpenter were compatible as singers and as brother and sister.

- Discover why Whitney Houston is such a musical phenomena.

Web of Relationships explores the karmic and mystical connections between child and parent, how friends support and understand each other, the significance of the horoscope as it pertains to connections and much more. Each chapter will bring you closer to your own web of relationships and the astrology of intimacy.

"Wherever you find people, you will find curiosity about interrelatedness. *Web of Relationships* is replete with formats and insights to stimulate and enhance one's development of practical equations for addressing this popular astrological requisite."
—Gray Keen, Consultant

Other Books in This Series

Forthcoming Books

Llewellyn's New World Astrology Series
Book 8

The Web of Relationships

Spiritual, Karmic & Psychological Bonds

Edited by Joan McEvers

1992
Llewellyn Publications
St. Paul, Minnesota, U.S.A. 55164-0383

FIRST EDITION

Cover Design: Christopher Wells

Library of Congress Cataloging-in-Publication Data

The web of relationships : spiritual, karmic, and psychological bonds /
    edited by Joan McEvers.
        p.   cm. -- (Llewellyn's new world astrology series)
    Includes bibliographical references.
    ISBN 0-87542-388-4
    1. Astrology.   2. Family—Miscellanea.   3. Interpersonal relations—
Miscellanea.   I. McEvers, Joan.   II. Series.
BF1729.F35W43   1991
133.5'81582—dc20
                                                              91-41814
                                                                    CIP

Llewellyn Publications
A Division of Llewellyn Worldwide, Ltd.
P.O. Box 64383, St. Paul, MN 55164–0383

THE NEW WORLD ASTROLOGY SERIES

This series is designed to give all people who are interested and involved in astrology the latest information on a variety of subjects. Llewellyn has given much thought to the prevailing trends and to the topics that would be most important to our readers.

Future books will include such topics as vocational astrology, various relationships and astrology, electional astrology, astrology and past lives, and many other subjects of interest to a wide range of people. This project has evolved because of the lack of information on these subjects and because we wanted to offer our readers the viewpoints of the best experts in each field in one volume.

We anticipate publishing approximately four books per year on varying topics and updating previous editions when new material becomes available. We know this series will fill a gap in your astrological library. We look for only the best writers and article topics when planning the new books and appreciate any feedback from our readers on subjects you would like to see covered.

Llewellyn's New World Astrology Series will be a welcome addition to the novice, student and professional alike. It will provide introductory as well as advanced information on all the topics listed above—and more.

Enjoy, and feel free to write to Llewellyn with your suggestions or comments.

Joan McEvers

Author of *12 Times 12* and co-author with Marion March of the highly acclaimed teaching series *The Only Way to . . . Learn Astrology*, Joan McEvers is a busy practicing astrologer in Coeur d'Alene, Idaho.

Born and raised in Chicago where she majored in art and worked as a model and illustrator for an art studio, she moved to the Los Angeles area in 1948 and continued her professional career in the sales field. This is where she met her husband Dean and raised their children.

Self-taught, Joan began her serious study of astrology in 1965 and in 1969 studied with Ruth Hale Oliver. About this time she started to counsel and teach astrology. She has since achieved an international reputation as a teacher and lecturer, speaking for many groups in the U.S. and Canada. An AFAN coordinator and member of NCGR, her articles have been published in several national and international astrological magazines.

In 1975 Joan and Marion founded Aquarius Workshops, Inc. with Joan as President. She also helped establish its quarterly publication *Aspects*, which is widely recognized for the wealth of astrological information packed in each issue. She continues to contribute to this periodical.

12 Times 12 details each of the 144 possible Sun/Ascendant combinations. Each description includes information about personality, appearance, health, likely vocational areas, interests and attitudes. Having always been intrigued with astrological/vocational potential, Joan and Marion presently are conducting a "Vocational Probe," seeking to establish a computer program which can be given to schools to assist young people in selecting work and career fields. They are collecting myriad types of vocational data for this program.

Co-winner with Marion March of the Regulus Award for contribution to Astrological Education, Joan also has been presented a Special Commemorative Bicentennial Award for the excellence of her published works from the *Astrological Monthly Review*.

Currently, she is editing a series of anthologies comprising The New World Astrology Series of Llewellyn Publications, working on a Horary Astrology book, and preparing for the fifth book in the March/McEvers ongoing series. She also reviews books and cassettes for Astro-Analytics Publications and writes their bi-monthly newsletter.

A double Aquarius with Moon in Leo, when she isn't preoccupied with astrological activities, Joan enjoys spending time with her husband, four children and five grandchildren, quilting and playing bridge.

Contents

INTRODUCTION

In *The Astrology of Intimate Relationships*, the companion volume to this one, the authors considered all types of intimate relationships. In this book, the range is much wider, taking into consideration familial and friendly affiliations as well as karmic and metaphysical ones. Our writers explore the connection between child and parent, how friends support and understand each other, as well as the significance of the elemental makeup of the horoscope as it pertains to connections. One author investigates past life relationships as shown in the chart. Another considers astrology as it relates with transactional analysis while yet another explains the mythological background of the planets as they pertain to relationships. A family tree is probed and the metaphysics of affiliations are discussed. All in all, a broad spectrum.

In most approaches to relationship astrology, certain houses are emphasized; the 1st/7th, 5th/8th in intimacy, the 4th/10th in parental connections, the 11th for friendly and social associations, the 5th in connection with those we love, especially children and the 3rd for siblings. But all the houses of the horoscope have significance in how we relate to, and get along with others.

The 1st House describes the basic outlook and personality, while the 7th portrays what is needed from the partner. This was already thoroughly discussed in the previous volume.

SECOND HOUSE SIGNIFICANCE

Very few astrologers refer to the 2nd House in dealing with relationships, but I feel it is very significant, since it mirrors our assessment of our own self-worth, our values and attitudes toward money. In any involvement with another person, these are important areas to be considered.

If a person who has Mars in or ruling the 2nd House with challenging aspects to Uranus or Pluto, teams up with someone who has Saturn in or ruling this house, there may be some difficulty in deal-

1

ing with financial matters or even deeper issues relating to values. The Mars person may have a need to earn, but will probably be a reckless spender unless other factors in the chart modify this position. Saturn in the 2nd traditionally expresses as a sense of financial insecurity and this can carry over into emotional insecurity as well. This person can be quite tight-fisted, since money may represent security and the need for it is a dominating factor in the life.

Obviously, these people will experience differences in values that must be considered before exploring a serious relationship. They may not even agree on what kind of household furnishings they like, let alone on a budget. This is not to imply that they cannot work out their differences and have a successful commitment to each other, only that 2nd House values should not be ignored in synastry.

THIRD HOUSE CONNECTIONS

In comparing charts of siblings it is important to look at the 3rd Houses in both charts, pursuing connections for communication and compatibility. Invariably there are strong astrological contacts between siblings. For example in the charts of sister/brother musical duo, Karen and Richard Carpenter, we find some fascinating cross connections. The Sun rules her 3rd House and trines Mercury in his 3rd. His 3rd House Sun sextiles her 3rd House Moon. Her Mercury (the communication planet)/Jupiter conjunction trines Moon/Uranus in his 10th.

They have some challenging aspects as well: her Venus exactly squares his 3rd House Jupiter, suggesting that they didn't always see eye-to-eye about communication matters. This aspect turns his T-Square into a Grand Cross, creating a sense of frustration that needs to find an outlet. Richard's natal Venus (ruler of his 3rd House) is unaspected; Karen's Ascendant/Uranus conjunction quincunx it, forcing him, as it were, to use Venus energy in a communicating way. Whenever someone has an unaspected planet, it can be activated by planets in another person's chart, making it easier to find an avenue for self-expression.

Her Jupiter/Mercury opposition Moon/Pluto is T-Squared by his Mars, obviously quite challenging as far as goals and friends are concerned, since the empty leg is in her 11th House. In any T-Square, the most obvious place to work out the energy developed is in the empty house. In comparison charts, when a T-Square is set up, the empty house shows where the stress may be.

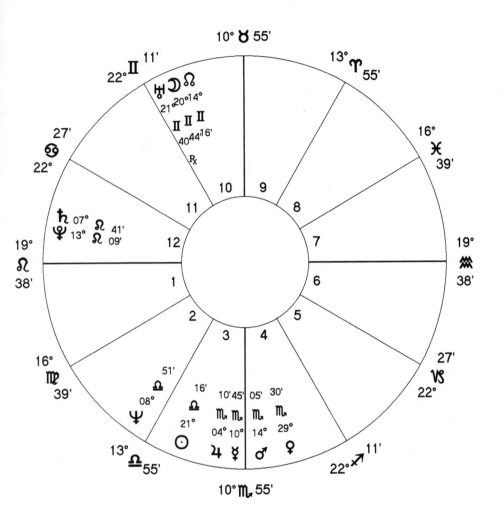

Chart 1
Richard Carpenter
15 Oct 1946 00:53:00 AM EST
New Haven, CT
072W55'00" 41N18'00"

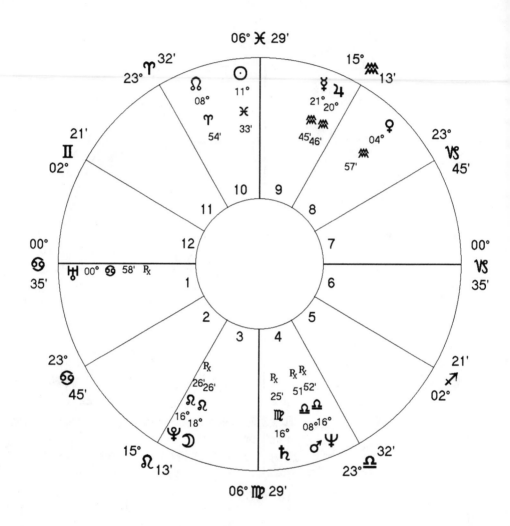

Chart 2
Karen Carpenter
02 Mar 1950 11:45:00 AM EST
New Haven, CT
072W55'00" 41M18'00"

Grand Crosses are much more difficult to resolve than T-Squares, as there is a tendency to run around in circles and become frustrated while trying to find an outlet for the energy. This can at times be quite devastating in a relationship, but we find it frequently in the charts of siblings. All of these planetary connections illustrate the ability of the Carpenters to make beautiful music together, but also mirror their different life styles. According to Richard, each went their own way when they were not performing.

If you are comparing your chart to that of a neighbor, the 3rd House represents your neighbor, also your teacher if you are a student, and your students if you teach. I place step-brothers and sisters in this house as well.

THE PARENTAL DILEMMA

The 4th and 10th Houses traditionally represent the parents. There is much disagreement among astrologers about whether mother is found in the 4th or 10th. Some say that in the chart of a woman, mother is the 10th and father the 4th and in a man's chart, mother is the 4th and father the 10th. Some astrologers feel that mother is always the 4th House and father is always described by the 10th. I feel that each astrologer must find his/her own way and use what works best.

I suggest to my students that children tend to see both parents in the 4th House and only as they become more mature are they able to differentiate which parent may be in which house. In counseling, I always describe both parents but ask the client which is which. Saturn is helpful in identifying the father, just as the Moon often characterizes the mother. But many times, these roles can be reversed. The astrologer finds challenging aspects to Saturn and suggests that perhaps there was difficulty with father and the client replies, "Oh no, it was mother who was cold, distant and disciplinarian."

In comparing charts of parents and children, refer to the 5th House in the parent's chart and both the 4th and 10th Houses in the child's. Also consider the Moon and Saturn as parental symbols.

Cousins related through the mother are located in the 4th House, while those of the father may be found in the 10th according to most sources. Sometimes both houses may have impact. Singing cousins Whitney Houston and Dionne Warwick have interesting cross aspects. Dionne's Sun conjuncts Whitney's Midheaven and certainly she helped pave the way for her cousin's musical success.

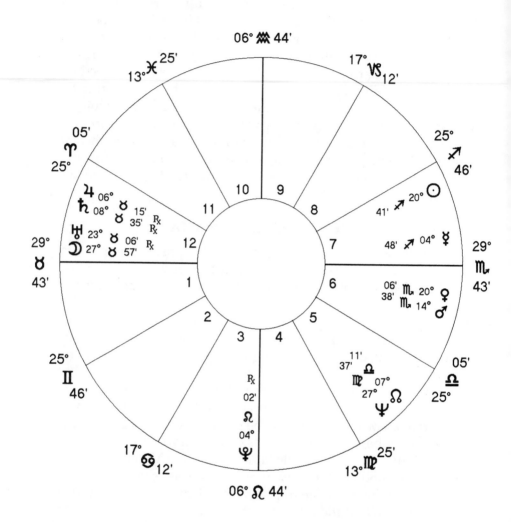

Chart 3
Dionne Warwick
12 Dec 1940 03:08:00 PM EST
Orange, NJ
074W14'00" 40N46'00"

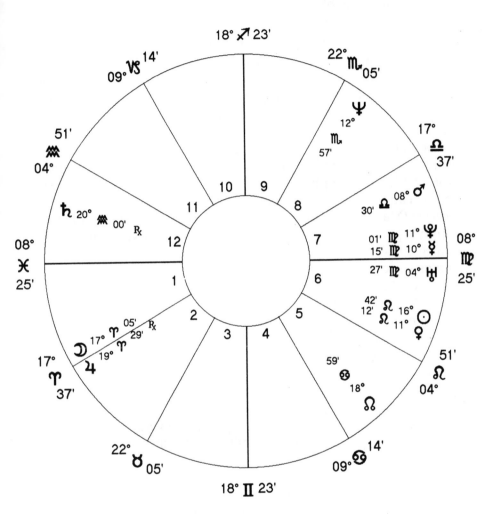

Chart 4
Whitney Houston
09 Aug 1963 08:55:00 PM EDT
Newark, NJ
074W10'00" 40N44'00"

Whitney's Mars trines Dionne's Midheaven and she always credits the relationship publicly.

WORKING TOGETHER

Traditionally the house of work, the 6th basically shows the attitude and aptitude for work, and in comparing charts of people who work together in any capacity, it is always wise to consider this house. A classic example is Johnny Carson and Ed McMahon who have worked together on "The Tonight Show" for almost 30 years. Mars rules Carson's 6th and is conjunct McMahon's 6th House ruler, Saturn, at 16 and 19 degrees Libra respectively. This conjunction sextiles Ed's Neptune and Johnny's Venus suggesting an easy rapport and genuine affection. However, it also triggers Carson's T-Square (Mars square the Moon/Jupiter opposition to Pluto). The empty leg of the T-square falls in Carson's 6th and McMahon's 9th, which could indicate possible differences of opinion on work and philosophical issues.

Ed's Mars falls in Johnny's 6th and Johnny's Moon and Jupiter are in Ed's 6th House of work certainly suggesting an enduring work oriented relationship. But theirs is also a friendly connection which is not surprising since both have Mercury ruling the 11th.

I feel cross sign/house placement is very important in long-term relationships of any type and this is verified by Carson's 12th House Sun and McMahon's Sun in Pisces. Because this is primarily a business affiliation, Carson's Saturn conjunct McMahon's Jupiter is very significant as these are business planets and when they are well aspected between charts they usually indicate success in a business relationship.

In their composite chart Uranus rules and is in the 6th House, which is quite apropos since Uranus also rules television, the medium through which they joined us five nights a week. Uranus is in Pisces in the composite as well as both natal charts and trines Pluto and Mars in the 10th House, suggesting fame, recognition and status connected with their work output.

Composite Saturn in the 2nd sextiles Mercury, Venus and Sun in the 4th, illustrating their ability to build on a firm foundation and become financially successful.

The 6th House also depicts relationships between maternal aunts and uncles and the individual. Paternal aunts and uncles are traditionally found in the 12th. But, it depends on which parental

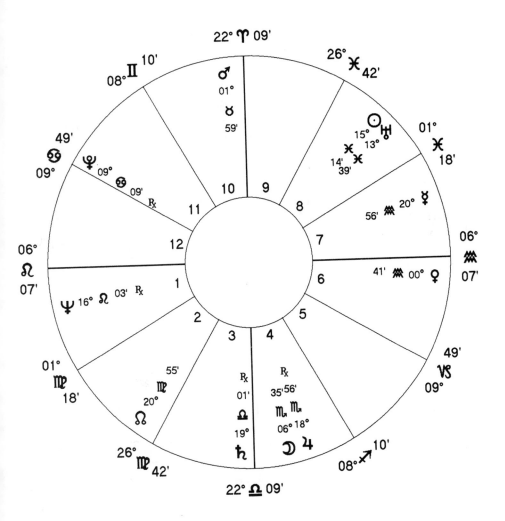

Chart 5
Ed McMahon
06 Mar 1923 03:00:00 PM EST
Detroit, MI
083W03′00″ 42N20′00″

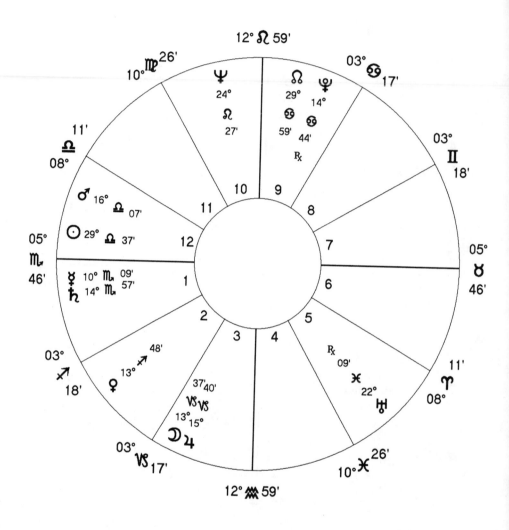

Chart 6
Johnny Carson
23 Oct 1925 07:15:00 AM CST
Corning, IA
094W44′00″ 40N59′00″

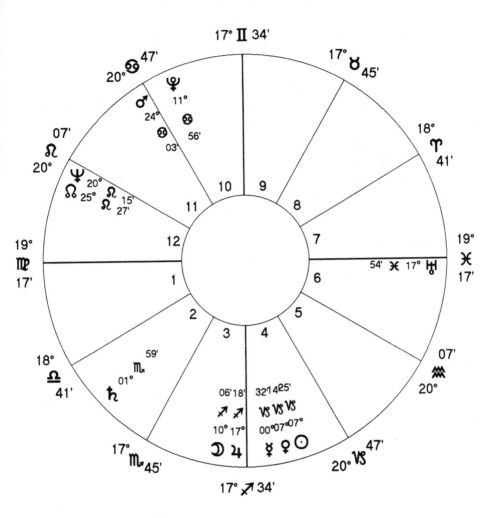

Chart 7
Carson/McMahon
Midpoint Midheaven
000W00'00" 40N45'00"

house you have decided represents which parent.

Tenants and landlords are also found here, as well as anyone who works for or with you or in your behalf, so if you are comparing these kind of charts, pay close attention to the 6th House, its ruler and any planets in it.

SOME OTHER SIGNIFICANT OTHERS

The 7th House, of course, is where we locate our significant other, but it also represents your doctor, lawyer and open enemy (though why anyone would want to compare their chart to that of an enemy is beyond my comprehension). However, if you want to know the way a relationship with your lawyer or doctor will proceed, consider a comparison with the emphasis on the 1st/7th Houses.

This house also signifies your second child, your maternal grandmother and paternal grandfather, as well as your nieces, nephews and legal adversaries. So if you are comparing your relationship to any of these people, be sure to consider your 7th House.

The paternal grandmother and maternal grandfather are traditionally placed in the 1st House.

IN-LAWS AND GRANDCHILDREN

Besides being the house that represents the second marriage partner and third child, the 9th tells us what we need to know about our in-laws (the 3rd from the 7th House) and grandchildren (the 5th fom the 5th), specifically the first one.

A word here about derivative houses: Your attitude toward and needs from marriage show in the 7th House, but it is helpful to consider the 9th House when looking at the second partner, the 11th for the third and so on, skipping a house for each marriage partner. Obviously, your primary partnership needs are discovered in the analysis of the 7th, but what you need from each succeeding marriage is uncovered in each alternating house. The information gleaned is added to that of the 7th for a fuller picture.

Just as the 5th House shows your basic attitude toward your children, the 7th adds information about the second child, as differentiated from the first, and the 9th House gives specific input about the third child, the 11th about the fourth, and so on.

Sisters and brothers-in-law are described by the 9th House and many astrologers look to this house to describe all in-law relations, but others use the 4th and 10th for mother and father-in-law. Since these houses are already beleagured by differing opinions, you might find it easier when comparing charts with a parent-in-law to take some notice of the 9th House in your delineation.

DECISIONS, DECISIONS

If your father is your 10th House, your mother is your 4th House; so if you have a step-mother, she is discovered in your 10th house, and your step-father shows up in your 4th. But, if your mother is your 10th and your father is found in your 4th, then step-father is in the 10th and step mother is probably located in your 4th House. Complicated, isn't it? I certainly have never been able to figure it out. In a comparison with a step-parent, you should probably try both houses and see where you find a correct interpretation of the way the relationship works.

There are other associations related to the 10th House. Anyone who has authority over you, or whom you respect is located here. If you are an employee and wish to know how you relate to your boss, look at your 10th and his/her 6th.

MORE CHILDREN, MORE IN-LAWS

Your in-law children, the spouses of your kids, are found in the 11th House; so are any foster children and spouse's offspring. This again relates to the derivative house system. Any relationship can be found by using this method of counting houses around the chart. Since your 5th House represents your child, if you count seven houses from the 5th, you find your child's partner in the 11th House. If your partner has been married before and brings children to the partnership, count five houses from the 7th and you find these children. Some astrologers place children you adopt here. I feel they are 5th House people, but in comparing charts, just as in all other areas in astrology, you must find what works for you.

THE 12TH HOUSE

This is not the easiest house to interpret, yet it is essential for any in-depth analysis. In comparing charts of any people, it is wise to look at the 12th as the place where each can be supportive and inspiring to the other. It has been said that if someone's Sun falls in your 12th House, they are your 'secret enemy,' yet, in practice this is rarely true. These can be people who teach you the deeper values of life. So, a careful analysis of this house can give deep insights into any relationship.

It is especially influential in clandestine relationships and if you are comparing charts of people involved in any kind of sub rosa affiliation, pay careful attention to this house.

OUR AUTHORS

When **Cait Hall** from Madison, Wisconsin first suggested that she write about mythology in connection with relationships, I was somewhat skeptical. But when I read her fascinating manuscript, I was intrigued with the connection between the Greek and Roman myths and the planets in the horoscope. I am sure you too will find this chapter both informative and thought-provoking. The concept that Jupiter may be more important than Mars in comparing charts is an exciting one and certainly worth exploring.

To get a handle on child/parent relationships, be sure to read the chapter by child psychologist/astrologer **Cornelia Hansen** from Los Angeles. She explores the charts of six problem children, pointing out astrological avenues that have proven helpful in her counseling of these children and their parents.

Many of you will remember **Spencer Grendahl's** contribution to *The Houses: Power Places of the Horoscope* earlier in this series. Leave it to Spencer to come up with a new approach to the old art of comparison astrology. His treatise on Astrological/Transactional Analysis describes a way of translating the horoscope into that format, a technique that is helpful in explaining an individual's or couple's inner psychology. You are sure to find this a stimulating approach to synastry.

Dickson Ward, from Palm Springs, California explains how he uses metaphysical principles in connection with his client consultations. He outlines his method of examining Mercury connections in comparison work which incorporates the elements in a most stimulating way.

If you have never considered a family tree from an astrological viewpoint, you are sure to be intrigued with the segment by **Lyn Greenleaf James** who hales from Lynden, Washington. Lyn had the good fortune to grow up in an astrological family, and the insights she gained are expressed beautifully as she explores the interaction of several generations.

Maria Kay Simms considers the elemental structure of the charts to be very significant in synastry. Her system of analysis is methodical and the illustrations she uses to explain her theories are well described and most interesting. In reading her chapter, you will discover a useful as well as practical tool for chart comparison analysis. Maria is from San Diego, California.

If you want to know how friendships work, you will be captivated by **Diana Chambers'** article on the interaction between several pairs of friends. Diana, from Eugene, Oregon feels that friendships come out of both the 5th and 11th Houses and confirms this position with some fascinating friendship stories. She also explores the impact of each sign pair across the 5th/11th House axis.

Bob Mulligan from Naples, Florida explores past life relationships and describes where to look in the horoscope to find what binds people together from one lifetime to another. He places a great deal of significance on certain karmic points which he defines in detail. Well illustrated with example charts, this is a very thought-provoking segment.

This is Volume 8 in Llewellyn's New World Astrology series and I am very pleased to have played a part in these informative books. This is my swan song and I wish to thank all the astrologers who have taken part in the series. I appreciate their contribution and many have become friends.

I will miss this interaction with my colleagues, but other fields beckon and I am on my way. The series will continue and I will look forward, as I am sure you will, to the books that follow.

Joan McEvers
Coeur d'Alene, Idaho
May 1991

Cait Hall

Astrology has been practically a lifelong interest for Cait Hall. From the age of seven, she has been reading about and studying this art and science and is primarily self-taught.

With a B.A. in English, Cait has been involved with editorial work, including newspaper, magazine and book publishing, for approximately five years, utilizing her Virgo Midheaven. Her future plans include pursuing a master's degree in Library Science.

Personally and professionally, she enjoys writing short stories and poetry—when she isn't learning a new musical instrument. With music as her first love, she has performed in piano competitions and participated in dance revues, choral groups, bell choir ensembles, and acted as an accompanist.

She also travels whenever possible and enjoys working with Amnesty International as well as transcribing manuscripts into Braille.

Her idea of bliss is retreating to her cabin in the woods with a classic or maybe even writing one of her own!

A HIGHER LOVE: THE RELATIONSHIPS
OF THE GODS

"With God for us, who can be against us?" This phrase seems particularly appropriate concerning the ideology of modern man, for we, at least in the Western world, live in a society brimming with self-confidence, believing in total self-control in this scientific, rather impersonal era.

If one were to ask a Greek in 500 B.C. the same question, he might reply, "Probably Hera." Although the Graeco-Roman pantheon was first and foremost divinity, the gods manifested common human feelings, traits, and talents, and above all, they related. Jupiter, the main god of the hierarchy, was called "the Father of gods and men" not because he created man but because he represented the moral values of his culture and he partook in numerous liaisons with mortals.

This human principle of the Greek gods may be what attracts us to their myths, for other commonly accepted religions maintain the supreme God as perfect and whole, without a need to relate to man. In fact, often believers must make the first move, "allowing" a relationship with God. Perhaps this is not so unsettling in a time where man is elevated as Man of Intelligence, and not particularly "godlike" or divine.

Our horoscope is, in fact, one map of relation since the planets we work with have been named after or associated with this band of humanistic communicators. Each god or goddess had his/her style of handling situations and relating to lovers, husbands/wives, children, etc., and this should be kept in mind in the combining of planets and signs when interpreting a chart. Every identifying feature of a planet, including its namesake's mythology and characteristics, gives clues as to how this power functions in your life. Relationships cannot just be aspects of Venus and Mars—all the planetary gods formed alliances, and some may surprise you. Thus, this chapter is devoted to the lives and loves of the gods and goddesses of Greece and Rome as well as their offspring, who provide insights into inherited characteristics of the deities, in the hope that it may shed a bit more light on planetary influences within the chart.

Although most of the myths surrounding the gods were based on the Greek deities, the Romans incorporated these divinities into their pantheon, often discarding their gods' original associations. Since we identify our planets in Latin, and it is rather cumbersome to go back and forth between Greek and Roman names, I will predominantly use Roman names when discussing the gods.

APOLLO

Since most astrologers use geocentrically based charts and Sun sign astrology is most common (but often misunderstood), it seems logical to start with the main "star" of a chart—the Sun.

Although Helios is the true god associated with the Sun, Apollo has come to be identified with this luminary, primarily for his characteristics of lightness, beauty, fairness, and intelligence. His many talents, including music, poetry and athletics (the Pythian games), represent a fully utilized Sun in a chart. Our Sun sign also points the way to health if we live in harmony with it, so it's no surprise that Apollo also ruled medicine. At Jupiter's order, he healed the fallen Hector, a warrior during the Trojan War. In addition, his prophetic powers reveal the inner knowledge our Sun sign holds for us, if we'd only listen to its teachings and respond to what we know to be true.

> "I am the eye with which the Universe
> Beholds itself and knows itself divine."
> Shelley, *Hymn of Apollo*

Our Sun sign represents our ego. As a self-directed god, Apollo was even forced to serve some time on Earth as a shepherd to King Admetus of Thessaly because of his overzealous actions against Uranus' sons. But without such conviction or such a strong identity, our Sun acts as if eclipsed, often to our detriment. Misuse of the Sun's action of the horoscope often prices the person to repeat lessons until they are well learned.

Apollo was the son of Jupiter and Latona and the twin of Diana. His mother was forced to wander the countryside in search of a birthplace by Juno, who was aggravated over Jupiter's indiscretion.

Finally, Latona alighted on Ortygia, a floating rock in the Aegean, and for nine days and nights she was in labor. Only after this agony did Juno allow Eileithyia, goddess of childbirth, to relieve her. Meanwhile, Jupiter had fastened the rock to the Earth, and it was then called Delos, or "the brilliant one," after the glorious birth of Apollo. Diana, his sister, was the first twin born, and she helped her mother give birth to Apollo. Soon afterwards, the god of light went to live among the Hyperboreans where the climate was always sunny and warm; and dancing, joy, and health prevailed.

Perhaps the first relationship to be discussed regarding Apollo is his love for his twin. While Apollo was equated with the light of the Sun, Diana was identified with the Moon, and since they were hunters, they both shared the common trait of killing transgressors with their arrows. In fact, Apollo was also called "Thundering Punishment." The myths concerning Apollo and Diana relate to the interaction of the lights (of the Sun and Moon) in the horoscope withe the Sun representing the male issues and the Moon confronting the female ones. One myth relates this god of music flaying his challenger Marsyas, an excellent flutist, for his presumption in even suggesting such a contest. (Remember the last time you felt like acting against your Sun's [ego] attacker?) The twins were so close that at times jealousy over the other's romances got in the way. Such was the case with Diana's love for the giant Orion. As they were traveling through the sky one day, Apollo spied a dark object in the water. Fully aware that it was the wading Orion, he incited Diana to test her archery skills, using her beloved as a target. Unfortunately, she struck him in the head, killing him instantly.

In spite of such an incident, Diana was very loyal to her brother, noted especially during his liaison with Coronis. Apollo met her while she was bathing in a spring, but a crow informed the god of Coronis' affection for and infidelity with Ischys, the Arcadian. Diana lost no time in killing her, but Apollo wanted his child, so he had Mercury retrieve the baby Asclepius from Coronis' womb as she lay burning on a funeral pyre. Asclepius went on to become a great healer since he was tutored by the centaur Chiron, noted for his medical expertise. It was said that Asclepius could even bring the dead back to life. This caused much distress with Pluto, god of the Underworld, since he was not receiving his due; thus, Jupiter struck Asclepius with a thunderbolt. Apollo's great affection for his son instigated his attack on the cyclopes, creators of thunderbolts,

thunderbolts, and it was this action against Jupiter which brought about his year of servitude to King Admetus.

Apollo's year as a servant discloses the strong relationship between this god of light and men. It is through the Sun's action in the horoscope that we come face to face with the major factors in relating to others ... and the aspects to the other planets show how. King Admetus fell in love with the enchanting Alcestis, but the conditions of her betrothal rested on her suitor's arriving at the palace in a chariot powered by lions and boars. This rather impossible feat was achieved by Admetis with Apollo's help. Thus, the god turned his supposed year of shame and toil into one of friendship and service, something to keep in mind when wrestling with difficult aspects to the Sun.

Apollo had more than one child graced with the powers of healing. His son Aristaeus was born in Libya, where Mercury had hustled his mother, the Bereid Cyrene, with whom Apollo had become enraptured as she fought a lion. The boy learned beekeeping, cheesemaking and the cultivation of olives from Mercury's nymphs, and in Boetia, the Muses, frequent companions of Apollo, fortified him with their hunting, healing and animal husbandry skills.

Musicians abound in Apollo's progeny, the most famous being Orpheus. This son was born to Calliope, a Muse, and his father gave him a lyre, which he learned to play magnificently. Orpheus did not lead such a charmed life, however, for after his beloved Eurydice died, he found no interest in the other available women. Incensed, they murdered him, and Jupiter, in recognition of Orpheus's greatness, placed his lyre among the stars. Linus, the musician was the son of Apollo and the Muse Terpsichore, according to Theban myths. He taught Orpheus and Hercules, but also fell to misfortune. Chione, the granddaughter of Lucifer ("bearer of light") and Apollo were parents of the musician Philammon, who began the tradition of female choirs.

Apollo passed on his prophetic powers to his children. His son Idmon was a renowned soothsayer, foreseeing his own death while on the Argonaut expedition. The brilliant god's child Galeotes also received the gift of divination and began the long tradition of soothsaying on Sicily. Apollo's lover Evadne bore the prophetic Iamus, while his son Mopsus, a soothsayer, was born of Manto, the daughter of the famed prophet Tiresias. But Apollo's prophetic gifts were not only bestowed on his progeny. He fell in love with Cassandra, who agreed to be his mistress if allowed one request. She wished to be able to prophesy. Once her wish was granted, she reneged and wanted nothing to do with Apollo. Enraged, he tinged his gift with bittersweetness, for although she would divine correctly, no one would believe her.

Apollo fathered the beautiful Hymenaeus, god of marriage, by a nameless Muse. He holds the bridal torch and it is believed he was named after the bridal song. Numerous other liaisons produced the ancestral parent of various cities and races, such as Dorus of the Dorians, as well as the famed architect Trophonius.

Of all the gods, Apollo seemed to have more than his share of trouble with romance, just as many Leos do. Leo, ruled by the Sun and associated with the 5th House of ten mirrors the mythological behavior of Apollo. One nymph, Castalia, jumped into the spring of the same name on Mount Parnassus to escape his embrace. The divinatory Sibyl would not consent to Apollo's desire unless he granted her a wish. Unfortunately for her, she wished to have as many years as grains of sand, not realizing that she would age along with them.

Perhaps the most famous tale of unrequited love concerning Apollo is that of Daphne. Cupid started this relationship by piercing the heart of the fair god with a sharp gold arrow, but Daphne was struck by a blunt, lead arrow. To make matters worse, Daphne was devoted to the virgin goddess Diana and had no intention of becoming Apollo's lover. As he pursued her, she cried out to her father, the river god Peneus, to save her since he knew of her wish of chastity. Just as Apollo nearly had her in his arms, she began to sprout leaves and her skin changed to bark—she became the sacred laurel tree of Apollo.

Apollo didn't have much luck with Marpessa, either. She had been won by the mortal Idas, and when forced to chose between either the god or the man, she picked Idas as her husband since she was aware of the god's likely desertion as she became old, when she lost her beauty of youth.

In keeping with the Sun as our ego in the chart, Apollo was the only god who truly rejected a lover. Her name was Clytie, and because of her worship of the god she was transformed into a sunflower so that she could gaze upon him all day long. This is, at times, typical Leo behavior at its worst. Its association with Apollo is well documented by this negative kind of action: egotism, pomposity, and imperviousness.

Apollo's love was not confined to the opposite sex. His most well-known male liaison was with Hyacinthus, son of the king of Laconia. They enjoyed athletics as well as fishing and hunting together. But Zephyrus, the West Wind, also had designs on the young man, and as he and Apollo held a quoits match, one of the god's quoits was blown off course, striking Hyacinthus dead. Where he bled a violet bloom grew, which was called "hyacinth," although it most likely was what we know as an iris or pansy. Hyacinthus was also loved by Thamyris, Philammon's son, who was a pupil of Linus. To get rid of Thamyris, Apollo told the Muses that the mortal had bragged of his musical and poetic talents in relation to theirs. They blinded him and ceased his singing. This story illustrates how occasionally our ego (Sun) will stop at nothing to get its own way. Apollo was also enamored of Daphnis, a son of Mercury, who with Apollo mastered the flute, and with Diana, acquired hunting skills. The hunter Cyparissus was another favorite of the god; Apollo transformed him into a cypress to alleviate the mortal's grief over the accidental killing of a prize stag.

Thus, Apollo represents a Sun of pleasure and health, loyalty, righteousness, knowledge, love of life, devotion to kin, occasional egotism and will, but above all, self-expression.

DIANA

Diana, the sister of Apollo, was the earthly personification of the Moon. Selene was equated with the Moon of the sky, with Hecate in the bowels of the Earth representing the dark of the Moon. Although the myth of the Moon's love for the shepherd Endymion may be told of Diana, it is generally believed to tell of Selene's love for the youth.

One of Diana's functions was to be a midwife. Thus, although she was a virgin goddess, she was a symbol of fertility and above all a protectress, especially of youth. The Moon in the chart often discloses what we fear and what we innately feel we should guard. The myth of Hippolytus, son of Theseus, speaks of treachery against youth, and perhaps this is one of the reasons Diana is involved. Hippolytus' stepmother Phaedra lusted for him, but told her husband Theseus quite the opposite. In anger, Theseus asked Neptune to rouse a sea monster to frighten the horses guiding Hippolytus' chariot. The chariot crashed, but Asclepius and his aunt Diana resuscitated Hippolytus with the Moon goddess ensuring his safety by having Egeria, the fountain nymph, watch over him.

As a huntress, delighting in sports and freedom, Diana cared little for men or gods (except Apollo) and passed time with her retinue of nymphs. Her sacred oak grove by Lake Nemi became the target of many a slave trying to gain liberty. In the midst of the grove stood mistletoe, and if the slave could seize a bough of the tree before being killed by Diana's current priest, he would gain his freedom. Her devotion commanded a rather high price since her priest would continually have to fight for his life.

Perhaps this type of relationship with the opposite sex explains why we have nary a myth concerning romantic love and the goddess Diana. Unfortunate Actaeon came to a much worse fate than her priests when he happened upon Diana and her nymphs bathing. Since her arrows were out of reach, she threw water at him, and he turned into a stag. Upon leaving the goddess's cave, his own hunting dogs ripped him to shreds. Her only true love appears to have been the giant Orion, her hunting companion who lived with her until she accidentally killed him as related in the previous section.

Chaste, modest, and determined to be true to herself, free to do as she pleased with no one to hold her back, Diana insisted that couples offer her a sacrifice on their wedding day. Perhaps because of her lack of partiality to nearly everyone, Diana listened to oaths, maintaining their binding property.

Thus: the Moon in the chart is based on a divinity of independence, fierce femininity, and emotion primarily founded on self-containment or self-preservation. It's no wonder the Moon has often been connected with our inhibitions, habits and the fears that impede our interaction with the world. The Moon's positive side reflects Diana's nurturing, midwifery, and fertility.

MERCURY

God of all forms of intercourse, Mercury flying by his petasus (winged cap) and winged shoes, served as the messenger of his father, Jupiter. He had many talents and ruled over such sports as wrestling and gymnastics as well as skills that require versatility and dexterity. The medical profession still utilizes one of his symbols which represented his abilities and his association with healing—the caduceus, which he received from Apollo in exchange for the lyre he had invented out of a tortoise shell. Mercury had given the instrument nine strings in honor of Apollo's nine Muses. Along with his connection with commerce (merx, "merchandise" and mercari, "to trade"), his verbal gifts and his quickness, both mental and physical, made him god of all thieves.

Since Mercury signifies communication, one of the most common types of relationships in mythology is that of the helpful friend. Whether rescuing someone, protecting youth, or delivering a mortal to the gods, Mercury works to bridge the gap, to correct or right a situation. In the horoscope, Mercury represents neighbors and siblings through its association with Gemini and the 3rd House, as well as co-workers through its rulership of Virgo and the 6th House.

Mercury was sent as a last resort to speak with Prometheus, who was chained to Mount Caucasus, in order to persuade him to reveal the secret of Jupiter's future. Jupiter also dispatched Mercury to alleviate the suffering of his current attraction, Io. Juno, in her spite, had commissioned Argus, a guard with 100 eyes, to ensure that Io, in the form of a cow, would lead a miserable life. Mercury, however, succeeded in lulling Argus to sleep by playing on his pipes and telling tales, and soon he had cut off the watchman's head, closing his 100 eyes forever.

In another tale, Ulysses was granted Mercury's favor when Circe had transformed many of his friends into pigs. As a god of intellect, Mercury befriended the hero and gave him a sprig of moly, a plant that thwarted any magical schemes of Circe, and upon the threat of death, Circe changed his comrades back into men. When Queen Nephele was disposed of by the king, she worried for her children with their new stepmother until Mercury stepped in, giving her a golden-fleeced ram that flew away with her children. Jupiter also expected Mercury to protect his child Dionysus from Juno by transporting the babe to the nymphs of Nysa. Mercury retrieved Proserpine from the Underworld for her reunion with Demeter; he also helped Hercules wrestle Cerberus up to Earth without the aid of weapons. In spite of his fondness for Venus, Mercury was responsible for bringing Psyche into the fold of the immortals when Cupid was hopelessly in love with her. In most of these experiences, Mercury seems to signify the communication that finally binds the relationship because he appears on the scene right before the action occurs that ends the story.

As a god of intercourse, Mercury is attributed as the father of all satyrs, the woodland creatures that were half man, half goat, and totally lascivious, terrorizing women whenever possible. In relation to these satyrs is Mercury's son Pan, whose mother is debatable. Some say the woman Penelope was approached by Mercury in the form of a ram or goat; others say Pan's mother was a nymph. At any rate, this son was surprisingly unattractive with his goat's horns and hoofs but very spunky and loud, amusing himself with woodland nymphs and his beautiful music. Pan was forced to live on Earth because the other gods would have no part of him. The word panic is derived from this god's habits since nighttime travelers would often be thrown into such a state from the strange, disturbing noises of the dark. Another son of Mercury's, Evander, was associated with Pan and was worshipped as such in Arcadia and is credited with introducing new laws and teaching Italians how to write.

Mercury had another wild son called Silenus. This jovial, portly, middle-aged drunk traveled on an ass with Dionysus and was considered a sage. He was born at Nysa and was Dionysus's mentor.

Some of Mercury's progeny made up a retinue of thieves or tricksters. With Chione, one of Apollo's lovers, he had a son Autolycus who coached Hercules in the art of fist fighting, when he wasn't stealing from others. Whenever he wished, he could make things invisible by a simple touch. Autolycus often disguised animals in other forms to make it easier to pilfer them. However, he also nursed Odysseus, his grandson, back to health when he was injured in a boar hunt. Another son of Mercury, Prylis, took part in creating the deceptive wooden horse, filled with men, used to invade Troy. Mercury often represents the thief, clown or entertainer in the chart.

Mercury's "courtship" of Herse is rather tragic, and one of their offspring didn't fare much better. Mercury bribed Aglauros to facilitate a romance between him and Herse, but when she rescinded, he turned Aglauros into stone and raped Herse. Herse gave birth to Cephalus, who thought it great sport to test his wife's faithfulness. He disguised himself as a suitor to see how long it would take for him to seduce her. Once she gave in, she left him in shame—but returned to play the same trick on him. Herse's other son Ceryx, "herald," was the proclaimer of the mysteries of Eleusis. Considered neuter astrologically, Mercury frequently is considered to be conscienceless, unless in an earth or water sign.

Mercury and the stream nymph Lara were parents to little Lar, the personification of dead souls. He was an adolescent and each Roman dwelling had a personal protective Lar that was passed down to successive generations. In the horoscope, Mercury is the significator of young people.

Mercury, of course, had other liaisons, but the tale of one in particular was related of his Greek equivalent, Hermes. Said to have loved Proserpine, Hecate and Aphrodite (Venus), the last goddess and he produced Hermaphroditus, a handsome youth who had captured the fancy of the nymph Salmacis. Unfortunately, the boy did not feel the same, but she persisted by embracing him to her at her spring. Miraculously, the two became one, displaying and using the traits of both sexes. The Mercury ruled sign Gemini is often highlighted in the charts of homosexuals.

Hermaphroditus seems to represent the modern concept of Mercury—adolescent, handsome, but asexual or perhaps bisexual. Yet, all one need do is remember Pan and a satyr or two and quite a different picture of this god communicator emerges. Luckily, the charm and good-natured personality of most Mercurians smooth over such impropriety so that we often forget such an association with this sparkling divinity. God of utility, even to the point of theft, Mercury in the horoscope serves as the acquiescent link in relationships of all kinds.

VENUS

The goddess Venus and her Greek counterpart, Aphrodite, have very little in common, but the Greek goddess' attributes and myths are generally accepted as part and parcel of the Roman goddess and will be treated as such here. In actuality, Venus was simply the vegetation goddess of small gardens, providing food and beauty for the home. She had to do with pure and simple love. Aphrodite, on the other hand, is of Near Eastern origin and is more concerned with all the wiles and games of love. Astrologically, Venus is the symbol of love, partnership, money, and social interaction.

Venus' birth is questionable. Homer states that she is the offspring of Jupiter and Dione, but the more common myth shows her born of the sea, created from the genitals of Uranus when his son Saturn castrated him. Her Greek name comes from aphros, meaning "foam." As she rose from the sea on a shell, the Seasons gave her soft, filmy garments, and she became the goddess of love and beauty with Cyprus as her sacred site. She also wore Cestus, the girdle that inspired love.

Most myths state that Eros or Cupid was her son, but, in fact, these gods are not one and the same either. Eros was the god of sexual desire who played the lyre; Cupid was the god of love who wielded arrows to induce either lust or repugnance in his targets. This corresponds to Venus' two fountains—one of water sweet, the other bitter and foul. The reverse or negative side of Venus is underindulgence, egotism, fickleness and dilettantism. Some say Eros was the son of Mercury and Venus; some say Penia (poverty) and Porus (expedience) begat Eros, or love. In fact, Eros was the attracting property responsible for love of any sex, and the soldiers of the Sacred Band of Thebes created quite a cult based on him. But the most logical myth states that Eros was not born by any god or goddess but was the existing force that causes all attraction and the reproductive urge. Thus is he seen as the companion of the goddess of love and beauty.

Pothos was another son of Venus who was related to desire, and Anteros was born because of the goddess' complaint over Cupid's childishness. When Venus consulted Themis (Law) about Cupid, she told the goddess that her son needed a companion. Anteros was either the avenger of unrequited love or the personification of mutual love.

As the goddess of affection, Venus often favored mortals in distress, such as Ariadne, who was saddened by the loss of the fickle hero Theseus. Venus promised that she would wed an immortal, and Dionysus did become her husband. It is said that at their wedding Hymenaeus son of Apollo (also believed to be the son of Venus and Dionysus) lost his voice, thus his relation to the bridal song. It also was Venus who promised Paris the most gorgeous woman on Earth because he gave her the golden apple to signify her surpassing beauty over all the other goddesses of Mount Olympus. The idealistic sculptor Pygmalion was granted his wish—his lovely ivory Galatea came to life to be his wife.

Other versions of this story show Venus annoyed with Pygmalion's lack of affection for real women and his need to resort to an idealization. When Hippomenes wished to win Atalanta, an athlete and a virgin who wasn't interested in marriage, Venus presented him with three apples to toss in Atalanta's path as they ran a race to determine if he was to be her future husband. Hippomenes outran her, and they were married. Unfortunately, because they forgot to pay Venus homage in their marital bliss, the couple were turned into a lion and a lioness. Astrologically, much depends on Venus's aspects. She seems to respond best to stressful squares and oppositions, because they often provide structure to her many times rather unstructured nature.

As kind as she was, Venus had a rather vicious and haughty jealous streak. Probably her most well-known act of cruelty concerns the beautiful Psyche, whom all felt to be at least as lovely as Venus. The goddess decided that although all would gaze upon Psyche, no one would ask for her hand, but her plan backfired when she sent her son, Cupid to carry out her ruse. He fell in love with Psyche and disobeyed his mother, eventually marrying the woman. Because of this rift between her son and herself, Venus did everything in her power to keep the two apart. For every little transgression Psyche committed, she devised torturous tasks for the girl. But Psyche finished all the chores successfully, identifying the existence of utility with beauty. Her final task proved to be her demise, however. She was sent to gather Prosperine's box filled with her beauty, but once above ground Psyche wished to see what this beauty looked like—the sleep of the Underworld. And Psyche was dead. Cupid finally was reunited with Psyche when Jupiter agreed to an immortal marriage, sending Mercury to fetch her from the realms of the dead.

The story of Hippolytus related in the section on Diana occurred because of Venus' disgust over the youth's attitude towards women. He really wasn't interested in relationships; thus, Venus induced lust in his stepmother. Venus also requested permission from Jupiter to punish the horse racer Glaucus because he would not let his mares mate. She poisoned a spring from which they drank, and from then on they ate flesh, eventually turning on their owner. Furthermore, the goddess of love withheld her favor from the Lemnian women; thus, they killed all the men of the area.

Jupiter gave Venus to Vulcan, the smith of the gods, in gratitude for his service, but she really didn't appreciate him. Mars, god of war, was more her style, and even though the two were caught in the act in an invisible bronze hunting net and made into humor for the gods, they still carried on and produced three children together. Two were Martian in character: Phobus (Fear) and Deimos (Terror). The third child was the lovely Harmonia (Concord). At her wedding to Cadmus, founder of Thebes, she was given a necklace fashioned by Vulcan. Whoever wore it would be deemed beautiful. Athena wove her a cloak, but as these gifts were passed around, it soon became apparent that they were a curse to the wearer's descendants.

Venus also had relations with Mercury (Hermes), which produced Hermaphroditus as discussed previously, Neptune and Dionysus. With Neptune, she bore Rhodius and Herophilus, of whom no myths still exist. With Dionysus, she became the mother of Priapus, who was given a rather large penis by Juno, becoming a god of fruitfulness, a protector of flocks, and taking on other attributes of his father. With her obsession with beauty and form, Venus left her son to fend for himself by the Hellespont.

One story of Venus' jealousy is truly bittersweet. King Cinyrass daughter Myrrha was proclaimed by him to be more lovely than the goddess. In a rage, Venus caused Myrrha to fall in love with her father, conceiving Adonis while he was drunk. The girl wished to kill her child, but Venus placed him in a box and gave him to Proserpine for safekeeping. The handsome Adonis stole the heart of the queen of the Underworld. On hearing this, Venus decided she wanted him. Jupiter decided that he would be split among the goddesses, sharing their company for half a year. Another version of this story states that Proserpine claimed Adonis after he was killed by a boar. Sometimes the boar is turned into a weapon of Mars. Finally, one tale tells of Venus getting in the way of Cupid's arrows and falling in love with Adonis, a hunter. The goddess acts totally out of character, roaming the woods like Diana and beseeching him to beware of beasts. Unfortunately, he is attacked by the boar, and Venus' tears and nectar mixed with his blood become the anemone.

Except for Adonis, Venus held herself above relations with mortals. That is until Jupiter decided to give her a dose of her own tricks. Anchises, prince of Troy, was to be her chosen man, so she dressed as a mortal woman and told sweet lies of Mercury whisking her to the prince's side when she was dancing in praise of Diana. She requested a meeting with his parents, but Anchises thought differently and consummated his desire. At this point, Venus revealed her identity. In fear, Anchises begged to be spared all the problems other men who slept with goddesses had experienced. But true to her basic nature, Venus was distraught over losing her insusceptibility to men and romantic superiority over the gods since she had succumbed to a mortal, so she warned Anchises not to brag of this encounter or Jupiter would strike him with lightning. But Anchises did not listen and broadcast his great fortune, causing his lameness or blindness by a well-aimed bolt from Jupiter. Their child was called Aeneas, whose name is based on the word ainon, meaning "cruel." Caesar claimed him as his ancestor.

Of all the myths pertaining to Venus, this last one makes her real for me. In this tale, she realizes she's no different from anyone else—she's not infallible and she, too, will experience abuse. This is how Venus acts within our charts and within our lives. We look to this planet to see what we hold as an ideal or the epitome of beauty, as well as to identify our charming qualities. But with these discoveries and typical intimate associations also comes the realization of disappointment and wounded pride as we realize our mystique will not enthrall another constantly.

MARS

The Roman Mars and the Greek Ares were perceived very differently in their respective cultures. Originally, Mars was a vegetation or fertility god because the Italian economy and culture was based on agriculture. Some believe that this forceful god was so important to the Romans because the people may have had to fight to maintain their fields and orchards. And, of course, as the Roman Empire grew, Mars became the magnificent brave conqueror. Ares, on the other hand, was not appreciated by the intellectual Greeks. In myths he is often shown as a wheedling coward and the laughingstock of the gods. (Remember his episode with Venus and the bronze net.) I imagine that when the Romans took over the Greek pantheon they ignored most of Ares' mythology, assimilating only his association with war.

In some cases Mars is said to be the son of Jupiter and Juno, but other tales state that he and his twin sister Eris (Discord) were conceived solely by Juno with the help of Flora. It seems that Jupiter's wife was jealous of his ability to produce Athena (Minerva) without any obvious feminine help, so she decided to do the same with her twins. When she touched a specific flower, Mars and Eris were born. In light of Jupiter's intense dislike of Mars, perhaps this parthenogenetic version is more in keeping with the relations of the gods.

As with Apollo and Diana, these twins shared similarities. Eris' duty was to visit battlefields to stir up hatred among the warring sides. She also created the scene with Paris and the goddesses since she gave him the golden apple. Thus, she was the instigator of the Trojan War. Among her children were Hunger, Pain, and Oblivion.

Mars is the symbol of war, yet, rather than being Aries or Scorpios, more generals and tacticians are ruled by Mars (Librans). So the polarity of these planets seems to be more impactive, at least astrologically, than Mars and Eris.

Mars also had a child who strode with him to the battlefield—Phobus. One of his children with Venus, this minor divinity created cowardice among warriors, causing them to desert. As mentioned under Venus, the pair also had Deimos (Terror) and Harmonia (Concord), so it seems that Venus provided a softening effect on his offspring, which was not the case in other pairings.

Mars often represents action and drive, and is the second most dominant male planet, after the Sun. Its energy is much like the Sun's but more direct, sometimes hostile. and occasionally violent.

Mars and the mortal Astyoche had Ascalaphus, a leader in the war at Troy who was killed by Deiphobos, a son of King Priam. The deceived King Oenomaus, who was killed when his chariot wheels were waxed by Myrtilus, a son of Mercury, was Mars' son by Harpinna, daughter of Asopus the river god, or Sterope, a Pleiad. One of the reasons why so many charioteers perished in their race for his daughter's hand was that Oenomaus' fleet of horses had been given to him by Mars.

The next two children of Mars seemed to have vendettas against Apollo. Perhaps these tales show us the Martian tendency to want to steal the Sun's glory in our charts. A son of Mars and Pelopia, Cycnus assaulted travelers journeying to Delphi to make an offering to Apollo. It's interesting to note that Hercules, son of Jupiter, killed him. Perhaps this relationship emphasizes the compatibility of the Sun and Jupiter in general. Mars and Chryse conceived Phlegyas, father to Coronis, the woman who bore the healer Asclepius to Apollo. However, Phlegyas in a rage destroyed Apollo's temple by fire and was sent to the Underworld for retribution.

Another son of Mars, Diomedes of Thrace, lured traveling strangers to his home to be fed to his horses. Mars's son Tereus took after his father in attempting to seduce Philomela, the sister of his wife. He was transformed into a vulture while Philomela became a swallow and his wife Procne turned into a nightingale.

Mars' female offspring didn't fare much better. With Agraulos he begat the lovely Alcippe, who was raped by Halirrhothius, a son of Neptune. In anger, Mars killed the offender, and when brought to trial by Neptune, the god of war was acquitted. Thus, Mars was the cause of the first trial regarding murder. One of his lovers, the mortal Aerope, actually died in giving birth to Aeropus, but miraculously the child suckled at her breast after death. It seems only Venus was truly immune to his deadly violent tendencies.

The one myth of Mars that appears to be truly Roman, in the sense that the god is regaled as a great ancestor, is the tale of Romulus and Remus, twin sons of the god and Rhea Silvia. She was forced to be a Vestal Virgin, circumventing the chance that she might have a legitimate son to overthrow the current king of Alba, her uncle. Once she became pregnant and gave birth, Rhea Silvia was buried alive while her babies were tossed into the Tiber in a basket. They landed on the shore where Rome now is situated and were nursed by a wolf. The shepherd Faustulus and Acca Larentia raised them until they grew old enough to vanquish their uncle, replacing their grandfather Numitor as head of state. They decided to build a city where they had washed up to shore, but in the arguments about the city's specifications, Romulus killed Remus. Romulus was also in favor of raping the Sabine women since his new city consisted mostly of men.

Mars also had more than a nodding acquaintance with the Amazons since he gave Hippolyta, their queen, a special belt. He likewise was related to Bellona, the goddess of war.

Thus ends my tale of the "great" god of war, who mistakenly, it seems, at least in light of the divinity's mythology, has been given too much prominence in discussing the facets of relationships. Yet Mars provides the spark and friction that first gets us involved and then keeps our interest intact as well as deep fires burning. But carried too far, Mars energy can dominate, stir up, agitate, and through hasty action can embroil the person in difficult situations.

JUPITER

The leader of all the gods of Mount Olympus was Jupiter, son of Saturn and Rhea. His parents were Titans and previous to Jupiter's ascendancy, Saturn and his brothers and sisters made up the "elder gods." Rhea was very protective of her child and placed him in the care of the daughters of Melisseus, king of Crete. There he was fed by the goat Amalthea, whose horn he broke to give to his caretakers. This is the first inkling of the benevolence and good fortune associated with Jupiter, for the horn gave its owner whatever s/he desired. As Jupiter grew he overthrew his father, claiming the throne for himself. He achieved this with the help of his first wife, Metis (Prudence), who, according to some myths, tricked Saturn with a drink that caused him to vomit his previously swallowed children. Thus, with the help of his brothers and sisters, this god of thunder became the chief power of the heavens with the Titans either thrown into Tartarus or punished severely like Atlas, carrying the world on his shoulders. Only Hecate, a Titan, was welcomed at Mount Olympus. Neptune received the ocean as his dominion, and Pluto was to be lord of the Underworld. Jupiter's attendants were Fortuna, Victoria, and Fides (guardian of promises).

This story of Jupiter's rise to fame and power (symbolic of his emblem, the eagle) is perhaps the reason why we associate this planet with success. Jupiter signifies the generational push for success that in the process rights the wrongs of one's elders. Evidence of his prominence in Greek and Roman culture, Jupiter held many titles, including Lucetius, god of light; Stator, the stayer of defeat and bringer of victory; Feretrius, the uniting force within the community; Soter, father and savior; Herkeios, guardian of the home; Xenios, maker of the principles of hospitality; Ktesios, property protector; Gamelios, divinity of marriage; and Eleutherios, ensurer of liberty. A couple of these titles might have surprised you. His association with wealth, justice, and victory is generally known, but most of us would not place Jupiter as the deity of marriage or unions within the community. When thinking of romance and potential partners, astrologers invariably check out Venus and Mars, but this seems rather short-sighted to me. A quick look at Jupiter's many liaisons compared to the love lives of Venus and Mars makes me wonder if we have indeed overlooked a very important aspect in relationships: the placement and activity of Jupiter.

Jupiter had quite a string of formal consorts, with many romances consummated in between. When Metis was his wife, Gaia and Uranus advised Jupiter to devour her if he did not wish to be overthrown by a child who would be blessed with both wisdom and power. This is why Athena (Minerva), goddess of wisdom, equity and handicrafts, sprang from her father's head as Vulcan cracked open his skull. Thus, he retained this wisdom, never needing to worry about patricide because she was truly "his" daughter. Indeed, she was his favorite child.

Jupiter's next wife was Themis (Law). Even after their marriage formally dissolved, she sat next to him as his counselor. The two produced the three Moirae, sisters of man's fate. Clotho spun, Lachesis dispensed every man's lots, and Atropos snipped the thread of life at the proper time. The pair also had the three Seasons, or Horae, which personified spring, summer and winter. Later legends number the Horae at 12, and one of these is called Irene, or Pax, and is the goddess of peace. Their other lovely daughters, Astraea and Pudicitia (Modesty) lived happily on Earth until men became greedy and evil. They then ascended to the heavens to become the constellation Virgo.

Jupiter's third wife was Eurynome, an Oceanid. They produced the Graces, female divinities of happiness and naturally, grace—Thalia, "flowering"; Euphrosyne, "joy"; and Aglaia, "radiant." These joyful deities were always at weddings. (Some tales state that they were the offspring of Jupiter and Venus.) The couple also begat the river god Asopus.

Jupiter's fourth official consort was Demeter, the goddess of corn and the harvest. Their son Iacchus carried the torch at the procession of Eleucis, bearing myrtle on his brow. Jupiter and Demeter also produced the beautiful maiden Proserpine, who was carried off by Pluto in a fit of passion. This portion of Jupiter's liaisons is very confusing and it's difficult to know just who bore whom. It seems that Proserpine also had relations with her father, and sometimes Iacchus is considered the reincarnation of their child Zagreus. Jupiter appeared as a dragon or a serpent and impregnated Proserpine with Zagreus, a form of Dionysus, god of the vine. At this time Jupiter was married to Juno, and she commanded the Titans to rip this child to bits. After assuming many shapes, a characteristic of his father, Zagreus finally became a bull and was devoured by the Titans. Jupiter's daughter Minerva retrieved his heart for her father, and one version of the story has either he or his current lover Semele swallowing the heart to conceive Dionysus.

Mnemosyne (Memory) was the mother of the Muses with Jupiter. There were nine of them, and together they represented love poetry (Erato), lyric poetry (Euterpe), comedy (Thalia) and tragedy (Melpomene), song and dance (Terpsichore), astronomy (Urania), history (Clio), epic poetry (Calliope), Hymns (Polyhymnia) as well as memory. They often kept company with Apollo.

Jupiter's next consort was Leto, or Latona, the mother of the twins Apollo and Diana. Her story is related under the section on Apollo.

The most well-known wife of Jupiter was Juno, who was also his sister. In fact, all Roman women had their Juno because she was regarded as the spirit of women as well as their protector. She was honored by each woman on her birthday. Jupiter made his first advances to the goddess in the form of a cuckoo who came and sat in her lap after a rainstorm. They had at least three children together. Eileithyia was the goddess of childbirth who assisted Hercules's mother as well as Leto. Hebe was the goddess who nourished the gods of Olympus with ambrosia, making them young and immortal. She eventually became Hercules' wife.

Jupiter and Juno also conceived Vulcan, the homely, lame, but extremely capable artisan of the gods who was the keeper of fire. He provided his father with thunderbolts as well as armor and royal furniture. There are a couple of stories that explain his removal from Mount Olympus. One states that Juno was so disgusted with his ugliness that she threw him into the sea, where he was cared for by Tethys. When he grew up, he constructed a magical throne for Juno, with a catch—she was unable to leave it until she admitted him back into the company of gods. The other version of the story states that Jupiter kicked him out of heaven for taking his mother's side in an argument, and he fell for an entire day before landing on the isle of Lemnos. Although some claim Mars to be their son, a different explanation of his birth is given under his section.

The nymphs, with the exception of the Nereids and the Oceanids, were purportedly the offspring of Jupiter and the Sky, falling to the Earth as raindrops and leaping as beautiful creatures from springs.

Along with his benign offspring Jupiter was father to the mischievous Ate, whom he exiled from Mount Olympus. Her mother was Eris (Discord), Mars's sister, and Ate followed suit in instilling infatuation, trickery, and guilt in the hearts of men and the gods. At one point she cajoled Juno into harassing Jupiter. Fleet of foot, she was always in front of the unfortunates she was to lead astray.

But, as if to alleviate or compensate for his pesky daughter, Jupiter also produced the Litae, known as the personification of prayers, which they offered to their father in return for his favor, thus our connection of Jupiter to religion. These daughters bestowed grace on those Ate had left in distress. Such was their burden that they appeared lame, elderly and squinting.

Another famous god was the son of Jupiter and Maia, the daughter of Atlas—Mercury. He was raised by Arcas, Jupiter's son by Callisto on Mount Cyllene in Arcadia. As his father's messenger, Mercury played a paramount role in one of Jupiter's romantic predicaments. In the story of Io, Jupiter seduces her by first sending her dreams that beckon the young woman to leave her bed for the meadow of Lerna. In order to hide his latest love from Juno, Jupiter transformed Io into a heifer. Unfortunately, Juno was not to be deceived and she demanded the cow, which she promptly put under the dreaded watch of the 100-eyed Argus, as mentioned previously. When Mercury had succeeded in killing Argus, Juno proceeded to pester Io with a gadfly, which sent her to many lands and countries until she was given mercy in Egypt. Here she regained her former shape and gave birth to Epaphos on the Nile, who became king of Egypt and founder of Memphis.

Callisto was another of Jupiter's lovers who met the same fate as Io. She was turned into a bear because of Juno. Ironically, Jupiter approached her in the disguise of Apollo, and some versions even say Diana since Callisto was a devoted follower of the Moon goddess. As Callisto went to greet her son, he, in fear of the rearing bear, nearly killed her. In light of the mother's grief, Jupiter placed them in the sky as the Great and Little Bear, but Juno had the last word, for she begged the ocean never to allow these bears to drink. Thus, these constellations never set.

Jupiter was the father of several famous heroes, the most notable of whom was Hercules, son of Alcmena. The fact that she was married at the time of his passion didn't seem to bother the god of the heavens. He just approached her as her husband, Amphitryon, who happened to be at war at the time, and their one night of love equalled three. Thus, she had twins—Hercules, son of Jupiter, and Iphicles, son of her husband. Instead of having Alcmena tend to her baby, Jupiter had Mercury fetch Hercules and then placed him at Juno's breast as she slept. When she discovered Jupiter's ploy, Juno flung the boy away, forming the Milky Way with her milk. But the deed was done—Hercules was now graced with immortality. But this of course, did not stop Juno from attempting to kill him in the form of his famous 12 labors. Eventually, he burned to death, and his father immortalized him in the heavens.

Perseus was another famous warrior son of Jupiter. Although the child's mother was locked in a brass tower to deter any chance of begetting a son to overthrow King Acrisius, Jupiter managed to reach Danae as a golden shower. Believing Perseus to be the product of Danae and her uncle Proetus, her father once again imprisoned her in a chest with the babe and sent them to sea. Perseus eventually went on to kill Medusa and transform Atlas to stone with his paralyzing shield.

A celebrated warrior in the Trojan War, Sarpedon was the son of Jupiter and Laodamia. He led the Lycian forces in this major battle and met his demise at the hand of Patroclus. But rather than be humiliated by the enemy, Sarpedon's body was sped away by Apollo into the care of Death and Sleep, such was Jupiter's concern.

Twins figure in another of Jupiter's romances. This time he appeared to Leda as a swan, who gave birth to Castor and Clytemnestra in the usual manner, and Helen and Polydeuces in an egg. But this story begins with an earlier seduction, according to some versions. It seems Remesis was intent on avoiding Jupiter and continued to alter her form. When she became a goose, he transformed into a swan. Finally, at Rhamnus Jupiter caught her, but she deserted her egg containing Helen. In this version Leda is only involved as a midwife of sorts when a shepherd gives her the egg.

More twins—Jupiter in the form of a satyr, loved Antiope and begat Amphion and Zethus. Because of her father's wrath, Antiope left for Sicyon, where a worse fate awaited her. Her brother Lycus attacked the city and held her captive, ordering her babies to be left on Mount Kithaeron to withstand the elements. She was then taken back to her homeland where her brother became king with his queen Dirce. Under unspeakable duress by Dirce, Antiope was finally rescued by her sons, who murdered their uncle and aunt. The twins founded Thebes.

The Palici twins of Jupiter and the nymph Thaleia were born in the Underworld since their mother feared Juno's revenge. It was said that their cradle was a volcanic lake, and tablets inscribed with oaths were tossed into its waters. If they stayed on the surface, they were regarded as truth. A somewhat similar story is told of Elara, mother of the giant Tityus, only here Jupiter places her in the Earth from his fear of Juno.

Perhaps one of the most famous transformations of Jupiter was his embodiment as a white bull topped with golden horns. In order to catch Europa's attention, Jupiter exhaled saffron, and soon she was riding the bull to Crete. There she gave birth to Minos, eventual king of Crete and judge; Rhadamanthus, another judge of the Underworld who heard the cases of Asians; and Sarpedon. The third judge of the Underworld, Aeacus, was also Jupiter's son, but his mother was Aegina, who was visited by Juipter as an eagle. This just dealer of fate received the dead of Europe and held the keys to the Underworld.

The most familiar tale of Dionysus involves Jupiter and Semele. Semele would be visited by Jupiter, but she was unaware of his identity—until Juno came on the scene as Beroea, her nursemaid. Soon, Semele had to know exactly who her lover was and tricked Jupiter in granting her one request. Unfortunately for her, she asked to see him in his divine form, and she died from the light. But his child was saved from death as he placed him in his thigh; three months later Dionysus was born. Cared for by nymphs, Dionysus became a god associated with wine, reveling and madness. Juno had a hand in the last attribute. Because of her extreme aversion to the illegitimate child, she forced him to wander from town to town until he reached Phrygia. There, the goddess Rhea tended to his sanity and instructed him in the art of ritual so that he began teaching religion as well as winemaking to the people of Asia.

Endymion, the beautiful melancholy shepherd, was the son of Jupiter and the nymph Calyce. It is said the Moon fell in love with him and would bend down each night to kiss him and watch him as he slept. Another form of the myth says that Jupiter granted him perpetual youth and sleep. In this case, the Moon watched over his flocks, assuring their fecundity. Endymion is the poet searching and dreaming of his ideal world, thus Jupiter's association with lofty aspirations.

As calm and soothing as this pastoral story is, the children of Lamia and Jupiter had much crueler fates. This couple's offspring were numerous, and jealous Juno decided to kill them all. At this injustice, Lamia began roaming the countryside eating nurslings. Incensed, Juno made it impossible for Lamia to rest, but Jupiter, in his kindness, gave her the power to remove her eyes.

The story of Jupiter's son Pactolus reinforces the god's connection with good fortune or wealth. This child dove into the River Chrusorroas, the "river that rolls in gold."

However, Jupiter, like Apollo, also had his share of rejection. The nymph Juturna was one of his conquests, and although her waters do heal, they also are very cold, symbolizing her coolness towards the god of all. And, like Apollo, Jupiter had homosexual liaisons. Euphorion was the winged son of Achilles and Helen, but because he spurned Jupiter he was struck by a thunderbolt and died. The story of the replacement of Hebe by Ganymede also points to Jupiter's interest in young men. In exchange for his son, Jupiter gave Ganymede's father fine horses, and the boy was carried to Olympus by a strong wind or in the talons of Jupiter as an eagle.

But Jupiter's relations with humans did not only consist of romance. As god of hospitality, he also walked on Earth to reward those of a generous and courteous nature. With Mercury, he traveled from door to door in a certain village, looking for food and shelter. Being turned down by many, at last they came to the modest home of Baucis and Philemon, who made room for their guests and prepared the best meal they could muster. Just as they thought their wine was to run out, it was miraculously refilled, and they then knew they were in the presence of gods. They were taken to a hill outside the village where they watched as the area was destroyed by Jupiter for its selfish ingratitude. Their poor home was changed into a temple, and their only wish was to depart from this life simultaneously as Jupiter's priests. Thus it came to pass that this devoted, selfless couple were revered by Jupiter and transformed into an oak and linden tree as they drew their last breaths. In recognition of such encompassing matrimonial love as this couple's and as a god of legal union, Jupiter allowed Cupid and Psyche to become married after all of Venus' peskiness.

With Jupiter we also see a certain amount of pride and self-defense. Prometheus, the famous Titan, was chained to Mount Caucasus at Jupiter's order because he would not reveal a certain truth about the god. Jupiter made a vulture continually eat the Titan's liver until he finally heard the secret. It seems that Jupiter was planning on marrying the Nereid Thetis; however, Prometheus knew that this marriage would produce a son who would be greater than his father. At this news Jupiter ordered her to marry Peleus and their child was the great hero Achilles.

Jupiter also had a very impartial side. Demeter and Iasion had a son called Ploutos (not to be confused with Pluto), who ruled over the allotment of wealth. Jupiter blinded him so that he would not judge anyone (unlike Pluto) but give freely to the worthy as well as the scoundrel.

This god of heroes is associated with Sagittarius, often referred to as the "bachelor" sign of the zodiac. This is somewhat odd considering the numerous formal marriages in which Jupiter engaged, but perhaps his myriad romantic encounters outside these ties suggest such a correlation. He certainly personifies the element of surprise in relationships with his many forms, as well as the importance of hospitality and discretion. He seemed to care deeply for his offspring of beauty, skill, knowledge and joy, and generally speaking, he looked after his paramours quite well. This planet represents all these things in addition to the god's breadth of experience, thus the expansionary property of Jupiter is understood, and honor and wisdom reigns.

SATURN

Although Saturn is often contemplated with dread and anxiety, the Romans held him in high esteem as ruler of the Golden Age when the world was wrapped in constant summer, health, contentment and purity. With the rise of Jupiter to power, man was forced to work for a living and the year was divided into seasons with barren times. As mentioned in the Jupiter section, once he reigned men became hungry for worldly goods and his daughter Astraea left men to become Virgo in the sky.

Saturn was a member of the "elder gods" made up of Titans. In some versions, his mother and father were Ophion and Eurynome and they also produced his wife Rhea. Other stories state Gaia and Uranus as his parents. From this version comes the tale of Uranus' castration and dethronement by Saturn. Thus, the association of power at any cost is sometimes bestowed on Saturn. What is often forgotten is the reason why Saturn ousted his father. Because Uranus despised and envied his children, he forced them to live in the Earth, or in Gaia, his mother. Because of her unbearable suffering, she pleaded with Saturn to do something about this condition and provided him with the sickle to carry out his deed.

As Saturn became ruler, Uranus warned him of experiencing the same fate. This prompted him to swallow all his children, which included Vesta, Demeter, Juno, Pluto and Neptune. It is symbolic that Vesta was the couple's first swallowed child because she signifies the fire of the hearth, or the beginning of community and balanced family life. Jupiter was also a child of Rhea and Saturn, but to obstruct the devouring of this son, Rhea gave her husband a rock to consume. After Jupiter had grown, some versions of the tale relate Rhea persuading Saturn to regurgitate his children and to laugh off his fears, which he did—until Jupiter with his siblings turned on Saturn, fighting for 10 years to gain control.

Some accounts state that Saturn was fastened to a boulder underneath the sea by Jupiter; others relate that Saturn traveled to Italy where he reigned over the Golden Age. Saturnalia was celebrated in remembrance of this benign era when all men were equal. With our restrictive, limited viewpoint of this god, it may come as a surprise that at this time of year an effigy of Saturn, which had been tied with wool cords to prevent his departure from Rome, would be freed of its bonds, and the revelry lasted for days.

It seems that Saturn had very few relations outside of his marriage to Rhea. Some myths have Saturn and his mother Gaia producing Dione, possible bearer of Venus. Another myth involves a son of Saturn, Picus. He was a Roman divinity of agriculture, but because he would not succumb to Circe's seduction, he was transformed into a woodpecker. He was said to have the gift of prophecy, especially concerning the imminence of rain.

Perhaps Saturn's most famous son (besides Jupiter, Pluto and Neptune) is Chiron. Saturn appeared to Philyra in the form of a horse so as to escape Rhea's watchful eye. Thus, their son was half human and half horse. He lived on Mount Pellon after his mother deserted him, and became well known for his healing and medical skills as well as his prophetic powers.

Up until now, I have never associated Saturn with prophecy, but perhaps he does rule over this realm with Apollo and possibly Neptune. His dominion over the Roman treasury, legal records, and Senate decrees is more logical and in step with our typical version of the melancholy Saturnine, paternal figure, always trying to maintain order in business and get ahead. Yet, we should not ignore his original mythological role of the supreme equalizer and protector of the Earth. Capricorn, the sign ruled by Saturn is often considered to mirror Saturnine type behavior patterns...somewhat cold and dense in nature, but the rock, dependable, responsible; also ambitious and, once you get to knew them, surprisingly social.

URANUS

Uranus, the Heavens, and Gaia, the Earth, were the primal pair, for before them there was only the void. Gaia parthenogenetically produced her son, and together they produced such larger-than-life beings as the Titans and Titanids, the Cyclopes, and the Hectatoncheires.

The Titans consisted of Oceanus, Coeus, Crius, Hyperion, Iapetus, and Cronus (Saturn). The Titanids were Tethys, Theia, Themis, Mnemosyne, Phoebe, and Rhea. Originally, the 12 were called the Uranidae. But their father was so disappointed in his offspring, as well as terrified of a rebellion, that he disowned them, throwing them onto the Earth.

The Cyclopes, three in number, were called Brontes ("thunder"), Steropes ("lightning") and Arges ("bright"). It's amazing to think that with only one eye shared among these huge creatures that they could make fantastic items from their forges, but they were renowned for their skill. They created Pluto's invisible helmet, and with Neptune's Telchines they are credited with forging the sea god's trident. They were eventually killed by Apollo since one of their thunderbolts struck his son Asclepius.

The Hectatoncheires were also gigantic, but they were "blessed" with a hundred hands. Cottus, Briareus, and Gyes were craftsmen like the Cyclopes and might possibly symbolize the waves of the sea.

As related under Saturn, Uranus' children were not to be kept "in the womb," so to speak, and Saturn castrated his father with a sickle for his extreme self-hate. However, Saturn's rule was not free from usurpment by kin. As previously discussed, Jupiter seized the throne from his father, Saturn, but not without a 10-year battle called the Titanomachia. Jupiter was aided by the thunderbolts of the Cyclopes as well as by the Hectatoncheires, and eventually replaced his father on the throne. Thus, the Titans found themselves imprisoned in Tartarus, but the Hectatoncheires were given the privilege of guarding them.

From Uranus' castration, the Giants were born. Frightful beings with tails of a dragon, they were volcano entities who waged a war against Mount Olympus by heaving mountains upon other peaks in order to reach Jupiter. Most of them were slain by Hercules. Another child of Uranus and Gaia was closely allied to the Giants—the nymph Aetna. She is often represented as the divinity of Mount Aetna, and in some myths this volcano is believed to be the jail of the monster Typhon and Enceladus, a Giant who survived Hercules' attack.

Other unusual children from Uranus' castration include the Meliades, who were ash tree nymphs that watched over infants left beneath their branches and guarded herds. The Furies were also his children, and it's especially fitting that these three sisters were retaliators of transgressions committed particularly against one's kin.

The most unusual child engendered at her father's castration is the lovely, docile Venus, born of the sea and Uranus' genitals, which Saturn tossed to the waves. She does not fit in with the rest of Uranus's progeny and this fact alone tends to give credence to the belief that the tale of the "woman on the half shell" is not a Greek or Roman myth at all but of Near Eastern origin.

Other disputable offspring include Mercury and Silenus, the wise but jocular and drunk son of Mercury or, in some myths, Pan. Although Uranus is considered the higher octave of Mercury, once again things don't quite fit. Mercury as the god of intercourse and communication as a son of Jupiter makes more sense, especially in view of the fact that Mercury was often his father's companion and messenger. However, Mercury did have his share of astonishing and not-so-lovely children!

At any rate, another somewhat startling relation to Uranus is man. Even though Jupiter is thought of as the "Father of god and men," Uranus' son Iapetus, a Titan, gave birth to Prometheus, who fashioned the first man from water and clay. True, Jupiter did present man with the lovely and talented Pandora, but there seems to be some debate over whether he did it in malice or as a grand gesture.

With so many unusual children coupled with just as incredible an aversion to them, it's no wonder Uranus is generally viewed as the planet of egocentric eccentricity. As the first male, he truly is unique, thus his placement in the horoscope most likely does show our idiosyncrasies or distinctive differences from the norm. The fact that his partner was his mother also lends credence to the interpretation of unusual liaisons when this planet is combined with other typical "relationship" planets.

But to me, he symbolizes man's inherent connection to this primal energy of inventiveness, dissimilarity, self-abuse or self-inflicted alienation and overblown personal reality. Necessity, the mother of invention, indeed!

NEPTUNE

God of the sea and shaker of the Earth, Neptune had quite an active social life, producing many offspring. He did, however, have a wife, Amphitrite, who was a Nereid. But he only became interested in her after he discovered, like Jupiter, that Thetis would produce a powerful son who might eclipse his dominion. Apparently Amphitrite was not too excited by his attentions, for Neptune resorted to sending Delphinus, a dolphin, to court her at her hiding place in the Atlas Mountains. She acquiesced and the two of them produced Triton, a trumpet-playing merman with a pair of fish tails. He blew a conch shell and was often a mediator between Neptune and seafarers. Amphitrite also gave birth to Benthesicyme who raised Eumolpus, a son of Neptune's by another liaison with Chione, daughter of Boreas. Another of their sons was Rhodes who gave his name to the isle, and gave birth to the Heliades who were well versed in astrology.

This god of moisture produced other sea creatures. With Tethys, he begat the famous Proteus, the "Old Man of the Sea." Second in importance to Neptune in terms of sea divinities, he ruled the seals and was quite a prophet. At noon he would doze by rocks, and this was the time to pounce on him to coerce him into telling the future. He would transform himself into many creatures, as well as the elements Fire and Water, before finally giving in.

The Telchines were considered descendants of Neptune. These creatures with tails and webbed feet inhabited Rhodes and at times even changed into snakes. They were great metalworkers, producing Neptune's trident, but their evil natures exceeded their good and eventually they were killed by Jupiter or Apollo.

In many of Neptune's exploits there is an element of deception;

thus, this attribute of the planet seems appropriate, as in the case of Amymone, one of King Danaus' 50 daughters. When she went to gather water for her family, she accidentally woke a snoozing satyr, who attempted to rape her. Neptune appeared on the scene as the heroic rescuer of the damsel and fired his trident at the satyr, but in the end he decided to rape Amymone.

Shapeshifting is very prominent in many myths concerning Neptune. In one such fable, the greedy Erysichthon stooped to the point of selling his daughter, Mestra, who in desperation, called to Neptune as she stood by the sea, watching her new owner approach. Neptune transformed her into a fisherman, so she escaped this fate but when she returned to her human shape, her father decided to try to sell her again. This pattern continued until Mestra had become a horse, a bird, an ox and a stag, among other forms. Some versions have her as the mother of Neptune's Bellerophon.

When Neptune asked one of his lovers to make a wish, she asked to be a man so that she would be invincible and able to protect herself. Thus, Caenis became Caeneus and battled against the Centaurs. Unfortunately, they drove him into the ground, but at death Caeneus was transformed once again, into a female bird.

The beautiful Theophane was beleaguered by suitors, so Neptune transported her to the island of Crinissa. Once there, he changed her into a ewe with the villagers as sheep, since her suitors were still tracking her down. Neptune changed into a ram and the couple begat a ram with golden fleece.

King Pterelaus, a son of Neptune, was deceived by his daughter Comaetho. The king believed Mycenae to be his territory because his ancestor Mestor Electryon, king of Mycenae, requested Amphitryon, his nephew, to battle Pterelaus to maintain their rulership. But, Amphitryon fell for Comaetho, and she cut the one Neptunian golden hair of her father that kept him alive. Unfortunately for her, Amphitryon was horrified at her deed and called for her death.

Neptune had more than his share of violent sons. With Gaia, he had Antaeus, king of Libya, a giant, who thought it great sport to wrestle with and kill strangers. He planned to build a temple of skulls for his father and feasted on lions. Because he was Gaia's son, the Earth revitalized him during and after each fight. But he met his match when Hercules came along, for the hero raised him into the air so that he could not touch the ground and he died of suffocation.

A very similar story is told of another son of Neptune's, Amycus the boxer. He would force strangers to fight to their death, until Polydeuces of the Argonauts extracted a promise from him to stop harassing travelers.

Another son, Sinis, also meddled with passersby, tying them to tree tops; then he'd bend them to the ground, fasten the unfortunate traveler and release the trees into the air. The hero Theseus did the same to him.

In some myths, Neptune is also believed to be the father of Sciron, the evil one who made travelers wash his feet after which he would toss them into the sea to a huge hungry tortoise. Theseus sent him to the same fate.

Neptune and Anippe begat the king of Egypt, Busiris, who at one point was having quite a time with drought in the land. Resorting to a soothsayer, he was told to kill a foreigner annually. Busiris started this tradition with the soothsayer and kept it up until Hercules came along and slayed Busiris and his retinue.

Along with Apollo and Mars, Neptune also had a son named Cycnus, who was believed to be unconquerable because of his lineage. However, Achilles killed him in the Trojan War by choking him with the strap of his helmet. Neptune transformed Cycnus into a swan.

All but one of King Neleus' twelve sons were slain by the son of Jupiter, Hercules. Neptune, in fact, had quite a time seducing Neleus's mother, Tyro, because she was enamored of Enipeus, a river god. In another act of deception, Neptune came to her in the form of Enipeus and their union produced the twins Neleus and Pelias. But the twins were deserted at the command of Tyro's stepmother, and they were raised by a caretaker of horses, which enforces Neptune's rulership of large animals. Eventually, they regained control of Iolcus. When Hercules rampaged Pylos, he killed all Neleus's children except for Nestor.

One of Neptune's sons was already mentioned in the story of Diana's real love—Orion. Born of Neptune and Euryale, a Gorgon, this giant hunter could walk on water. He was in love with Merope, but her father would not allow their union. Finally, Orion became violent and tried to capture Merope. Furious, her father decided to entertain Orion until he became so drunk he could blind the giant. He wandered along the seashore to Vulcan, who gave Orion Kedalion to take him to the Sun, who would give him back his sight.

But not all of Neptune's children were so impassioned. Some were great soothsayers, such as Euphemus who sailed with the Argonauts, utilizing his divinatory skills. Another already mentioned in relation to other sons of Neptune is the great hero Theseus, born of Aethra.

Some of Neptune's offspring and liaisons are interesting simply because they are so monstrous or unusual. One of his lovers was Medusa, the Gorgon with snakes for hair who turned all onlookers to stone. This relationship caused distress for Minerva because Neptune romanced Medusa in her temple. Perseus killed the Gorgon and Neptune's sons, the lovely winged Pegasus and Chrysaor, were born from her blood.

The Molionids were the offspring of Neptune and Molione. They were twin sons who burst through a silver egg. They were so identical that they shared a body but each had a head, a set of arms and a pair of legs. Hercules also did away with them.

Neptune had a fancy for Demeter, but she changed into a mare to elude his embraces. However, Neptune became a stallion and the two produced Arion, the swift talking horse/man. The couple also had a daughter, but like many other wives or children of Neptune, she is enshrouded in mystery.

With Theia, Neptune had the Cercopes, devilish gnomes of thievery. They decided to assault Hercules, who found them so amusing that he (surprise) didn't kill them, but Jupiter finally changed them into monkeys.

Among Neptune's monstrous offspring is Charybdis, daughter of Gaia. She had such a healthy appetite that she took some of Hercules' cattle for a meal. At this offense, Jupiter threw her into the Strait of Messina where Scylla, a hideous lover of Neptune, lived. Charybdis was known to intake huge mouthfuls of water thrice daily and cause roaring whirlwinds to terrorize seamen. Three times a day she'd regurgitate the ships she'd capture in her storms.

Another well-fed child of Neptune was Polyphemus, a Cyclops, born of the nymph Thousa. He only had one eye and ate humans. A shepherd by trade, he spent his time strumming his lyre. His most well-known myth centers around Ulysses and his meal of the hero's men. Neptune eventually sent a storm to the escaped hero since he had burned the Cyclops' eye.

Unlike Juno, Amphitrite handled her husband's infidelity rather well, except in the case of Scylla. Once a woman of incredible beauty, Scylla, became the victim of Amphitrite's jealousy as she entered a bathing pool poisoned by her lover's wife. She instantly became a creature with six heads, a dozen legs, and a yelp like a small hound. She lived to capture traveling seamen that were attempting to steer clear of Charybdis, for then she would eat them.

Like Apollo and Jupiter, Neptune's head was also turned by attractive young men. The deceitful Pelops was one such fellow, and his chariot and horses were gifts from Neptune for his success in winning Hippodameia, the daughter of King Oenomaus.

And finally, Neptune is associated with the mythical, mysterious Atlantis. Here he resided with a woman named Clito and they produced 10 children. However, in later years, the descendants of these leaders of the island became consumed with greed and exploitation, ruining the land's natural resources. Although they had built a land of beauty and prosperity, the inhabitants' haughty ways were too much for Oceanus, and he spread his waters over the land, burying it forever.

The most apparent attribute of the planet Neptune regarding the god's relationships and children is the ability to disregard the ugly or unappealing factors of a partnership. It's obvious that the sea god's violent, destructive children were not a source of concern for him. Neptune not only alters his own shape but he transforms his lovers into whatever they wish to become. This quality always seems to be operating in relationships, so perhaps it is not so unusual that this deceptive god appears to have surpassed the other gods and goddesses in liaisons, with the exception of his brother Jupiter. Just as Neptune in mythology was shapeshifting, so it is astrologically... being considered vague, indefinite, but compassionate, creative, and beauty loving, as is reflected by the sign Pisces ruled by Neptune.

PLUTO

At last we come to Pluto, that "grisly god, who never spares, / Who feels no mercy, who hears no prayers" (Homer). As the Greek Hades, he was known as "The Unseen" and accorded great respect for his identity within the realms of everyone's future manifestation. He was not thought of as a devil or punisher of sins but just as one beyond measure. In the Underworld, he reigned in the company of three judges: Minos, Rhadamanthus and Aeacus, all mentioned earlier. After crossing either the river Styx or Acheron, most of the dead would exist as shadows in the Plain of Asphodel. Those who led near-spotless lives dwelled in Elysium, or the Islands of the Blest. The few doomed unfortunates inhabited Tartarus.

Pluto was labeled the "father of wealth" and represented the abundant gifts of the Earth. It is small wonder, then, that this god would primarily be associated with Proserpine, a divinity personifying the youth and life of spring. Pluto was traversing the countryside to survey the damage done to the Earth's surface from war when Venus decided that this serious god should not be allowed to escape the entrapment of love. Up to this point, it appears that Pluto had no consort. Cupid aimed well and Pluto was so enamored with the young Proserpine that he carried her off to his dark realms of death, a blow of his trident cracking open the Earth. The maiden's mother Demeter (Ceres), the goddess of the harvest, continuously searched the land for her daughter until a nymph of the River Cyane, near Pluto's entrance to the Underworld, floated Proserpine's girdle toward the distraught goddess. At this point, Demeter blamed the Earth for her great loss and neglected its sustenance. Eventually, the goddess came upon Arethusa, a fountain that originally had been a nymph pursued by the river god Alpheus. With her plea to Diana, she was transformed into a stream that passed through the Earth, where she saw Proserpine. Thus, Demeter learned of her daughter's fate and immediately turned to Jupiter for aid. He agreed to Proserpine's release from the Underworld only if she had not eaten a morsel of otherworldly food. An agreement was reached where the maiden, now Queen of the Underworld, would spend half the year on Earth, delighting in its vibrant riches, and half the year with her husband with his mineral and judicial wealth since she had eaten of the pomegranate. Proserpine was identified with the poppy because its somatic properties represented the fall and winter months in the company of Pluto.

The story of Theseus and Pirithous gives a clue as to how relentless (and territorial) Pluto actually was. Pirithous, an overzealous son of Jupiter, thought it would be a great lark to travel to the Underworld and seduce Proserpine. But, of course, he never got the chance, for the two of them were permanently attached to a rock at the entrance to the lower realms. Other versions of the myth place the two in deep chairs from which they could not rise. Theseus was finally released by Hercules, but Pirithous is there to this day.

Besides acting as messenger to Jupiter, Mercury was also the right-hand man of Pluto, ensuring safe passage of souls to the Underworld. In this capacity, Pluto's kindness is clear, for he implored Mercury to place his gold staff across the eyes of the departing so that they would sleep gently as they journeyed to his world of eternity.

Of all the "mature" gods, Pluto seems to be the most faithful. One love interest of Pluto was a nymph, who Proserpine drove into the ground. In respect to her, Pluto changed her into his beloved mint plant, and she was known as Minthe. His other lover was Leuce, who became the white poplar of the Elysian Fields after her death. While Apollo wore laurel leaves in remembrance of Daphne, Pluto wore sprigs of the poplar. Lastly, it was believed that all maidens who died would "marry" Pluto in the world beyond.

The god's long-standing association with Proserpine points to the enduring, strong principle most astrologers assign to Pluto. His kidnapping of the young woman also lends credence to the obsessive tendency that Pluto can manifest in a chart. But his mythology likewise reveals a harsh, just side to his personality tempered by a genuine kindness and care for the new inhabitants to his realm. He was very protective of his wife as well as his domain. Just like Pluto, Scorpio, the sign it rules, is also deep, mysterious, tenacious, but supportive and sensitive.

And there you have it—a quick re-creation of the major myths of relation surrounding each of the gods represented by planets in the birth chart. In fact, the tales are endless as the Greeks and Romans altered their myths with their lifestyles and prevailing points of view and their deities reflected this.

With Jupiter participating so heavily in all types of alliances, I compared the onset of significant influential relationships (discounting relatives) and Jupiter transits to my natal chart. I found that 76 per cent of the time Jupiter was transiting either my 5th, 7th, 8th, or 11th Houses when these important people—friends, lovers, mentors, associates—came into my life and major experiences for growth presented themselves. Unfortunately, most clients cannot remember when they first met someone who notably altered their lives or mental/spiritual outlook, so I have not found such success concerning others' experiences. But the point I hope to make is that as a god of good fortune, religion, knowledge, and relationship, perhaps Jupiter is the force that brings these experiences and relations that blossom under other planetary influences. Look back at your life and see if this is in fact the case. Such transits may help to explain why we seem to have periods when great development and rich new experiences occur to offset more typical or ordinary acquaintances. At any rate, let's acknowledge Jupiter as the Great Benefic he is, and may you embrace the gifts he offers.

By becoming familiar with the myths of the gods and goddesses, you can gain a better understanding of the signs and planets in the chart.

BIBLIOGRAPHY

Bulfinch, Thomas. *The Age of Fable or Beauties of Mythology*. Rev. Philadelphia. PA: David McKay, 1898.

The Enchanted World: Gods and Goddesses. Editors of Time-Life Books. Alexandria, VA: Time-Life Books, 1986.

Hamilton, Edith. *Mythology: Timeless Tales of Gods and Heroes*. New York: Meridian, 1989.

Lefkowitz, Mary R. *Women in Greek Myth*. Baltimore, MD: The Johns Hopkins University Press, 1986.

New Larousse Encyclopedia of Mythology. Trans. Richard Aldington and Delano Ames. New York: Crescent Books, 1987.

Schmidt, Joel. *Larousse Greek and Roman Mythology*. New York: McGraw-Hill Book Company, 1980.

Stapleton, Michael. *The Concise Dictionary of Greek and Roman Mythology*. New York: Peter Bedrick Books, 1986.

Van Aken, A. R. A., Ph.D. *The Encyclopedia of Classical Mythology*. Trans. D. R. Welsh. Englewood Cliffs, NJ: Prentice-Hall. Inc. 1965.

Cornelia Hansen

Since receiving her master's degree in Early Childhood Development at the California State University at Northridge, Cornelia Hansen has been a pre-school Director and Los Angeles Children's Center teacher. In 1982 she returned to school, this time to Antioch Univerity for a second master's degree in Clinical Psychology. Cornelia was associated with the Hollywood Counseling Center four years while working toward her license as a Marriage, Family and Child Counselor. While there, she taught "Mommy & Me" and parenting skills classes. At present, she is in private practice with Encino Psychological Associates. She began studying astrology in 1976 with Joan McEvers and Marion March through Aquarius Workshops. In addition to her therapy practice, she has a busy astrological practice and also writes a column for *Aspects* magazine called "Kidwheels."

CHILD AND PARENT
A Study of the Developmental Matrix

The horoscope or natal chart, as a diagnostic tool, represents a means of studying and interpreting an individual's psychological beginnings as well as how s/he functions in his or her life. Viewed in its entirety, the chart is symbolic of a psychic structure, a map that acts as a guide to the inner model of the external world the person has constructed over time including an image of himself and how he fits into that world. This is why I feel it is incorrect to speak of the 4th House or the Moon as representing the actual mother. More properly, they reflect the individual's perception of the mother, the experience of her. In viewing the chart as a whole, it is easy to see the principle of polarity at work, for everything has a negative as well as a positive influence. In addition, each sign and house has its opposite but related meaning and significance. It is more helpful then, to talk about the parental axis than it is to attempt to resolve the disagreement over which house represents which parent, particularly in an age when traditional roles have become blurred.

We are born into a matrix of physical, mental, emotional and social factors which are best described by the angles of the chart, the Ascendant/Descendant and MC/IC axes, but we arrive with a temperament fully intact which influences our parents' responses toward us which in turn affects our behavior. Temperament is the behavioral style of the child, the *how* rather than the what and why of behavior. Although temperament consists of many components, a simple description is derived from the emphasis in a chart on the elements and qualities. For example, Mutable/Earth could be one type of temperament. If the child's temperament is in harmony with his environment, development proceeds constructively. If, on the other hand, there is a stressful interaction between child and environment, problems in development may appear. For instance, a child with a strong Fixed/Fire emphasis who has Pisces on the 4th

House cusp will have some adjusting to do since Leo and Pisces have little in common. A great deal depends on how willing and able the primary caretaker is to accept a child who is fundamentally different than herself.

Ancient astrologers ascribed the first four years of life to Moon rulership. In one sense, this appears to be quite accurate because the child suffers separation anxiety up to the age of four and after that seems to handle leaving his mother without much problem. However, developmentally speaking, this "Lunar Period" would more accurately cover approximately the first eighteen months of life. Since each child develops at his own rate and stages tend to overlap, it would be impossible to pinpoint the exact time a child moves from the symbiotic, dependent state with mother and begins to establish himself as a separate individual. Somewhere between eighteen months and two years, the child begins to express his will in no uncertain terms. His interpersonal relations are almost completely dominated by taking what he wants and saying "No" to parental requests and demands. By age two, he settles down a bit and gives the parents a rest before the stormy period to follow, from two-and-a-half to three. The two-and-a-half-year-old is subject to violent emotions, difficulty making decisions and often shows amazing perseverance. Whatever he enjoys, he wants to do over and over again. While he is energetic, enthusiastic and vigorous, he is not an easy person to have around. The attention he pays to other children is greater than at age two, but it is usually to protect anything he considers his property. His ability to share, take turns, to wait, or to give in is extremely limited. The three-year-old, on the other hand, likes to share, things as well as experiences. People are more important to him and he would rather conform than resist.

From the foregoing descriptions, there appears to be a strong connection between these various stages of development and the energies symbolized by some of the planets and houses. All are present at once, of course, but at each stage, a particular one may predominate. As the child moves from the Lunar Period, the individual will (the Sun) begins to assert itself (Mars). At two-and-a-half, the idea of "me" and "mine" exerts itself which is connected to the Taurean aspects of Venus. At three we see the cooperation and sharing aspects of the more social Libran side of Venus.

To understand the relationship between parent and child, a thorough examination of the parental axis, the horizon, the Angular

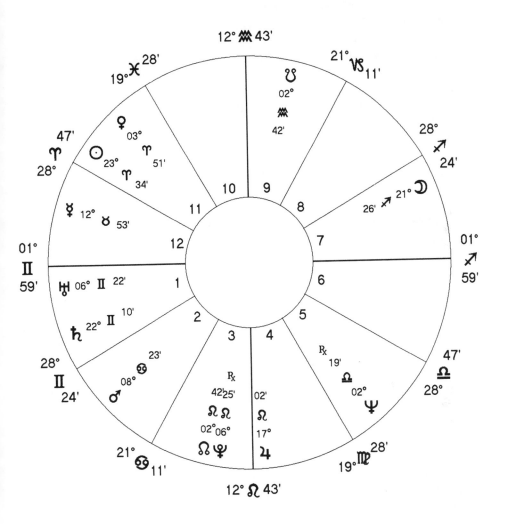

Chart 1
Tom
13 Apr 1944 08:27:00 AM PWT
Los Angeles, CA
118W15′00″ 34N04′00″

houses and their signs as well as planets in them is necessary. Bruno and Louise Huber have developed an excellent technique they call the "Life Clock" which is very useful for understanding the patterns that are constructed in those important early years.[1] According to them, each astrological house covers a period of six years. As the Age Point progresses through the Signs and Houses, it aspects the planets and changes are brought about in our development. Any planets in the 1st House will be contacted by the Age Point in the first six years of life. In addition, any planets in the Angular houses will be aspected by square or opposition and their energies will affect development.

For an example of how this technique works, examine Chart 1. Tom has Uranus very close to the Ascendant. When the Age Point contacted it around his first birthday, his parents split up and went their separate ways. Between the ages of four and five, he experienced first the Moon by opposition and then Saturn by conjunction. His mother was forced to place him and his brother in a foster home for a period of time. He experienced the separation as abandonment and felt isolated, alone and depressed. This experience set up a pattern which has affected his relationships with women ever since.

We begin life at the Ascendant, but we are born into the 4th House. Words associated with this house include home, birthplace, heredity, parents, environment, persons living in the home, spiritual security, even the words breasts and milk. The 4th House is a "field of experience"[2] in which we are nurtured, cared for and supported by those in the home. Here is the past, the very roots and soul of our being. In a metaphysical sense, it is the sea from which we arise and to which we return in the end. It is where we are connected to others in the Universe by the simple occurrences of infancy of being fed, changed, washed, held and comforted. Here is the part of the mind that remains unconscious but is the creative source of symbols for dreams, fantasies and the arts. In this house we find that part of the individual referred to variously as the Real Self, the True Self, the inner child, and, more recently, the "child within."[3] The temperament of the child and how it is shaped and supported by the container of the 4th House represents the child within. The "persona" or false self that we project to the world is the 1st House.

Signs and planets connected to the 4th House describe the atmosphere in the home. The psychologist, Erik Erikson, labeled the first stage of development as the time when we learn to trust or mistrust the world.[4] If the home is a supportive, nurturing, caring, loving place, we proceed through the following stages of development with trust and confidence. If, on the other hand, the home represents a place of deprivation, hostility, and frustration, our perceptions will color all subsequent experience and affect the course of progress through the other stages.

While the 4th House provides the nurturing we need, the 10th House provides the structure, the boundaries, the discipline, and the goals to strive for. The 4th/10th axis reminds us that both parents provide love and tenderness, affection and closeness but at the same time make boundaries, set limits and provide some form of discipline. They also make known their expectations of the child and set up a structure of beliefs, morals and values. While the 4th House provides the nurturing, the 10th House provides the experience of authority which colors our experiences of future authority figures. As the 4th House represents the private family, the 10th House is the public family, the face the family presents to the world, the status the family holds in the community. The 10th House also contributes to our sense of identity in the form of goals, where we identify ourselves in terms of what we do.

Major questions regarding the parental axis concern how the parents carry out their functions. Are the parents acting as a team or are they in conflict? Are they rigid and dogmatic or they flexible and democratic? Are they consistent in speech and action or erratic or confused? Do they accept the child as an individual or are they controlling and manipulative? The signs and planets connected to the 4th and 10th Houses provide information to answer these questions. For example, Aquarius and Uranus are erratic; Pisces and Neptune inconsistent; Scorpio and Pluto controlling; Capricorn and Saturn authoritarian; Aries and Mars are angry. These, of course, are the negative attributes. There are also the positive expressions: Uranus is independent; Pisces spiritual; Saturn responsible; Pluto resourceful; Mars assertive.

Chart 2 is an example of a strong temperament, in this case Mutable/Earth, born into a family represented by Aquarius on the 4th House cusp and Saturn there in Pisces. As Steven Arroyo describes in his book, *Astrology, Psychology and the Four Elements*, any relationship depends on the interaction between energy fields. In this case a Fixed/Air atmosphere in the home would not feed the energy field of this girl, Mary. In fact, her natural energy was blocked and frustrated and her already nervous temperament developed into extreme anxiety. The Leo/Aquarius parental axis describes well her parents, both of whom were involved in the entertainment industry. (I have charts of several other people with this axis whose parents are in entertainment.) Mary's father was egotistical, egocentric and narcissistic with a flair for the dramatic. He loved attention and encouraged his daughter to "perform." He was also unpredictable, having a violent and sudden temper. Mother was an actress, extremely vain and very controlled. The parents, being "Fixed" in their ways, were overwhelming to this child and she adopted many of the mother's co-dependent ways of relating. Mother had an alcoholic father, a narcissistic first husband, and after divorcing him (when Mary was seven or eight) married an alcoholic. The Moon in this chart aspects every planet except Saturn, Venus and Mercury. However, it relates to Saturn since it is in the (lunar) 4th House and the Moon is in Capricorn. Neptune in the 1st House indicates the confusion around Mary's identity and the feeling of being out of touch with her own body. She has had a hard time separating from her mother and saying anything negative about her father without feeling terribly guilty.

Along with the 4th/10th axis, the child experiences the 1st/7th axis. In the 1st House, he is establishing a body image. He plays with his feet, examines his hands, explores his body and practices all forms of motor movements. He sees himself in the mirror for the first time. As he begins to move more and more into his environment, he becomes the explorer, an ever-curious learning machine. As he emerges from the Lunar Period and its dependency, the ego begins to form as does the will to exert itself. The individual identity as separate from the parents' becomes established.

As the self-image is developing in the 1st House there is a simultaneous experience of the "other" in the 7th House.

It requires a significant other to help establish a sense of oneself. The human baby responds more rapidly to a human face than to any other object and it quickly learns to discern mother's face from any others. As astrologer Robert Hand aptly points out, self-awareness arising from encounters with others is symbolized by the 1st/7th opposition.[5] As children we are very vulnerable to the reflections others offer of ourselves. If we are told that we are good, pretty, smart and capable, we believe it. Unfortunately, we also believe the opposite if we are told that often enough.

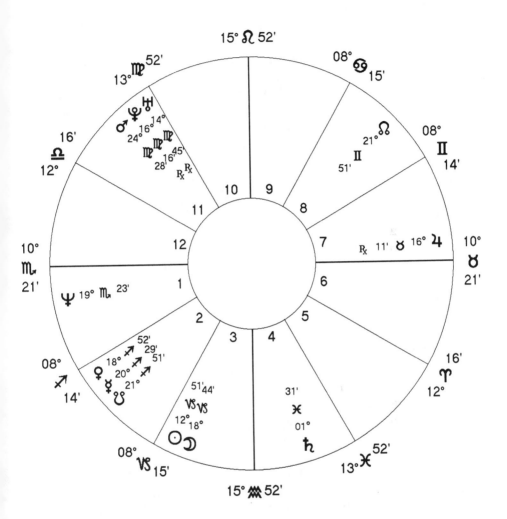

Chart 2
Mary
03 Jan 1965 02:15:00 AM PST
Los Angeles, CA
118W15'00" 34N04'00"

Since the 1st/7th axis is a relationship axis, it is here, in our home and early life that we learn to relate. Some families stress the importance of individuality and assertion (Mars). Others value co-operation and conformity (Venus). In Mary's chart the rulers of the 1st (Mars and Pluto) square Venus, ruler of the 7th and though she has no trouble in attracting people to her with Jupiter in the 7th, she does experience difficulty in her intimate relationships. She tends to be a "people pleaser" and has trouble asserting herself. Neptune in the 1st House clouds the interaction between her and others and is the source of her co-dependent issues.

Another way to study the angles of the chart is to study the relationship between the Moon and Saturn, the natural rulers of the 4th and 10th Houses, as well as between Mars and Venus, the natural rulers of the 1st and 7th Houses.

In Freudian terms, the Moon represents the emotional energy, the survival needs of the baby who depends on others to care for it. As the child begins to move out of the Lunar Period, the ego, represented by the Sun, appears to mediate between survival need (Moon) and desires (Mars) and the reality principle (Saturn). The child now begins to understand that he cannot always have what he wants, that others have rights also, that sometimes there are severe consequences for putting his own needs and desires first. Saturn and the reality principle are necessary if the child is to develop from his egocentric state where he feels he is the center of the universe, to a recognition and appreciation of the rights of others. Too strong a Saturn influence can create a sense of alienation, loneliness and depression. Too little can leave wrong dependency needs which delay maturity.

As the ego develops, there is an attempt to balance the instinctive needs (Moon) with the drives of the ego (Sun). An examination of the relationship between these two bodies gives clues as to which predominates. If there are many aspects to the Moon, the relationship with mother can be very complicated and requires working through because those patterns were set up so early in life that they remain unconscious. Many aspects to the Sun on the one hand suggest a more complicated relationship to the father. Aspects between the two bodies indicate the nature of the relationship between the parents while aspects of other planets are more indicative of the child's relationship to each parent as an individual. Rulers of the 4th and 10th Houses add to the picture.

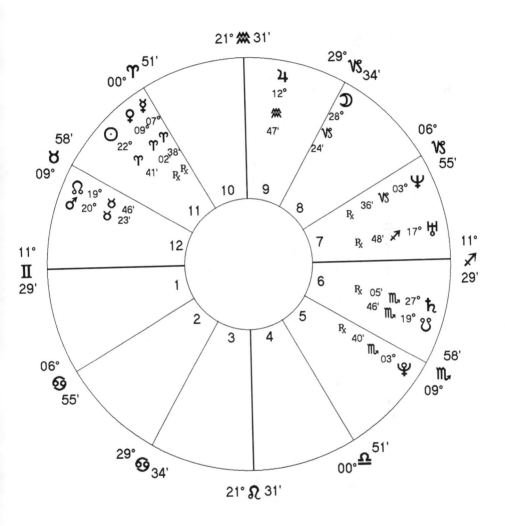

Chart 3
Female
12 Apr 1985 08:05:00 AM PST
Pasadena, CA
118W09′00″ 34N09′00″

In Chart 3, we have a girl with a Cardinal/Fire temperament born into a home and family with Leo on the 4th House cusp and the ruler in Aries. She feels at home here, supported and cared for. The Sun trines Uranus, the ruler of the 10th House, which is in Sagittarius, another fire element. The Sun is in the 11th, the natural house of Aquarius. Her parents work as a team, their child-rearing practices are in harmony for the most part, and they share the same values and goals. The father is in the entertainment industry, the mother is a teacher. The Sun squares the Moon suggesting the parents do have some emotional conflict which at times creates tension in the home. The child exhibits conflict between ego and emotional needs. The Moon has four aspects while the Sun has two, suggesting a stronger relationship to the mother. Mars opposes Saturn and quincunxes Uranus. The father has an explosive and unpredictable temper which the child has witnessed, although he has never been physically abusive toward her or the mother.

During the Lunar Period, those first eighteen or so months of life, there is usually a primary figure the child attaches to. This doesn't have to be the mother but it usually is. It could be a relative, a foster mother, even a father, but whoever the person is, that is where the child forms his first bond and this primary association colors all his relationships from then on. This is not the same as social relationships which are ruled by Venus but it is the process we all go through of bonding to an individual on the most intimate emotional level.

The attachment process goes on all through the first year and it is usually with one person. The child quickly learns to discriminate Mom (or the primary caretaker) from others, and a pattern of interaction emerges. The pattern will persist through the next few years and remain relatively stable unless there is a concerted effort by one or the other to change it or some unexpected environmental event causes a change. This primary attachment is most significant because it is how we learn to form bonds in the most intimate way and it persists through life because it remains virtually unconscious. It's not something that you remember. You may recall some of your third year and have flashbacks to some event of the second but the patterns of the first two years are beyond conscious memory and it is for this reason they have a strong influence on all future relationships.

What is attachment behavior? From the studies of British psychiatrist John Bowlby, a great deal has been determined about attachment, separation and loss. When a child is crying and the mother picks it up it will stop crying for her, but will not for others. When there are other people in the room, the child follows mother with his eyes and if she should leave the room, he cries. If the child is crawling on the floor, he will crawl toward her. When the child is upset, hurt, frightened, sick or tired, he will move toward mother above all others. The mother becomes an anchor from which the child will move out and explore his environment. He returns occasionally to make sure she is still there and then he's off again. If the attachment is secure, the child feels free to explore his envi-ronment but will flee to mother if he feels threatened. These are the kinds of things that are called attachment or bonding behaviors.[6]

The question then becomes one of how does this affect other relationships? When we become involved in an emotional relationship, many of these security, dependency needs are triggered and patterns from the unconscious exert themselves without our understanding the connection. The Moon rules the emotions and also the unconscious, the habit patterns laid down in early childhood. It is enlightening to work with two-year-old children and watch what is going on, how much is being learned and yet how little is remembered. While the child is building a relationship to mother, he is simultaneously building a model of what the world is like. If he has a secure attachment to Mom, then the world is a safe place. Using Mom as a base, he moves out into the environment and when he returns, she is consistently there. She gives him love, praise and encouragement. This strong foundation of trust, as Erikson called it, establishes the confidence that he can take risks. "I am able to master this. I'm successful, so in every new situation, I have this optimistic view that I will succeed, that my needs will be met."

The other part of the internal model of the world he's building is not only how the world is but also how he fits into it. "If my needs are taken care of, I must be lovable and acceptable." The other side of the picture is the child who is internalizing a hostile world, a world in which his needs are neglected or ignored, where he cries for long periods of time without comfort, where he is frightened but nobody comes to his aid. This is a world he does not trust, a place where he feels unacceptable and unloved. There may be strings attached and he has to behave in certain ways in order to get his needs met.

Planets in the 4th House or closely aspecting the Ascendant affect this sense of trust. Saturn especially can create a feeling of isolation and mistrust that is hard to overcome. Pluto here may indicate an undermining of self-confidence and strong feelings of guilt. Uranus can indicate a home that was unpredictable and gave a sense of insecurity. Neptune interferes with boundaries and damages identity and self-image. Jupiter and Venus in the 4th can indicate emotional support providing other things in the chart do not show a tendency toward too much dependency.

The child's perceptions are now colored by his experiences. He engages in perceptual activity which means that he compares, analyzes and anticipates what is happening now with what happened previously. He is not perceiving reality now but is building a model which may or may not fit reality. His reality is the only one he knows. It isn't until many years later that he will begin to compare his parents and home life to those of his friends.

He is also building a method of forecasting, which means that if he tries something, his expectations are that it will succeed ... or it will fail. If his needs have not been met up until now, the chances are they won't be in the future so why even try. This "failure syndrome" is established and perpetuated in the school system where he is constantly being compared to other children. The "success syndrome," on the other hand, says "I'm confidant, I have good self-esteem, I have a secure foundation emotionally and I'm willing to take risks because I know I can master whatever tasks are put in front of me." These two ways of being in the world become established in the first few years of life.

Of course, the child forms other bonds as well. There are other siblings, father, grandparents. The more figures there are available to the child for bonding, the less stress is felt if tragedy strikes. There is usually a hierarchy of attachment figures but there is always a primary figure the child prefers. Other attachment figures can be seen in the chart by any rulers of the various relationship houses which are in Angular houses or in strong aspect to the chart ruler. For instance, I have the ruler of the 6th House, aunts and uncles, conjunct the ruler of my chart. I was left with an aunt when my mother died and later spent my summers with her. She had a strong affect on my life.

It is the pattern of interaction with the primary caretaker that is observable by the end of the first year and this persists into adulthood. Some of these patterns of interaction were the subject of study at Harvard University some years ago in preschool children who had been categorized as "A" and "C" children as far as performance in school.[7] Observers went into the homes of these children and studied the interaction between the mothers and their children. They came up with five prototype mothers and how they affected the child's learning in school. As you will see, these categories sound very much like planetary energies.

I have ascribed aspects of Jupiter, Saturn and the outer planets to the Moon to describe these categories of mothers and the patterns of interaction they demonstrate with their children.

MOON/JUPITER

Jupiter aspecting the Moon describes the "Supermom." She takes a lot of time with her child and interacts with him a by carrying on a running dialogue and labeling things. She's the kind of mother who buys many educational toys but does not leave the child alone to play with them; instead she joins in his play. She shows him things and encourages his thinking by talking and asking questions. Nurturing in this Jupiterian sense, provides the encouragement to grow and expand, to assimilate experience with a sense of mastery and accomplishment. Jupiter aspecting the Moon is less concerned with detail than with building whole "gestalts" or patterns of information, seeing connections between things. Negatively, Mom can carry her teacher role to extremes. She can be so eager to help that she doesn't allow enough room for the child to do anything for himself and so a strong pattern of dependency is created. Too much success can be as deleterious as too little. In this case, there is often a fixation or arrest at the emotional level and little impetus to move out of a stage in which the child is enjoying the benefits of success into a stage of new uncertainty and tasks to master. When Mom takes the position that her child is the best at whatever he attempts no matter what the actual truth of the matter, she is not mirroring a realistic picture of who and what he is. As the child moves out into the world, he is ill-equipped to handle competition or rejection because he has built an internal model of the world in which he is the Ring and others support his position whether he has earned it or not. There may be a spoiled, self-centered arrogance that is difficult for others to accept. If all his whims are indulged by Mom, he becomes self-indulgent whether it takes the form of food, drink, emotions or possessions.

The harmonious aspects between the Moon and Jupiter are "form-maintaining," a concept of Arroyo,[8] which means that they have a lot of stability and strength, consequently there is little tension and impetus to move out of them or resolve them. Trines and sextiles can be problematical if there are no squares or oppositions to provide some tension, The squares, oppositions, quincunxes and sometimes the conjunctions are called "energy-releasing" aspects. They are not always stable and can involve a tension which takes an effort to overcome. The optimum would be to have a balance in the chart of both these types of aspects. A person with tension-producing aspects to the Moon at some time in his life, if he is lucky, will have to confront his difficulties in relationships by taking responsibility for his part in them and learning how to resolve them. With the Moon, there usually has to be some sort of counseling help since the patterns are unconscious and it takes time and effort to bring them to awareness. Aspects to these patterns by transit or progression usually present the opportunity to work on them.

The energy of Jupiter can provide the foundation of optimism and trust that encourages growth and expansion. But with growth there must also be some form of limitation, some establishment of boundaries so that the child does not remain fixated at the narcissistic, egocentric stage of development.

MOON/SATURN

Saturn provides the complimentary energy needed for the child to begin to separate from mother. Saturn represents reality, not in the philosophical sense, but the reality of the environment in which the child finds himself, the boundaries and limitations of that reality. In one sense, it is the social or cultural reality as it is filtered and interpreted through the family system. Every culture, society and era has expectations of children and forms of discipline by which it molds the child's behavior. The balance of Moon and Saturn, the healthy integration of these two polar energies, is needed for the individual to reach maturity without sacrificing the "inner child."

The "Zoo-Keeper Mother" as defined by the Harvard study, is one that manifests an abundance of Saturnine energy. She is highly organized and disciplined and, while the child's needs are met physically, emotionally he is pretty much on his own. He may have educational toys but he plays by himself. There is little interaction between mother and child so that the child has a highly stereotyped way of behaving. There is not much in the way of spontaneity or freedom of action. What is provided is structure, whether the set of rules and duties or a religious dogma. Fear of intimacy is suggested with Saturn contacts, particularly the hard aspects. Even the softer aspects manifest as an aloofness, an emotional reserve which requires some time to overcome before trust can be established. Too much Saturn energy affecting the Lunar Period damages the self-esteem and creates a sense of alienation, separation and fear of abandonment. There's a deep longing for close emotional contact that can provide the safety and security that was missed in childhood, but the fear of rejection and abandonment stifles the ability to get those needs met.

Examine Chart 1 again to see how Jupiter and Saturn have influenced this chart. Tom has a strong Fire/Air temperament which was supported by the environment he was born into (Jupiter in Leo in the 4th, Moon in Fire in an Air House, the ruler of the 4th is the Sun in Aries in an Air House). Jupiter in the 4th gives a strong foundation of faith and optimism, trust in the world. It also forms a Grand Trine with the Sun and Moon reinforcing strong self-confidence and self-esteem. A Grand Trine could be apathetic and lazy but the opposition to Saturn provides the tension to bring about accomplishment in his life. He is a very successful business man. There is a strong tie to his mother which is still present; also a strong idealization of her which affects his relations with other women. The Sagittarius influence is further emphasized by the Neptune opposition to Venus. The Moon in the 7th House is also impacted by the ruler of the 7th (Jupiter) in the 4th. All of this manifests through his multiple relations with women. He married early, mostly for security reasons. Married three times, he longs for that close, secure relationship to mother he lost at an early age when she was forced to place him in a foster home. Later he was sent away to school and hated it. Saturn manifests in his chart as disdain of intimacy based on fear of eventual abandonment. He is extremely generous financially in relationships, but not emotionally. As soon as he begins to feel close to a woman, tension becomes so overwhelming that he starts to sabotage the relationship and eventually breaks it off. His

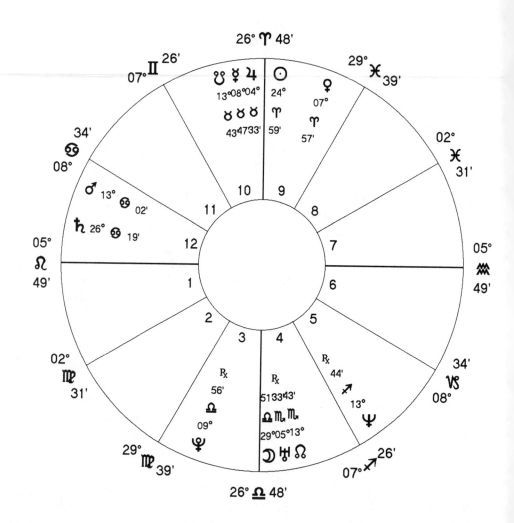

Chart 4
Bill
14 Apr 1974 00:00:00 PM PST
Los Angeles, CA
118W15'00" 34N05'00"

last relationship ended when the woman became tired of his "come here, go away" behavior.

MOON/URANUS

The next planetary energy in relationship is Uranus. Here we have the "Overwhelmed Mother" because she has so much going on in her life that she doesn't have much time for her child. She could be working or just totally involved in a lot of activities or organizations. Whatever the reason for her unavailability the result is that the child is forced into an early independence. He has to learn to function on his own. What he learns is that others are unreliable and unpredictable. This is similar to the concept of intermittent reinforcement—sometimes my needs will be taken care of and sometimes they won't, but I can't tell or make safe predictions. With Uranus, the attachment process is hit and miss so that the qualities of nonattachment grow out of the process. This is seen quite often in children of military personnel where the family is frequently uprooted and the child learns that if he gets close to someone, the chances are he will have to move so he learns to attach in a shallow way so the disruption of the bond will not be as painful. The same thing is happening in the bonding process with the mother, where one moment she may be hugging and kissing him and in the next moment it's "don't bother me." In the softer aspects of the Moon and Uranus, there's an emotional independence that requires freedom in close relationships. With the harder aspects there is an element of tension and unpredictability which is very hard on the nerves. With Saturn there is a longing to attach but a fear of it. With Uranus you fear attachment itself because of the belief that people generally are unpredictable and unreliable.

In Chart 4, Bill has a Water temperament which could be Cardinal or Fixed depending on the interpretation. He has five Cardinal planets including the ruler of the chart. On the other hand, there are four planets in Fixed signs and the angles are Fixed. Whichever way you look at it, Bill does not feel a very strong sense of belonging at home. Aquarius on the 4th House plus Uranus conjunct the Moon indicates the disruption in the early home. Father and mother separated although they kept in close contact. His mother went to work (in the computer business). Jupiter is in exact opposition to the Moon/Uranus conjunction so any benefits of Jupiter have been overwhelmed. In this case it shows the tendency of the mother to foster a dependency in her son which she defines as being "helpful." The father is very involved in his son's life even though he married a woman with a girl Bill's age and has a new child. If there is any problem between Bill and his father, Bill uses his mother as a go-between to express his needs. Bill has a high I.Q. but is an underachiever in school. Given to irritability and outbursts of violent temper, on the surface he can be out-going, charming, witty and articulate, but he expresses little feeling and remains emotionally distant from his family and friends. Bill seems unable to take responsibility for his actions and projects blame onto others. Diagnostically, he tests as paranoid. He has a difficult T-Square involving Pluto with Venus and Mars. The Scorpio Moon and Pluto/Venus opposition show the tendency of the mother to be very controlling. His anger is a way of keeping her at a distance.

MOON/NEPTUNE

The "Almost Mother" involves Neptune. She may enjoy and accept the child but she's confused and frequently unable to meet his needs. She may lack the capacity for intellectual input and waits for the child to initiate things and then she doesn't quite understand what he needs. Quite often this mother is self-involved either because of illness, mental problems, alcohol or drugs. She may be incapacitated in some way and cannot meet the child's needs. At a very early age, the child begins to feel that mother needs him more than he needs her and he tries to help, taking on the parental role.

Another possibility is the very permissive Mom who doesn't know how to say "No," doesn't set up boundaries, and the child has difficulty in separating himself from her. There is a symbiotic immersion where the child has a problem in discerning the difference between his needs and hers.

Sometimes he creates an ideal picture of this relationship and goes through life looking for the "ideal woman" who will satisfy all those unmet needs. He projects this illusion onto anyone who seems to fit the bill, but after a time reality shatters the illusion and he's left with disappointment, frustration and anger. In some cases, the child grows into a "rescuer" searching for someone who needs to be rescued, an alcoholic or drug abuser; then he becomes the victim. The problem with Neptune is that it clouds the boundaries so the person avoids any situation that presents him with the harsh reality of his position, because he's convinced that if he tries hard enough, sacrifices enough, eventually he'll get what he wants.

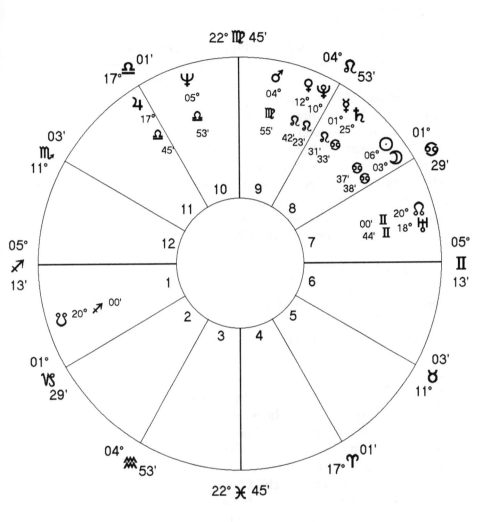

Chart 5
Jack
28 Jun 1946 06:00:00 PM CDT
Joliet, IL
088W05 41N32

Chart 5 is a difficult chart with all the planets packed into a tight wedge pattern, with no oppositions and both the Sun and Moon squared by Neptune. Jack also has three planets in Cancer and three in Leo. Divisions like this can cause problems because so much energy is split between signs that have so little in common. Another difficulty is the lack of oppositions, while there are three planets in the 7th House. Jack requires a partner in order to feel complete, but he has no inner model for relating. The rulers of the 4th and 10th Houses, as well as the rulers of the 1st and 7th are unrelated by sign and aspect. The Sun and Moon are conjunct but dominated by the Moon which is in its own sign and is the dispositor of the whole chart. Mother has played a very strong and unhealthy role in Jack's life. His father was critical and physically abusive. He was killed in a car crash when Jack was eight. Until the age of twelve, Jack had Mom to himself and when she remarried, he bitterly resented it.

His relationships with women have been physically abusive, overly possessive and intensely sexual. Following his mother and step-father's example, he is a heavy drinker. He has very little insight into himself or his responsibility for his marital problems. His relationship with his mother still dominates his life.

MOON/PLUTO

In the "Smothering Mother" we see the force of Pluto at work. This mother raises a child who is an "A" in learning ability but emotionally shy or very infantile. She is discontented with where the child is at any moment and is constantly involved in molding the child to her vision of what she wants him to be. The issue with Pluto is one of control and as the child begins to establish his identity he finds himself involved in an intense power struggle in which his chances of winning are minimal. Future relationships are colored by control issues. Rick's Chart 6 is an interesting one because of the complexity in relation to the Moon. It aspects every planet except Uranus but it is connected because Uranus is in Cancer in the 4th House. The Gemini/Sagittarius parental axis describes his foreign-born parents who adopted him at birth (Uranus in the 4th), the profession of the father (a writer who travels quite a bit), and the emphasis on communication, language and learning in the home. Rick's Fixed Air temperament feels some sense of support in the home, but more on an intellectual than a feeling basis. The ruler of

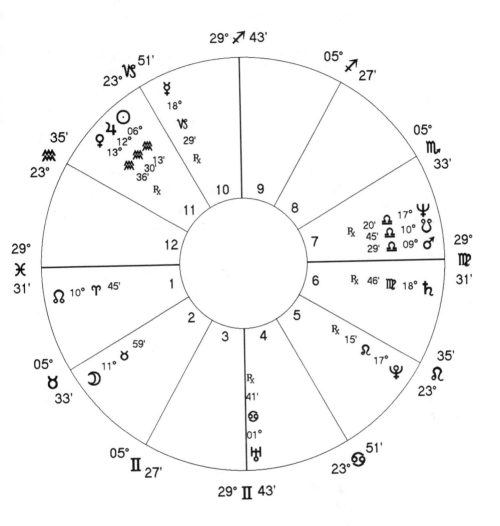

Chart 6
Rick
26 Jan 1950 09:30:00 AM PST
Los Angeles, CA
118W15′00″ 34N04′00″

the 4th in the 10th shows how the mother assumed the role of both parents since the father more or less abdicated his role both by choice and by travel. He used the son as a buffer to keep his wife from running his life. The rulers of the two houses are unrelated by sign. The Sun square Moon indicates the emotional conflict between the parents. The Moon forms a Grand Trine with Saturn and Mercury in Earth signs and houses. There was no lack of material things while he was growing up—in fact, the mother controlled him to a large extent by money by fostering a dependency on the "good things" in life.

Though Rick believes he would have been better off if his mother had gotten a lap dog instead of adopting him, he was never able to develop enough strength to break away from her, even going so far as to be her nurse for the year it took her to die from cancer. Rick has never been able to sustain an intimate emotional relationship. He quickly begins to feel smothered and has to break away. He suffers from what has come to be known as the "Madonna/Whore Syndrome." Sexual fulfillment comes only with strangers, usually with women he feels are "beneath" him. Sexuality in relationships is present as long as the relationship is in the beginning stages but it fades rapidly. Pluto in this case squares the Moon and opposes the Venus/Jupiter conjunction. This chart reflects a Moon dominated personality with a strong mother complex while the "father" representation is weakened by the Sun in its detriment and Mars conjunct Neptune and the South Node.

SUMMARY

In summary, to understand the relationship between child and parents, it is necessary to study the natural temperament of the child and the interaction between him and his environment. The matrix from which the adult will develop includes the angles (the 4th/10th axis and the 1st/7th axis) their signs and rulers and the planets in them. For further confirmation of the picture the relationship between the Sun and Moon, the Moon and Saturn, and Venus and Mars should be examined. The chart represents an internal map of the world and his place in it but it is important to keep in mind that this is his perception of the world and his interpretation of his experience, not necessarily reality. To understand the child is to understand the adult.

Endnotes

1. Huber, Bruno & Louise. *Lifeclock*, Vol I. Maine: Samuel Weiser, 1982.

2. Arroyo, Stephen, M.A. *Astrology, Psychology & the Four Elements.* Davis, CA.: CRCS Publications, 1975.

3. Whitfield, Charles L., M.D. *Healing the Child Within.* Deerfield Beach, FL: Health Communications, 1939.

4. Erikson, Erik, *Childhood and Society* (2nd Edition). New York: W. W. Norton, 1963.

5. Hand, Robert. *Horoscope Symbols.* Rockport, Mass.: Para Research, 1981.

6. Bowlby, John. *Attachment.* New York: Basic Books, 1969.

7. Pines, Maya. *Why Some Three-Year Olds Get A's ... and Some Get C's In As the Twig is Bent.* Ed: Robert Henry Anderson & Harold G. Shane. Boston: Houghton Mifflin, 1971.

8. Arroyo, Stephen. M.A. *Astrology, Karma and Transformation.* Davis, CA: CRCS Publications, 1978.

Spencer Grendahl

Writer, speaker, radio, TV and party entertainer, TV producer, educator and personal and corporate consultant, Spencer is well–known for his varied skills. His books include *Romance on Your Hands*, Simon and Schuster; "The Third House," a chapter in *The Houses: Power Places of the Horoscope*, Llewellyn Publications; *Secrets of Love*, New Moon Press, and *Mad Dog* (a novel), G. P. Putnam and Sons.

A riveting speaker, he has been active at conventions, on video tape, radio and television. His background includes being a consultant to corporations and individuals on broad matters of timing and communication as well as metaphysical topics relating to stress.

Spencer has a teaching background in English, writing, speech and history and has been active in leading seminars and small group activities. His show business activities include "Swami Spencer," "Sir Spence" where he shows off his hypnosis skills as well as his astrological expertise.

He was a Peace Corps Volunteer in Nigeria, is a graduate of Harvard University (1969) Ed.M. and Brown University (1967) A.M. and has been published in several magazines.

ASTROLOGICAL/TRANSACTIONAL ANALYSIS

When an astrologer decides to forego predictive work and get deeply involved in dealing with human relationships, it is very useful to experiment with ways of translating the traditional natal wheel into a psychological model which can be readily understood by clients. Such adjunctive charts do not replace the natal chart. They must be considered an educational supplement, giving the natal data a new communicative framework which makes astro/psychological insights more readily understandable to the client. Experimentation in my astrological practice has evolved a way of translating a chart into the format of transactional analysis. This technique yields excellent results in diagnosing and communicating an individual or couple's inner psychology. It opens the door to an intense and successful growth experience by providing a sharp perspective of their relationship to their inner self (or selves) and to others.

My approach in this essay is to show a method for drawing up a supplemental transactional analysis chart based on a client's planetary placements. It will be shown how this approach makes astrological concepts more understandable to clients and enables the astrologer to be more effective in showing how individual relationships work. The procedure will review the bare bones of transactional analysis, then translate a natal chart into a transactional format and finally demonstrate how this information can be utilized in counseling situations involving both individuals seeking better interpersonal relationships, and couples seeking to work on their specific relationship challenges.

HOW TRANSACTIONAL ANALYSIS WORKS

Eric Berne's two pioneering volumes, *Transactional Analysis in Psychotherapy* (1961) and *The Games People Play* (1964), provide a succinct exposition of the basic principles of transactional analysis (hereafter referred to by the initials, TA). The essential position of TA is that at any given moment every individual's consciousness fluctuates in a shifting dynamic of three "ego states," a parent, an adult and a child. These ego states reflect attitudes which were formed in the maturation process and are an integral part of the personality.

These three states are diagramed in a three tier stack which is sequenced from top to bottom as Parent, Adult, Child (see Figure 1).

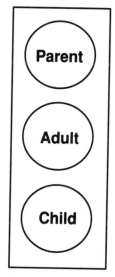

Figure 1

The parent reflects those aspects of an individual's consciousness that can reproduce ego states experienced from their parents. These parental attitudes can be activated under certain circumstances. Thus there is a kind of *in loco parentis* in every person which is a repository of the parenting techniques experienced when being raised. These techniques include survival skills, reality formation and the philosophical matrix from which one views the self. These may be positive or pejorative. For example, a parent may counsel a child to be careful when crossing a street, always good advice. Yet the same parent may also scream in anger "You're an idiot, I'm ashamed of you!"—hardly a positive affirmation. Perhaps the best summary of this ego state is that "everyone carries his parents around in his mind on memory tapes which are constantly playing."

The Adult represents the mature individual's capability for objective coping skills. The adult's behavior patterns can adapt to the fluctuations of reality. Berne calls the adult a partially self-programing probability computer designed to control the consequences in dealing with the external environment. The adult is organized, diagnostic, adaptable and intelligent. The adult of a factory worker and that of a Fortune 500 executive may be different, but each will demonstrate mature coping skills for their environment. Learning opportunities will be utilized, successes and failures identified, and a sense of constructive identity will emerge through this interaction.

The Child should always be considered "child-like" not "child-ish." Berne refers to the Child as that ego state in which we find intuition, creativity, spontaneous drive and enjoyment. Whereas "childish" is a negative judgmental term for an immature or poorly functioning Child ego-state. In contrast, the Child in TA is meant to describe those early states of mind and instinct which are yet to be molded by the environment and maturation process. This is best exemplified by the common saying that there is a little of the child in all of us, which means that in each person there is an ego state which, when tapped, brings out the creative, the intuitive, the emotional and the spontaneous.

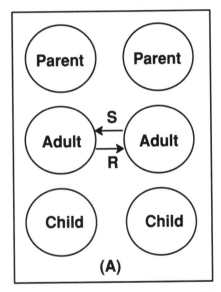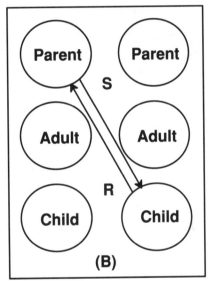

Figure 2

TA INTERACTIONS

These three states of consciousness interact in a variety of ways, and two of the most important of these will be examined before we turn to how astrology can adapt this psychological system. The first and simplest form of transactional interaction is designated Complementary (Figure 2) where the interaction is give and take (stimuli and response) between just two spheres.

In Figure 2-A, one Adult interacts with another Adult in a complimentary fashion, the receiver responds to the sender. This type of communication is possible between any two spheres (Figure 2-B), as long as the lines of stimulus and response are parallel. The Parent speaks to the Child and the Child speaks to the Parent, the Spheres interact one on one. When this one on one, complimentary pattern is broken, mis-communication or a crossed transaction is the result.

Crossed Transactions (Figure 3) are disruptive because more than two spheres of consciousness are involved and the lines of communication get literally crossed. The situation is no longer one on one communication. More spheres get involved.

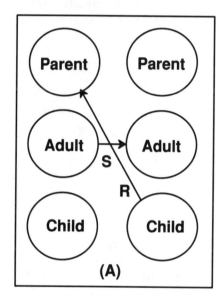 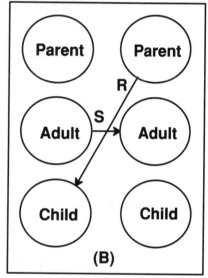

Figure 3

In Figure 3-A an Adult speaks to another Adult, but the response is from the receiver's Child to the sender's Parent. The lines of sending and receiving intersect, making this a "crossed" communication. This is a perfect example of individuals getting "their wires crossed." For example, a wife asks her husband to mow the lawn. Instead of saying, yes, he will do it or, no, he doesn't want to do it now, (for whatever reason) his response is that his child gets angry and attacks the wife's Parent by saying, "Get off my back, you're always nagging me! You're just like my mother, pick, pick, pick." Of course this response to the wife's Parent will set off another chain of exchanges and usually an argument will follow.

In Figure 3-B, the wife's concern for the lawn mowing will be met differently. Her Adult request is made to the husband's Adult, yet his reply is by his Parent, who will say something like, "What do you know about mowing the lawn? You can't even put gas in the lawn mower. I know when the lawn needs a mowing and when it needs it I will do it. So stop crying about it." This response is guaranteed to cause the wife to regress to her Child and respond in an immature way. Another argument will probably ensue.

THE BRIDGE FROM TA TO ASTROLOGY

What is interesting is why the Adult or any other ego state involved in a crossed transactions reacts that way. And this is where astrology can work with TA to simplify communication with clients.

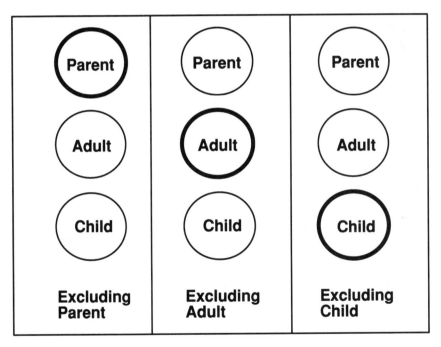

Figure 4

Berne explains that there are different psychological or emotional powers in each sphere or ego state which will lead to one's pejorative domination of the others. This causes distorted personal growth as one sphere calls most of the shots, blocking the free expression of the other ego states. Berne calls this negative ego state an "excluding" sphere (Figure 4) which results in crossed transactions.

The sphere with the name spelled out and the accentuated circle represents a dominating or excluding ego state which arrests the growth of the whole individual.

The key to understanding an individual is found in identifying and understanding the nature of these various dominating ego states and their affect on the personality. Some have an excluding Parent, some an Excluding Adult, or an Excluding Child. Therapy consists of discovering and balancing the unique powers of each client's ego states through a process of careful interviewing and counseling. This process can be time consuming and expensive.

However, Astrological TA can give the astrological counselor a quick and usually reliable format to pinpoint how a client's TA ego states are functioning as well as an effective way to communicate this information with the client. Let's see how this can be done.

ASTROLOGICAL TA

The key to transforming Berne's TA model into one based on astrological data requires putting selected elements of the natal wheel (which will always be close at hand) into the creation of a TA chart. Like most adjunctive charts (harmonics, secondary, etc) the TA chart's strength lies in its focus on specific planetary functions which give a succinct diagnosis and lends to clear communication.

Figure 5 illustrates this author's efforts in translating radical chart relationships into a TA chart.

Before proceeding, it is acknowledged that only by knowing the house and aspects of any planet can its impact in the individual's personality be known. This is why the natal wheel remains the astrologer's first arena of analysis. The astrological TA chart focuses its scope on a planetary adaptation of the concept of ego states. This planetary model stresses the

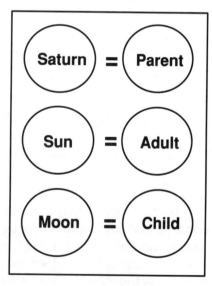

Figure 5

valuative powers of aspects to yield a specific insight into personality analysis. The graphic and easy to understand TA format promotes a definite ease in astrologer/client communication. The popularity of TA makes the three circle psychological presentation recognizable by a wide number of our population and is easily explained to those who are encountering it for the first time.

Let's continue by demonstrating how to convert a chart in to an Astro/TA graph. We will proceed by agreeing that for these purposes Saturn symbolizes the Sphere of the Parent, the Sun that of the Adult and the Moon that of the Child.

Certainly Saturn is a viable candidate for the Parent. Cronos, the definer of time and space, the giver of boundaries, is the teacher of our hard lessons. With a good Parent, it is supportive and strong with a negative one it can be a destructive, castrating critic. Liz Greene calls Saturn the architect of the ego. It follows that if there is a positive Saturn then the ego is strong; if Saturn is negative, personal growth is distorted.

The Sun for this author's purposes is the Adult ego state. It is the center of the chart, the focus of the greatest energy in the solar system. Aspects to the Sun carry very strong impacts. In *The Only Way to ... Learn Astrology* (1981) March and McEvers define the Sun as representing the inner self, the personality and the ego. These astrological teachers often refer to the Sun as symbolizing that state of consciousness or ego state to which we are evolving. The Adult ego state is precisely this flow of awareness to a better expression of the inner self which the Sun symbolizes.

The Moon is the child. It represents the emotions and the instincts, the creative urges and the fluctuations of feelings that can totally animate a personalty. When Berne writes of the Child's intuition, creativity and spontaneous drive for enjoyment, no better symbol could be found than the Moon. One's sensitivity and inner spontaneity, one's first initiation and exposure to the rule of authority are the domain of the Moon or Child ego state. The power of the Moon is inspiring; it is our closest sister, our closest emotional and astronomical relationship.

ASTRO-TRANSACTIONAL
EVALUATION OF THE EGO STATES

Determining the power of these ego states is the key to under-standing how these different aspects of our personality interact. As-trology is very helpful in estimating their varying strengths. The ba-sic technique developed to provide such a "ranking procedure" is to "weigh" Saturn, Sun and Moon, with their primary and secondary aspects. This is done by first noting all the aspects that are those made directly to a planet symbolizing an ego state. For example, if Mars squares Saturn, this is considered a primary aspect and Mars is graphically attached to Saturn or the Parent ego state by a line with a square. However, we do not stop here. Aspects to Mars are then noted, for these (secondary in relationship to Saturn) aspects reveal more of the true flavor of the Mars square Saturn. Mars which squares Saturn and also trines Jupiter is a different form of energy than a Mars which squares Saturn and also has a tight quincunx to Jupiter. The Mars trine Jupiter and Mars quincunx Jupiter represent two different secondary aspects to the Saturn. Mars squares Saturn in primary aspect in both examples, but what a different Mars en-ergy in each case due to the secondary aspects to Jupiter.

To review, primary aspects are made by a planet making direct contact to Saturn, Sun or Moon. Secondary aspects are not directly involved with the Saturn/Sun/Moon matrix, but are aspects to those planets involved with a planet making primary aspect. This tracing of energy back to two levels indicates a deeper understand-ing of the planetary filters which focus and shape its nature. It is also possible for advanced astrologers to work with progressed aspects to the Sun, Moon and Saturn to develop a progressed perspective.

MEET KAREN

The result of this astrological transposition is three circles, each with various spokes representing primary and secondary aspects. To see how this works in a real relationship, let's take a look at the example of Karen (Figure 6). The MC and the Ascendant are also used as points of importance and included in the graphics utilized in this technique.

The key astrological elements in Karen's chart are: a stellium in Leo consisting of Mars, Saturn and Pluto; a Grand Fire Trine which is also a kite with Mercury opposed to Mars; a Yod with the Sun as the finger quincunx Neptune and Pluto, a T-Square with the

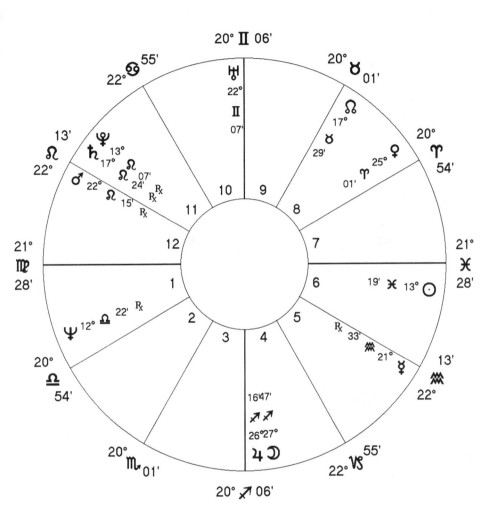

Figure 6
Karen's Chart
03 Mar 1948 06:27:00 PM EST
Patterson, NJ
074W10'00" 40N55'00"

Ascendant as the arm involving the Moon, Jupiter and Uranus; a second Yod with the Ascendant as the finger quincunxed by both Mercury and Venus; the Mercury/Mars opposition which is also a small learning configuration with the quincunx of Mercury to the Ascendant and the semi-sextile of Mars to the Ascendant.

This data will take a seasoned astrologer time to digest, let alone embark on the delicate journey of explaining its meaning to a client who has no astrological training. Let's see how TA makes this communication process easier.

The important thing in creating an astro-transactional diagram or adjunctive chart is the weighing of the astro/energies affecting each of the circles representing the three elemental ego states. This is done by diagraming the planetary aspects to these circles. If one can remember diagraming sentences in English class, it may help. Once the principles are learned it's actually very easy.

Let's examine Figure 7, Karen's chart translated into this new format. Note that all primary or direct aspects to Saturn, Sun or Moon are presented by lines to the respective circle, and the type of aspect is presented in conventional astrological symbolism: square, trine, etc. To further dramatize and understand the subtle relationships of the energies involved, the other planetary (if any) aspects to these planets which make contact with Saturn, Sun, Moon are also diagramed with dotted lines and are considered a secondary influence. For example, Karen's Mars which conjuncts her Saturn is involved in a Grand Trine that is graphically included as a "secondary" factor and fine tunes the type of Martian energy interacting with Saturn. Her Mars wants to flow and go, then it runs into Saturn and seeing how this Saturn/Mars works makes this format dramatic and revelatory.

This process becomes a "self weighing" procedure which makes analysis very simple. The rule of thumb is that the contour of the planets graphically delineates the strength of the ego states. A heavy Saturn configuration emphasizes the strength of the Parent ego state. The Sun's configuration reveals the amount of positive, decisive, self-accepting and other accepting qualities so often attributed to the Adult. The Moon's aspects reveal the Child's emotional qualities, or how an individual's feeling base was programed in childhood. With this in mind, let's interpret Karen's chart.

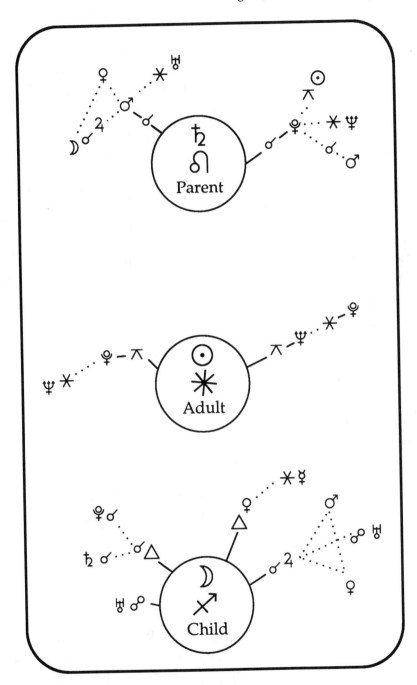

Figure 7

HOW KAREN'S CHART WORKS

It does not take long to arrive at some basic thoughts about Karen after looking at the TA transposition of her natal chart. Each planet that makes an aspect to one of the ego state planets is given an energy vector—a line connecting that planet to the ego state with an accompanying angle. Note that Karen has Moon conjunct Jupiter, so Jupiter is attached to the Moon with a vector line and a conjunction sign. The secondary aspects of Mars, Venus and Uranus to Jupiter are indicated by dotted lines. It is very important to note that Mars and Venus are involved with both Saturn and the Moon ego states, by either primary or secondary aspects.

The most obvious visual clue to Karen's chart is the Sun's lack of any really hard aspects. Compared to the Moon or Saturn, the aspects to the Sun are few and insecure, a quincunx forming a Yod. But from even a common sense look, the Parent and the Child seem to hold the power in this individual. If this true, who suffers? The Adult suffers, for calm logical decisions are rarely made. Either the Child is making an emotional decision, or the Parent is ranting and making new decisions, new schedules that even a super human couldn't follow, let alone Karen.

This TA image of two competing mental states would appear to be true in Karen's personality. The creative Child manipulated by a practical Parent (Moon/Saturn) is reflected in Karen's work, advertising, where she has done everything from marketing and sales to design and "rip-off photography" (taking pictures of children at a department store). Her dress is a broad spectrum of very crazy L.A. hip to very straight, cocktails at the elegant Four Seasons.

When Karen came for a consultation, it sometimes seemed as if she was often acting out her Child's drives for a spontaneous and creative life, the "live-it-as-it-comes" and "be free-spirited" attitude. Yet, on other days, Karen would be very hard on herself; she would be busy making plans to reeducate herself, to get back at foes in office politics, to develop more discipline.

Karen talked and acted about men in a very conflicting way. On the one hand she wanted to marry money and class. However, she ended up dating married men who had money but were unavailable, while dating single men who had dependency problems which prohibited commitment.

It was pointed out that the Adult in her Astro-TA was weak. Karen at first couldn't believe this diagnosis because she "perceived the Parent as Adult (no wonder she didn't want to be an adult). Realism is the domain of the Adult, good decisions are another trademark, whereas the Parent is often a rigid, self-judgmental critic who is never satisfied. When Karen made this distinction, she did an "Aha" double take. Her problems didn't stop instantly, but she did get new insights, especially into the nature of the Child as well as the Parent.

"I thought being strict on myself was being good to myself," Karen said. "I wanted to do well. So I'd be strict, so strict that my Child would rebel and foil the plans of the parent. Wow!"

Please note the amount of personal insight she has gained from seeing a diagram which shows her Astro/TA graph. There is a lot more information about her family's loud and violent environment which gave her low self-esteem. See how Saturn makes primary or secondary contact with every planet in her chart except Mercury. Her super ego is so powerful as to be inhibiting. The point of this is to show how the Astro/TA chart communicates important issues very clearly without astrological mumbo-jumbo. It is a wonderful marriage of astrology and psychology.

This method can be used to better understand how the inner life is a mix of several competing personality or ego states. In the act of self-individuation these different states must be integrated into a functioning whole. The astrologically weighted symbols for the TA ego states gives immediate insight as to which ego state is dominating, and how. The Astro/TA practitioner is able to quickly cut through resistance by short-circuiting the laborious task of the repetitive, therapeutic interview which takes so long for insight to develop, often because the very nature of client resistance makes it so.

The basic strength of this Astro/TA method is that it brings a client into a format (TA) which they understand because of the wide spread popularity of Berne's Transactional Analysis. Not only are there popular books on TA, but articles in current magazines as well. The result is that oftentimes clients are pre-conditioned and pre-educated to grasping this format. This enables the astrologer to utilize this methodology in developing communication and awareness.

IT TAKES TWO. . .

The Astrological/TA weighing method works in relationship counseling by creating two Astro/TA Ego State Maps and working with their interaction. Let's turn our attention to how a romantic relationship can be mapped and analyzed in the light of the principles learned so far.

Carol presented herself as a client with a strong inner drive to make her mark in Hollywood. A model with a distinct look, Carol wanted to find a path for herself. She wasn't exactly naive, but she was a sincere seeker of a "good" life as opposed to the "sell out" life. Carol's first husband lost her and his business to a cocaine addiction (it was during her Saturn return). She knew the roller coaster that life could sometimes become and she was seeking stability. Here is Carol's chart, Figure 8.

Carol has several interesting configurations. Her Fire Grand Trine Venus/Jupiter/MC as well as Mars conjunct the MC and trine the Jupiter/Pluto conjunction, give her very powerful sexual charisma, a strong camera presence and charming appeal. Her two tightest aspects are Mars quincunx Uranus and Mars trine Jupiter/Pluto, placing all this fiery energy in a "gitty-up/whoa" double bind. The trine provides easy flow to achievement, the quincunx makes her feel uneasy as her ambition and creative abilities take her into new grounds. Saturn squares her Sun in the 12th House suggesting a distorted sense of self-awareness and a self-critical inner life. Her Moon in Virgo opposes the Pisces Ascendant, inconjuncts Mercury and Venus. Though grounded in Earth, this position for the Moon is unsure of the deep emotions she feels and how to communicate them.

The information an astrologer would like to communicate to Carol about her chart is complex and dynamic. Let's see how Carol's chart transposes into an astro-transactional analysis chart (Figure 9).

Carol's Parent/Saturn sphere shows the only release from difficult squares is a trine to Uranus, underlining her tendency to jump into new situations to avoid the problem of an immediate conflict. Her Parent is a powerhouse. The Parent dominates the Adult/Sun sphere. The Adult finds release only through a trine to Neptune, an escape. Thus her Parent and Adult spheres show a tendency to leap into anything new and fanciful.

Her Child/Moon sphere has no easy outlets, no flowing trines or sextiles. Her Child has always met with difficulty in expression. Life is a serious endeavor with constant seeking for the "way" and then dealing with the pot holes encountered. Enter Larry.

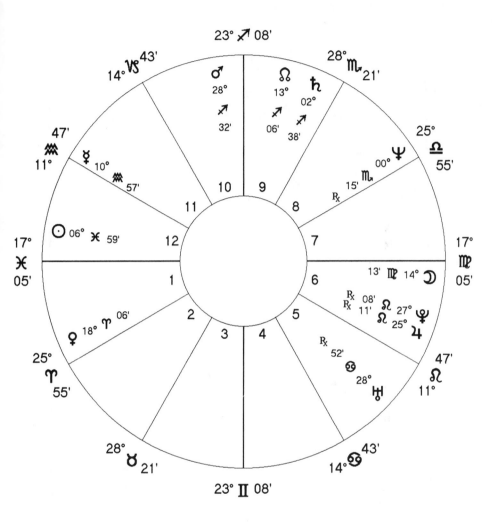

Figure 8
Carol's Chart
26 Feb 1956 07:36:00 AM MST
Salt Lake City, UT
111W54'00" 40N46'00"

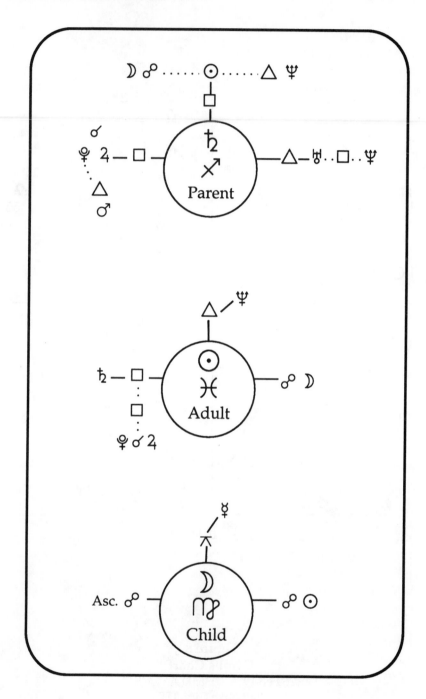

Figure 9

When Carol met Larry at a Beverly Hills night club, she was open to some change, to some fantasy. She was looking for security. Larry immediately pursued her. She refused to give him her phone number, but he somehow got it. Larry swept her off her feet. He was a media agent and knew how to put the rush on.

What did Carol do? She got Larry's birth data and asked her astrologer to evaluate the potential of the relationship. She wanted to know if it was in the stars. Figure 10 shows Larry's chart.

Larry has no planets in Earth signs to ground himself. His T-Square—Mercury, Mars, Moon, with the opposition in the 1st and 7th Houses and the finger in the 5th spells out compulsive creativity and love affairs, especially when Jupiter (which is the point of a Yod, quincunx the Moon in the 1st an Uranus in the 3rd) is exactly conjunct the South Node in Scorpio in the 8th House. This only adds fuel to a growing diagnosis that Larry is a player. His Aries Moon and Ascendent give great initial passion, but where is the follow through? Neptune conjunct his Sun indicates his difficult illusions. His Venus opposes the Ascendant and receives relief only through sextiles to Pluto and Saturn in the 5th, the house of love affairs, and creative speculation, at both of which Larry excels. Would you want your client to date this character?

Now that this basic, but complex astrology has been perused, let's translate this into an Astro/TA chart. See Figure 11.

There is a lot of power in each of Larry's Ego States. His Parent is dominated by Saturn conjunct Pluto, suggesting a dark and oppressive side to his need to be controlling, both to himself and others. Pluto's presence hints of trauma when growing up, trauma which may now be reenacted on others.

Larry's Adult is ruled by the Sun conjunct Neptune, a sign of compulsive behavior at best and illusions at worst. Neptune also conjuncts Venus which ties Larry's love life into one of his illusions.

Larry's Child is disruptive. The square to Mars which squares Mercury makes for a mean mouth. This man could regress and say biting words, aggressive childish things. The Moon's quincunx to Jupiter suggests a reluctance to mature.

Each of these traits was carefully discussed with Carol. Larry looked like a very negative emotional risk. Carol could see what the Astro/TA diagram expressed about Larry's inner nature. Larry

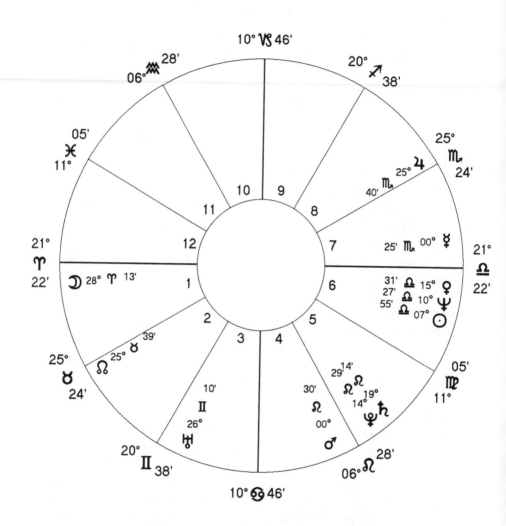

Figure 10
Larry's Chart
01 Oct 1947 06:01:00 PM EST
Ottowah, Canada
073W22′00″ 43N39′00″

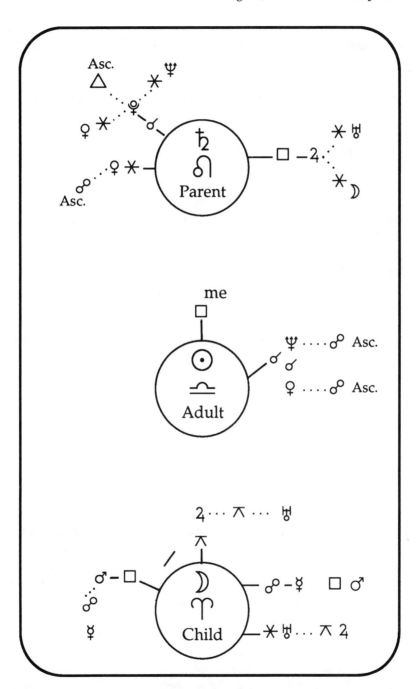

Figure 11

seemed overly ardent. Could all these flowers and displays of affection continue? Still, it seemed so exciting for her to be at the center of such dramatic attention.

The underlying connection was that each adult in this relationship was under the power of Neptune. The romantic dream was the reigning need. Larry's power hungry Parent (Saturn conjunct Pluto) was easy to see in his business dealings, where he was known to be ruthless. He was also very bitter about his divorces. One of his ex-wives threw all his clothing in the swimming pool and promptly went out and deliberately wrecked his Rolls Royce.

Like most clients who receive less than positive news from their astrologer, Carol chose not to listen to the offered advice, which was to keep Larry at arm's length. If he was still around in eight months (two light years by Larry's Hollywood agent's time) she might think more seriously about him. Larry continued to court her passionately, bought her a car, begged her to move in with him, and bought a ring. Carol called to ask her astrologer about Larry's proposal. It was pointed out that what she and Larry were doing was letting their unstable Adult Spheres flood their lives with passion. When the fog of Neptunian romance lifted, Larry would not seem so great. Carol listened politely, but married Larry. The wedding was held at a big wealthy country club, important people attended. Carol looked great.

Carol was married to Larry for three-and-a-half years and had two sons. She got a house as a divorce settlement. Shortly after the marriage, Larry's personality changed. He became cruel, mean. On two occasions he beat Carol. Responding to a call from their home to talk to them after a fight, this astrologer recommended a good female therapist. Larry took off into therapy as if looking for gold. He had an illusion to chase. He stopped therapy when great changes were not immediately forthcoming and chose not to save the marriage. Two weeks after he left Carol he was busy pursuing a beautiful actress.

Carol is still consulting her astrologer. She has had a lover since the divorce, but she works much more with what the Astro/TA has revealed about her and her own inner needs. She is careful. She listens to self improvement tapes, reads astrology and pop psychology books, always with the view of getting in better touch with herself before trying marriage again. For her, the third time has to be a charm. Also being a mother has opened her eyes to how raising children can reawaken memories of one's own youth and the programming one received. She is developing better connections with her inner child. She is growing.

SUMMARY

Astro/TA is a very effective way to communicate complex astrological data to individuals who have limited knowledge of astrology. The key to good counseling is to plant a seed for future growth. While neither Karen or Carol made miracles work out of their situations, they were able to grasp the key issues of their charts and continue to work with these issues even though the immediate results were the continuance of poor judgement. However, the seeds planted by the Astrological/TA enabled them to see key psychological concepts, to perceive tools of insight and to continue working with them. This led to experiences of personal awareness which precipitated growth. Gradual change is the way these clients responded to the challenges of life experiences.

One of the hurdles of being a practicing astrologer in these final years of the 20th century is translating our discipline, whose roots predate modern science, into a form that can be understood by a population inundated with a barrage of media information. To answer this need astrologers have advanced "mythic" astrology, spiritual astrology, transcendent astrology; the list grows and grows. Still the fact is most clients know more about Madonna the actress/singer than Aphrodite or Venus. Similarly, they know more about the strong arm of a professional football quarterback than the thunderbolts hurled by the arm of Jupiter. The astrologer's task continues to be that of seeking ways to enable people to understand astrology, themselves and their relationships through some common ground.

Astro/TA is an important contribution to this growing effort to facilitate astrological communication. Used as an adjunctive measure to the natal chart, Astro/TA can be an effective bridge from the astrologer's insights to the receptive understanding of the client. Productive communication of the energies that surround personal relationships can be expressed through Astro/TA. The relationship between astrology and TA is sharply prolific and deserves a broader study by more astrologers and psychologists alike.

Dickson Ward

In May of 1972, when transiting Saturn made a conjunction to Dick's Gemini Sun, his television production company in Hollywood was sold prematurely by the financial backers. His astrologer, Betty Collins, advised him to start studying astrology at The First Temple of Astrology in Los Angeles. That was the beginning of his astrological journey. He subsequently studied with such luminous teachers as Marion March and the late Carroll Righter.

Dick practices astrology in Palm Springs, California where he also writes for television and produces television commercials. He has had his own local radio astrological forecast show and was one of the early writers for Star Scrolls. In the Fall of 1989, he was awarded his practitioner's licence at the Palm Desert Church of Religious Science. Earlier that year, he started to incorporate his metaphysical knowledge into his astrology work.

Dick attributes his multi–faceted career to the dual sign of Pisces on the Midheaven. Natal Uranus is in the 9th House trine the Ascendant and part of a Grand Trine with Jupiter and Pluto. The dual sign, Sagittarius, is on the cusp of the 6th House and his Moon is in Sagittarius as well.

THE METAPHYSICAL/ASTROLOGICAL
APPLICATION TO RELATIONSHIPS

Once upon a time there was an astrologer who was having a difficult time marrying astrology and metaphysics into any kind of meaningful relationship. So I took the sensible way out and decided to take a sabbatical from my astrological studies and practice. That was in late 1984.

My entry into the realm of metaphysics began during a period, a phase, when nothing in my life was working, and when I resisted change at every turn. What an admission for a mutable Gemini, who's supposed to be flexible and adaptable to change! My cop-out is that my Venus—value system, life-style—is in Taurus and, consequently, I am rooted in doing things the way I have always done them. Of course, a Cancer Ascendant didn't help matters any. I've always had to try a little harder to live in the now and pry myself out of the past.

At that time, I had been on the Alcoholics Anonymous program for about four years, and was not getting that message either. I was clean and sober, but I was still rooted in the old ways of thinking and doing.

One Sunday, I went to a service at the Hollywood Church of Religious Science in Los Angeles, where the minister reminded the congregation: "What you think about, you bring about!" This idea is adapted from the teachings of Jesus: "It is done unto you as you believe!"

The mind is the most powerful instrument in our beingness. Through the right use of it, we can bring abundance where there is lack, health where there is sickness, joy where there is sadness, and PRODUCTIVE, HAPPY, AND LOVING RELATIONSHIPS where many, if not all of the qualities of anger, jealousy, possessiveness, resentment, and low self-esteem existed before. Until we acknowledge this "metaphysical" philosophy, we can go on assessing all the supposed wonderful effects of the trines and sextiles of transits to natal planets until the Sun freezes over, but we will just be spinning our wheels!

I returned to my beloved astrology with great enthusiasm in the beginning of 1989 with a new awareness and an understanding of how to use my metaphysical knowledge in the interpretation of astrological phenomenon. As a prime example, I believe there is a "Divine Plan" for all of us, and everything is a part of that plan, including relationships. Astrology goes a long way in helping us understand "The Plan" and what it is.

To people well-schooled in the "New Thought" (metaphysical) movement, the idea "if we change our thinking, we can change our life" is accepted and practiced on a daily or even hourly basis, depending on how long we have been carrying garbage around in our subconscious. The more deeply imbedded it is, the more work there is to get rid of it.

Ernest Holmes, the founder of Religious Science and one of the key people in the New Thought movement, said: "Life-long habits of wrong thinking can be consciously and deliberately neutralized." But, we must replace worn-out, wrong thinking with active, positive thinking. He said we must become actively constructive and happy in our thinking—not merely passively so.

MERCURY

The planet of thinking / communications, MERCURY, should be the first thing we look to in our analysis of a relationship. Even when I studied comparison astrology, before my metaphysical studies, I was fascinated with the importance of the role that Mercury plays. Talking, communicating, intellectualizing—realizing how vital and important these are in order for any two human beings to remain mates, lovers, friends, business partners or whatever. After I got the metaphysical/astrological message, I went back through my files of clients who had come to me with relationship problems, and the importance of Mercury made more and more sense.

For the sake of simplicity, let's just look at MERCURY in the qualities or modes as they are sometimes referred to: Cardinal (Aries, Cancer, Libra, Capricorn); Fixed (Taurus, Leo, Scorpio, Aquarius); and Mutable (Gemini, Virgo, Sagittarius, Pisces). The Fixed and Mutable qualities bear the greatest consideration as to how easy or difficult it will be for us to change our thinking and move into a compatible, harmonious, relationship, but for the sake of the more traditional astrologers, Cardinal will also be included in our discussion.[1]

If, for example, two people with negative thinking and approaches to the relationship both have Mercury in Fixed signs, the relationship is probably doomed to fail. Both may be stuck in a rut and unwilling to change their thinking. On the other hand, if both parties have Mercury in Fixed signs and also have a very positive approach and thinking toward their togetherness, the relationship could last. A determination may exist to make the partnership work. One thing to remember, though, is that when two people have their Mercuries in the same quality, there is always going to be a certain amount of mental gymnastics, a challenge to bring harmony into the relationship when the signs are square, opposed or conjunct each other.

As to how much "positive" or "negative" we can expect from the partners, a lot depends on the natal aspects between these signs in each individual chart. The major difficulty in the conjunction of two fixed Mercuries is that the lack of flexibility can be a roadblock to the growth of the relationship.

David Viscott, the noted psychiatrist, said: "If a relationship is to work, each person has to have the room to grow. Growing cannot be isolated from the relationship." To grow or to expand brings the planet Jupiter into the arena. But more about that later.

If we want to experience a harmonious and loving relationship, we must first embody the idea of freedom and, at the same time, commitment. Freedom with space to grow and commitment to each other and the entity of togetherness. And in the bargain, we must each maintain our individuality, each being special emissaries of God, with a Divine Purpose while we're here.

Let's consider a Fixed/Mutable couple.

I observed conflict and discord come into play with a female client (Susan) with Mercury in very Fixed Scorpio. Her lover (Randy) has Mercury in very flexible (Mutable) Sagittarius. Scorpio

---

1. I chose not to include Mercury in the Elements for purposes of this discussion. Remember our premise: "If we change our thinking, we can change our lives." The Qualities—Cardinal, Fixed, Mutable—allow us to analyze two charts of a relationship, directly, easily, and without confusion. The comparison factors of how Fire or whatever other element, gets along with the other elements has been dealt with in great detail in other works and is not pertinent here.

and Sagittarius may be next-door neighbors in the zodiac, but that proximity is about all they have in common when it comes to how they think and how they communicate. Until Susan was willing to let Randy be his own person, to give him room to grow, to let go of her jealousy and possessiveness, the fur flew on a fairly regular basis. Of course, no sign has exclusivity on the traits of jealousy and possessiveness, although this is often an indicator of low self-esteem.

Randy with his Mutable Mercury loved her a lot, maybe because she directed so much of her thought to her sex drive and his; but overall, his way of thinking brings to mind the old song "Don't Fence Me In." Randy could be flexible until his freedom was impinged. Oh yes, her Scorpio Sun and his Sagittarius Sun only serves to emphasize the opposing qualities of fixity and the mutability in the relationship.

When I first met Susan, she had been living with Randy for three years. The basis for their togetherness is probably attributable, to a great degree, to the fact that both have their Moons in Cancer, hers conjunct his Ascendant. However, when transiting Pluto conjoined Susan's Mercury, her thinking transformation was under way. Pluto also trined her Moon and, for the first time in her life, she wanted and needed the freedom to express her own feelings. She realized that it was now safe to experience all her feelings, to express them and let them go.

She was ready to hear some metaphysical truths, and make affirmations like: "I am willing to change," and "I'm willing to release the need for an inharmonious relationship." I advise clients to repeat affirmations as many times a day as they get stuck in their old self-destructive, negative ways. All astrologers know how difficult it is to get people with heavy placements of planets in Fixed signs to either accept or make changes in their lives. Don't get me wrong, some of this Gemini's best friends AND past lovers are of the Fixed persuasion—Taurus, Aquarius, and Leo.

As a reminder of what I said earlier, the mind is the most powerful instrument in our beingness, and when we change our beliefs, change our thinking, then, and only then, can we change our lives for the better.

One of the old time astrologers, Charles E. O. Carter, in his book *The Principles of Astrology* (1925), wrote: "The Mutable signs are intermediate between the two other qualities, having something of each. They stand for THOUGHT and the impartial attitude toward things, seeking to understand without bias." He said they are sometimes referred to as "common signs" because they have something in common with the other two qualities. Too much mutability and little or no fixity in one chart needs a partner with some fixity to ground them, to help them, by example, not to change their mind every five minutes. As always, in astrology, we need to seek a balance of the energies found in the natal chart.

Next, let's consider a relationship with Cardinal and Mutable Mercuries. Active and ambitious, independent and initiating, the Cardinal signs are usually the movers and the shakers. Progress for Cardinal people is usually embodied in change and movement. If we transfer those traits of character to Mercury, we will quickly get an idea of how the Cardinal mind works.

I am thinking of two gay clients who are lovers—one with Mercury in Capricorn, Andrew, the other with Mercury in Pisces, Michael (not their real names). Andrew is CEO of a large design firm and Michael, a successful dancer with Broadway and movie musicals to his credit. Andrew is also business manager for Michael, guides him, and helps him avoid the pitfalls of New York and Beverly Hills talent agencies. In the very personal and intimate aspects of their relationships, an impasse arose because Andrew wanted to apply his talents (for running things) to their home life, as well as business matters. There was "trouble in River City" as the man said in the musical, "Music Man."

I urged Andrew to rest his brain and to let Mike take charge in certain areas, and I gently insisted that he needed to practice flexibility. The Cardinal signs are much more easily convinced to try something if they think a goal or an objective can be accomplished. And change was okay as long as it contributed to the longevity of the relationship. He soon realized that Michael could provide the whimsy and fantasy and harmless escapism that is so lacking in his own thinking. In a word, Michael could get Andrew to stop and smell the roses. The partnership works very well now because Mike is naturally flexible when it comes to accepting the strengths of the real business man and Andrew has become adaptable when it comes to letting Mike take over for much of the leisure time.

If you want an example of flexibility in nature, observe the palm tree as it bends low toward the ground in a heavy wind, then springs back to its upright position when the wind dies down. Trees with more rigid trunks often break in times of stress and pressure. We need flexibility today more than ever because things are changing so fast. Such changes are not a problem for the person who understands and believes that he or she lives in the flow of life, whose foundation is a strong belief in the unchanging goodness of God. At the heart of such a belief is the idea that all things work together for good, as St. Paul explained to those of his time who were perplexed by the changes and uncertainties of their day.

When we are flexible, we can truly live in the NOW. The past is gone and tomorrow isn't here yet. There are other rewards to living flexibly like being open to spontaneity and adventure, seeing another's point of view, enlarging our own horizons, and seeing more of the infinite possibilities that life has to offer. I love the Helen Keller quote: "Life is a daring adventure or it's nothing!"

At the end of a session, I often ask my client to say out loud with me affirmations like: "TODAY I AM OPEN TO THE NEW AND WONDERFUL THINGS THE UNIVERSE (GOD) IS BRINGING INTO MY EXPERIENCE. I AM FLEXIBLE AND TRUSTING, KNOWING GOD'S WILL FOR MY LIFE IS ALWAYS FOR ULTIMATE GOOD". . . (or) this good advice: "CEASE THE ENDLESS CONTEMPLATION OF WHERE YOU ARE AND START CONTEMPLATING WHERE YOU WANT TO GO. IT WILL WORK EVERY TIME."

Out of all this must emerge the underlying principle that we can only change our own thinking, and NOT the thinking of the other person in the relationship. You may be aware of the PR slogan: "Attraction rather than promotion." In a one on one partnership, that means our mates will change their negative thinking easily or not—according to whether they're Cardinal, Fixed, or Mutable—by observing our example of being a positive, loving, non-judgmental person.

If that doesn't happen, the person isn't on our level of consciousness. Then we know that we are in the wrong relationship. This attitude has nothing to do with ego or the old-fashioned social snobbery, I'm simply talking about a metaphysical truth.

By this time, maybe something is becoming obvious to you, just as it hit me. Neither astrological principles nor metaphysical principles stand alone. Everything is energy and vibration as we travel on our quest for spiritual knowledge. Everything in the Universe is inter-connected. Metaphysics, in particular, addresses itself to the energy of the universe, which, in turn, translates to the God-power within our higher power, as referred to in the 12-step programs. I call it the highest power.

Sixty years ago the great astrologer Evangeline Adams said, "The Sun is the image of God in our universe. All the planets are children of the Sun, and are but specializations of ONE POWER!" Bringing that idea forward to the present time, it easily follows that each of us, as the children of God, is the individual and unique manifestation of the power and energy of God. And when we listen, in a quiet moment of meditation, we can hear the guidance of our highest power.

SOME KARMIC NOTES

Key bodies, like the Sun and the Moon, in a key position in another person's chart is, to me, an indication of the possible existence of the relationship in another lifetime. My close friend and one of my metaphysical teachers, Dr. Valjean McGinty, has Jupiter in the exact degree of my Cancer Ascendent. She is, in many ways, my spiritual benefactor.

Eleanor Roosevelt is reported to have said: "I don't think it any more bizarre to have showed up in another life than to have showed up in this one."

I have examined charts of people in a bitter divorce or even more violent separation and was astonished, at first, to NOT find any sign of karmic ties. Equally interesting to me are charts of people who break up for no particular reason, suffice to say they didn't want to stay together, and again, I found NO significant planetary contacts between the two charts. I am currently doing research on the karmic compatibility of two charts, particularly where two people believe they have found their soul mate.

Edgar Cayce believed that whatever kind of relationship we may experience in this lifetime, we come together with that person for a specific purpose in the evolution of our soul, perhaps for the transfer of knowledge, the gaining of information that contributes to our growth. He felt that when the purpose of our coming together is over, completed, the relationship will end, sometimes by death of one of the participants, or some other kind of separation.

I have used that explanation with much success to comfort clients and help them get centered after traumatic separations and terminations. I have used it following a death, divorce, loss of employment, and the breakup of lifelong friendships and business partnerships.

As far as the word "death" is concerned, the true metaphysician doesn't use it, doesn't believe in it. God is a God of Life. When we leave this temporary house (body) we live in, we make a TRANSITION to another plane of existence.

THE DIVINE PLAN

Earlier in this article, I alluded to "The Divine Plan." I believe that there are no accidents, no coincidences. We do have free choice, but the course our life takes is dependent, to a large degree, on how we handle or react to inevitable changes. If we can just get out of our own way, go with the flow of the energies in our chart, we will recognize THE DIVINE PLAN unfolding, guided by the supreme power for good in the universe. If, on the other hand, we choose to stand still—to keep moving down a road that no longer serves our purpose, all the king's horses and all the king's men will have a lot of trouble putting Humpty Dumpty together again.

Whether or not we choose to call it by that name, we see the indication of the Divine Plan in many different ways in the chart. How about the transits of Saturn to natal planets and sensitive points in the natal chart? In a relationship, for example, when Saturn makes a square or opposition to Venus or the ruler of the 7th House, if the relationship isn't working, maybe it's time to let it go, or to approach it differently. This transit definitely indicates some changes are necessary . . . and they have to start with you. Remember, Saturn is the teacher and its lessons should not be treated lightly. Saturn is sending a message and the bottom line is that the relationship can't continue as is!

Was the Divine Plan unfolding when transiting Saturn conjoined President Richard Nixon's Midheaven (Watergate and subsequent resignation from the Presidency)? He was obviously going "down the wrong road." Was the Divine Plan unfolding for Harry Truman (and the United States) when transiting Neptune came to his Ascendant and he was elected President of the United States (everything in his life came into focus)?

How about the transforming power of Pluto as it contacts a natal point, causing us to change course in our lives or make a move that we, otherwise, never would have made?

When we need to know the right steps to take in making a decision, the "Divine Guidance" may be right before our eyes! I believe astrology plays one of its most important roles in this instance, because it gives us clues as to what the Divine Plan is or has in store.

I'm reminded, as I write, of the incredible role HORARY astrology plays as it provides answers to questions about major events in our lives.

The real challenge is to have the FAITH and COURAGE to really let the Divine Plan unfold, and to take the action so that it will unfold.

JUPITER

As discussed previously, it's impossible to have a study or discourse on the application of metaphysics to astrological relationships without bringing the planet JUPITER into the picture. It would be difficult to experience real, sustained growth for the entity or for the two people involved without a consideration of the expansion planet. Look for Jupiter in one of the charts trine, sextile or conjunct the Sun (identity) and/or Mercury in the other. See how Jupiter in one chart aspects the ruler of the 7th House in the other. There are many other indications but these will certainly give us the clues as to the opportunity for growth between the partners.

Jupiter deserves a thorough study. I also look at Jupiter aspects in each individual chart. Robert Pelletier calls Jupiter "The higher mental faculty that seeks meaning in the affairs of life. . .every process that urges growth and expansion of consciousness is given a spiritual value." Jupiter determines what that value will be, according to the ease or difficulty of the aspects between the two charts. If the growth factor looks strong and fairly rapid, then the participants in the relationship can expect to enjoy a high spiritual rating.

If a Jupiter/Saturn square or opposition is present between the two parties, I would wave a red flag because growth of each in the relationship is going to be tested at best, and restricted at worst. Jupiter expansiveness will feel confined and frustrated. Saturn testing may strengthen Jupiter's confidence and hope, but only after an intense inner struggle.

SELF-WORTH, SELF-ESTEEM

One of the major barriers to a healthy relationship is low self-esteem on the part of either participant. In fact, it is unlikely that "togetherness" can ever really get off the ground; and if it does, the low self-esteem person will do what s/he can to sabotage it for the simple reason that s/he THINKS s/he isn't worth it. The 2nd House will always be a good barometer of a person's self-worth. What's your attitude, your outlook about what you possess?

It has been my observation that 99 and 44/100's of all people who come to any of the 12-step programs such as Alcoholics and Narcotics Anonymous, Overeaters Anonymous, or whatever, arrive with little or no self-esteem. In other words, s/he doesn't know s/he is a valuable, worthwhile person! We all know the obvious effects of substance abuse in any relationship, but in reality, lack of self-worth is the most insidious enemy. It would be interesting to research a sample group of people with admitted or known low self-esteem and see how many of them are members of or candidates for "anonymous" programs.

Let's consider the charts of two known alcoholics. (In any discussion of addiction, alcohol should be classified and included in the "drug" category.) Chart A has one of the classic alcoholism indicators, Jupiter square Neptune, too much fantasy and/or escapism. Jupiter rules the 2nd House and opposes the Moon in the 2nd House. The Moon there indicates fluctuating opinions and attitudes toward the self and any possessions. Mars, co-ruler of the Scorpio Ascendant, squares Venus which rules the 7th House (other people). Venus represents values, personal and otherwise, and it was certainly true that the owner of this chart didn't value himself very much. He has been in and out of AA, but there is evidence that he is trying to control his drinking.

The following powerful affirmations are very much a part of his recovery:

1. I AM CHANGING FROM MY OWN WORST ENEMY TO MY OWN BEST FRIEND.

2. WHAT I'M LOOKING FOR, I'M LOOKING WITH.

3. I APPROVE OF MYSELF.

4. THERE IS NOTHING IN ME THAT CRAVES ALCOHOL. I AM NOT SEEKING TO ESCAPE FROM ANYTHING.

5. I HAVE NO MEMORY OF EVER HAVING RECEIVED ANY PLEASURE OR BENEFIT FROM ALCOHOL.

Chart B had more serious consequences. He has a Jupiter/Neptune conjunction in the 2nd House square Mars in the 11th. I find that Neptune in the 2nd creates confusion over financial matters, what we own or what we're worth. An astrologer acquaintance says: "Neptune in the 2nd means that money slips through your fingers," and it would certainly apply that we don't know what we're worth. This man was a major drug dealer-drug addict, got caught and went to prison when a solar eclipse (Sun rules the Ascendant) made a conjunction to Uranus in the 10th (career and standing in the community). Uranus rules his 7th (in this case "hidden enemies") and the arrest came like a bolt out of the blue. His marriage was in a shambles at the same time.

I had advised him to quit dealing when I saw the approaching eclipse. He declined to take my advice. Intellectually, he understood my warning, but subconsciously, he didn't think he deserved to be "saved." Also, in addition to his low self-esteem, his Neptune in the 2nd manifested as an unclear concept of how to earn his money.

I counseled him when he was in prison, he was paroled early for good behavior, and he is a loyal client today. He is an active member of Alcoholics Anonymous. I currently advise him, astrologically, regarding his trading in the stock market. A composite chart of our business relationship reveals a Sun/Pluto conjunction on the Leo Ascendant and Jupiter (ruler of the 5th) trine Venus in the 11th. Time will tell about the karmic implications of that chart. He expresses in many ways now, if not in so many words, I AM A VALUABLE, WORTHWHILE PERSON.

In my own chart, I have Neptune in the 2nd square Jupiter in the 4th House. Jupiter opposes Venus. Saturn rules the 7th House of relationships and is square the Ascendant from the 4th. (No, in my early years, I did not have a good relationship with my father.) Saturn in the 4th often indicates a reverse relationship with the father and that was true for me. Further cause of low self-esteem: The idea that I was not worth a normal childhood with normal parent-son relationship.

As I shared earlier, I am a recovering alcoholic and I have a lifelong task of improving my self-esteem (currently well under way). Notice I said I am a RECOVERING alcoholic, rather than "I am an alcoholic," the usual way of identifying one's self in an AA meeting.

Two of the strongest words in metaphysics are "I AM." When we say I am _____, we perpetuate what we say we are! Emerson said: "Tell me what you talk about all day and I'll tell you what you are!"

CONCLUSION

In my relationship-counseling work, as a metaphysical/ spiritual practitioner at my church, I make it clear from the beginning that I will not pray, or "treat" (as it is called), for restoration of a relationship. Rather, I suggest that everything is coming together for "the highest good" of both parties, and that he or she let go and let the Divine Plan unfold. How I work with these people, of course, is much more involved, but that is the underlying theme. Sometimes a relationship may have to change form, take on an entirely new look, in order to continue to exist. I remind the couple that a healing will take place only if they change their thinking, and their attitude toward and about the relationship.

From the pulpit, the occult sciences including astrology are still disavowed. That's true of all churches, New Thought or Traditional. With some of the ministers, it may be ignorance of what astrology is all about. Others condone astrology, recognizing that everything in the universe is inter-connected, although there are many people in their congregations who have not reached the level of consciousness to embrace this philosophy. For those of us in astrology, it doesn't take a Nostradamus to predict that we are embarking on a stage in its development that is so exciting, that life on this planet will absolutely not be the same as we've known it in the 20th century.

Wayne Dyer said that a spiritual revolution is taking place in the 90s. Man's mind stretched to a new idea never returns to its original dimension. His greatest line: "It's the silence between the notes that makes the music." In the Universe, there's one song and we're all connected.

That idea that nothing stands alone, everyone and everything in the Universe is connected needs to be said over and over again. I know I need to reminded. It will probably happen slowly, but on second thought, since everything is changing so fast, maybe the new, enlightened state of man's beingness will take form before those of us over fifty make our transition.

Religion, medicine, psychology, philosophy, metaphysics and yes, the occult—all these tools to guide us on our journey to find the perfection and wholeness of our souls—are gradually becoming intertwined. We all need each other to make our lives better and happier. As Joan McEvers and her partner, Marion March, wrote in Vol. 1 of the series *The Only Way to ... Learn Astrology*, "We should try to understand astrology as a philosophy which helps to explain life, and not as a predictive art or science."

The dictionary defines a "pollyanna" as one characterized by irrepressible optimism. If that's what I am or what you think I am, so be it. The world consciousness not withstanding, our minds can carry us to greater heights than we ever thought possible. We can't afford the luxury of a negative thought.

What we think about, what we create in our imagination about our lives, we bring about. I'll bet you never thought Mercury would be the hot planet of the 90s, with some help from Neptune. Build an idea in your mind of the perfect relationship, perfect health, true prosperity. Build it by thinking of it, having faith in it and acting the part. And finally, come to understand the Power of the Highest Power. It's like a light switch in a dark room. The lights won't go on till you flick the switch.

Lyn Greenleaf James

Lyn Greenleaf James, while exploring the theoretical, has a no–nonsense approach to astrological consulting. She integrates modern scientific information and methodology with ancient wisdom and philosophy. A student of astrology since age 12, her background includes a degree in Medical Zoology (genetic research) Kinesiology, crystals and stones, hypnosis, body language and the philosophies and sciences of ancient civilizations.

Having grown up in an astrological family she has been able to observe family relationships firsthand, personally and astrologically. Lyn, her husband and son live happily outside of Lynden, Washington where they continue to experience their own family ties.

Having studied astrology most of her life, Lyn Greenleaf James has practiced professionally since 1982. She has lectured for international conferences, gave five years of dedicated service to Astro Computing Services where she was a founding astroconsultant. She currently writes astrological columns for *Inner Quest Magazine* (Chicago, IL) and *Fishwrapper!* (Bellingham, WA).

FAMILY TIES

It doesn't take a Psychology Ph.D. to recognize that much of the way we interact with other people in our adult lives is directly related to conditioning we received as children. Yet, family ties are one class of relationships we don't have the luxury to choose for ourselves. The relationships we have with our mothers, fathers, grandparents and siblings are all thrust upon us as a function of birth, whether we like it or not. Their personal viewpoints, biases, scars from their own childhood, and their general nature all have a direct effect on us and shade the interpretation of our horoscopes. The cycle continues as we in turn have this same effect on our children and grandchildren.

Astrology offers us a unique advantage in understanding the complexities of our family ties. This understanding can help us recognize our family's idiosyncracies and bypass childhood programming if needed. Astrology can help us keep a watchful eye on the development of our children, to nip potential developmental problems in the bud. We can even have happier relationships with spouses and other people when we no longer have the need to replay scenes from our family's past. Because our perspective about our own families is completely biased we can use an analysis of the horoscopes of our relatives to more objectively diagnose the effect of our family members on our past, present and future life; and our effect on the past, present and future of others. We can better understand the interactions of family members and how they relate to each other and us to them.

This chapter:

- Presents a unified field theory of Astro*Genetics, bridging the gap between the seemingly unrelated forms of inheritance, Biology/Genetics and Astrology.

- Focuses on the astrological interconnectedness between family members
  - astrological research to verify astrological inheritance
  - affinities as a model of astrological inheritance
  - delineating the time*space midpoint chart

- Discusses traditional and contemporary systems of analysis which can be used in conjunction with traditional synastry.

- Shows a family tree dating back 140 years and the influence each generation has had on subsequent generations.

THE COLD WAR OF INHERITANCE
ASTROLOGY VS. BIOLOGY

Before entering into a discussion of astrological signatures evident in any family tree let's look into a means of bridging the Grand Canyon of a gap between the concepts of genetic inheritance and astrological inheritance. This chapter on family ties wouldn't be complete without a statement about the biological legacy parents leave their children, since these synastries are unique because of their blood connection. The principle of genetic inheritance precludes any possible astrological inheritance. And vice versa, the central most principle of astrology discounts genetic inheritance since one's birth place date and time is independent of one's parents.

Astrologers will tell you astrology works. Doctors will tell you genetics—biological inheritance—work. So where does that leave us? To answer this let us take a little stroll down memory lane to our very beginnings—conception. A person's genetic make-up or body blueprint is determined at conception when Dad's sperm "moves in" with Mom's egg. (Wow, what a party that was . . .) The outcome of the egg-sperm genetic blending is the establishment of physiological and behavioral characteristics of a unique individual from head to toe.

By the time this unique individual is born there is a great fascination in the scrutinizing of all his or her physical features. Does the baby have Daddy's nose, Mamma's beautiful blue eyes, Grandad's quiet temperament and a tendency to Great-Great-Gramma Fergie's diabetes? The inheritances which are not evident shortly after birth sometimes show up as the child grows. Some behaviors are now even thought to be genetically predisposed and encoded in our bodies' molecules as well. The behavior of alcoholism, our scientific community has told us, leaves a genetic legacy, the tendency for alcoholism, to the next generation.[1] Again, all of this is theoretically outside the realm of the horoscope, and negating any possible interpretation about the moment of birth.

Whether the discussion focuses on behaviors or physical characteristics, it all stems back to the moment of conception and the blueprint for a unique individual in the single cell formed from the fundamental union of egg and sperm.

At this time, in this single cell is everything essential and all the knowledge necessary to create a Homo sapiens, a human being. All the tools and computers, all the energy generating devices, all the architect's plans AND a complete—enormous—library containing every aspect of the construction, development, operating manuals, reference tables and time tables to build a person—one cell at a time. This library database is encoded in the structure of a molecule called DNA (Deoxyribonucleic acid, now you know why they abbreviate it). You could call DNA your own private Library of Congress, plus the personal diaries of all of your ancestors clear back to the time humans crawled out of the first swamp, were created by God, or airshipped in by UFO's. Nothing happens in your body, since before the time your Dad's sperm met your Mom's egg, that hasn't been designed, built, managed and predicted by the library of information stored in the matrix of your DNA in EVERY cell in your body.

The whole body is made up of single cells, trillions of them, each complete in themselves, but working together as a whole unit—the person. To compare the wonders of life to the wonders of societies would be like expecting complete cooperation between all persons of 125,000 cities the size of metropolitan Los Angeles.

As complex as DNA and genetic inheritance is astrology can match it in its intricacies. Competent astrologers can spot the tendencies for alcoholism more easily than a doctor can test for the presence of the alcoholism "gene." While the cells of our body contain a blueprint, our horoscopes also can describe all aspects of us. Popularized astrology divides the world into twelve neat packages, but the astrologer knows that a horoscope is more unique than a fingerprint and won't be replicated for more than 25,000 years. Astrological technology is so versatile as to be applicable to Wall Street,

---

1. Fitzgerald, Kathleen Whalen, PhD. *Alcoholism, the Genetic Inheritance*, 1988. Doubleday: New York, p. 13.

brain surgery, volcanos, horse races, religion and philosophy geo-
political forecasting, and any other aspect of life on the planet, or an
individual's life that one wishes to better understand.

After describing the incredibly complex systems of astrology
and genetics it becomes clear that we as humans beings have two in-
tricate, apparently unrelated, systems of inheritance. The biological
or genetic inheritance we receive from our parents is perceived as
being outside of the dominion of our horoscopes, even though our
horoscopes can describe it. Our pattern of DNA is not a function of
the moments of our births. But there are at least two reasons why
biological and astrological descriptions of inheritance don't contra-
dict each other:

1. Because we are complex by nature it takes more than one system of inheritance to fully describe us. If we are body with no mind
or spirit then genetic inheritance is all that should work. If we were
light beings, where part of who we are transcends the physical
body, than biological inheritance would have no meaning. Astrology or some other multidimensional system like it would be the
only factor of inheritance. Since we are mind, spirit/soul AND
body, we need both astrological and genetic inheritance to describe
ourselves more completely. No fight need take place between biol-
ogy and astrology as they represent two ways of describing the
same individual. It is being "in tune" with our horoscopes more
than listening to the signals of our bodies which is easier for most of
us to use as a tool to give us a means for self understanding and
growth as well as a tool for tracking the cycles and rhythms of our
lives.

2. Astrology and genetics only conflict upon superficial analysis. What a funny coincidence it is that we have TWO very complex
systems for understanding ourselves. Many events we refer to as coincidences are much more closely related than just being two simultaneous but unrelated events. Upon close scrutiny a linking factor
can be found. I present the molecule DNA as the linking mechanism
between biological and astrological inheritance. Ok. So why make
such a fuss over one molecule? The functioning DNA molecule
stores the mechanism which integrates and aligns patterns of genetic inheritance with the astrological archetypes and signatures of the
natal horoscope.

We know DNA to be the physical mechanism of transference from parent to child. DNA has as of yet undocumented functions in creating a living imprint of a picture of the universe within our very being. I've heard many astrologers refer to the natal horoscope as being stamped on one's forehead. Well, that isn't quite right. It is stamped on the *Essential Substance* of the fabric of our being, in every cell of our bodies. This doesn't say the astrology is a function of genetics but that astrology is so powerful that living beings have a way to personally imprint themselves with it. That is, to be a living example of what we analyze in our solar system and in space. All this means that in addition to the beautiful symbolism and mythology in astrology, the spheres of the planets, stars and constellations etc., (not to leave out the black holers or the asteroiders) are a part of the makeup of every cell in our bodies, which we can access and utilize at any moment. The electromagnetic field of DNA and its vibrational frequency may be responsible for sending, receiving and storing information on the galactic plane as well as the earthly everyday plane.

While a longer essay on the intricacies of DNA isn't appropriate for this book it does open up new vistas for astrological theory, genetic theory and a unified field theory of Astro*Genetics which allows family astrology to be a vital living system which incorporates both biological and astrological inheritance, where the two systems work in harmony instead of contradiction.

ASTROLOGICAL INHERITANCE RESEARCHED

Anyone who has studied astrology enough to have copies of family member charts will see patterns (or sometimes a lack of obvious patterns). At astrological gatherings I have often heard stories of "astrological" inheritance:

- a preponderance of one Sun sign. "I'm the only one in my family who isn't Leo."

- a repeated planet placement (by sign or house). "Everyone in my family has Pluto in the 1st House."

Is this experience true of ALL families in the world, or just the ones that study astrology? Does it just seem like all families of humanity have some sort of astrological common thread? One of the earliest and most complete studies which examined the recurrence of astrological phenomenon in the human population was conducted by Michel and Francoise Gauquelin in the 1960s. Their original measurements were of a more astronomical than astrological nature (however, the astrological implications are obvious). They were testing for the correlations of occupation/vocation and diurnal planetary motion: planets rising, setting, at the upper culmination and at the lower culmination. In astrological language this parallels (but is not identical to) the Ascendant, the 7th House cusp or Decendant, the Midheaven and the 4th House cusp respectively. Their research, over time, involved 30,000 charts and documented that various planets rising or at the upper culmination did correlate significantly with the vocation of individuals. They established a slightly weaker, but similar correlation to the 4th House cusp and the 7th House cusp (Descendant). These Gauquelin sectors, as they are called, extend into the Cadent houses from the Angles.[2]

Another phase of their research more pertinent to the discussion at hand involved the hypothesis that planets in the four Gauquelin sectors were somehow transmitted to offspring. The data matched parent/child Gauquelin planetary placements. The number of father/child matches were statistically significant as were the number of mother/child matches. This implied that the matches were a product of some form of 'inheritance' rather than a product of pregnancy or labor.

When both parents had the same planet in the same sector the inheritance effect was nearly doubled. This involved testing 3,487 sets of Mother/Father/Child—more than 10,000 individual charts.

At this point one could say, "Astrological inheritance works!" This could mean a possible confirmation of the theories of the previous section of this chapter. But before you start counting the number of Sagittarius family members consider further research of the Gauquelins. In later studies, looking for more astrologically oriented factors the argument for astrological inheritance lost ground. The inheritance of the sign placement of the Sun, Moon or Midheaven was not statistically significant. Aspects were similarly researched by determining planetary placement within a 10 degree sector (instead of the traditional definition of an aspect by its angular separation and orb of exactness). Again, no statistically relevant correla-

---

2. Gauquelin, Michel. *Planetary Heredity*. ACS Publications: San Diego, CA, 1988.

tions were noted.

Other earlier studies had similar results:

> At the beginning of the 20th Century, the French astrologer Paul Choisnard (1867-1930) announced that he had statistically proven the laws of astral heredity: "The birth charts of blood relatives demonstrate a more frequent similarity than the charts of unrelated persons (1919)." Choisnard's law implies that there is a strong tendency for children to be born with the Sun, Moon, Ascendant and MC in the same zodiacal position as their parents.
>
> Swiss astrologer Karl E. Krafft (1900-1945) subsequently put emphasis on some of Choisnard's statements in his *Traite' d'Astrobiologie* (Astrobiological Treatise) published in 1939. This led astrologers to believe that zodiacal heredity had been proven by statistical studies. In 1960, for instance, the well-known Austrian astrologer Wilhelm Knappich stated: "Like Kepler, we consider as heredity factors the Sun, Moon, Ascendant and MC in the zodiac, the Houses and the Aspects."
>
> In *L'Influence des Astres* (The Influence of the Stars), 1955, [M. Gauquelin] put Choisnard and Krafft's claims to the test using large samples. [M. Gauquelin's] results showed that their astrological laws about heredity were based on faulty procedures.[3]

A 1984 repeat of their astonishing research of the 60s involved three years of hard work and 50,942 births. Surprisingly, it yielded results which contradicted the original study. In M. Gauquelin's words the differences between the two studies was a setback and hard to reconcile.

In English: the fact that Baby Jane has a Scorpio Sun just like Mommy is coincidence. This type of similarity isn't likely to occur in the majority of families in the world. The same holds true for aspects and house placements (Placidus houses as per the Gauquelins).

INHERITED AFFINITIES

So if the Sun sign doesn't consistently get transmitted from parent to child, what does? My comment on the last phase of the Gauquelin research is that the hypothesis being tested was slightly off the mark from the start. The extremely obvious chart placements

---

3. Ibid. pp. 41 & 42.

like parent Sun sign becoming child's Sun sign are not necessarily inherited. Any one of a number of themes in a parent's chart will appear in the child's chart, not just the one involving the Sun, Moon, Ascendant or Midheaven. We, as an astrological community cry out against the propaganda of Sun sign astrology, yet when we begin to statistically quantify our methods we have mostly tried to analyze Sun signs, planetary placements and aspects. What is transmitted is what Connecticut astrologer, Richard Roess, calls "affinities." Many other astrologers like Ann Toth have researched this idea under various names. Affinities represent astrologically related chart phenomenon linked through the natural Aries wheel and rulership rather than through traditional synastry. While the synastry between my husband and me includes Sun sesquisquare Sun (normally a less than congenial aspect) he has a 9th House Cancer Sun and I have a 4th House Sagittarius Sun. The sesquisquare aspect is evident in our marriage, of course. But the affinities of his Cancer to my 4th House and my Sagittarius Sun with his 9th House describes our Sun/Sun interaction very realistically. As you may have already guessed, there are 12 basic groups of affinities:

> 1st House—Aries—Mars
> 2nd House—Taurus—Bacchus[4] (or Venus)
> 3rd House—Gemini—Mercury
> 4th House—Cancer—Moon
> 5th House—Leo—Sun
> 6th House—Virgo—Chiron[5] (or Mercury)
> 7th House—Libra—Venus
> 8th House—Scorpio—Pluto (or Mars)
> 9th House—Sagittarius—Jupiter
> 10th House—Capricorn—Saturn
> 11th House—Aquarius—Uranus (or Saturn)
> 12th House—Pisces—Neptune (or Jupiter)

---

4. Bacchus, also called Transpluto is considered by the author as the ruler of Taurus, refer to Hawkins, *Transpluto or should we call him Bacchus, ruler of Taurus*. Dallas, TX: Hawkins Ent. Pub., 1978. As the polarity of Pluto it is very powerful. In mythology Bacchus/Dionysus, born of fire, is the benefactor and bestower of riches. Keywords: Generous, solid and steady, prophetic, charismatic, transformation to higher spiritual levels, self worth, obstinate, cantankerous, stubborn, tremendous release of destructive energy, bullheaded, possessive.
5. Many references are available about Chiron, especially in relationship to Virgo. The best: Clow, Barbara Hand, *Chiron: Rainbow Bridge Between the Inner & Outer Planets*. St. Paul. MN: Llewellyn Pub., 1987.

The best way to get comfortable with the idea of affinities is to look at a few. Consider a father with a Sagittarius Moon. Neither of his two children have Sagittarius Moons so traditional astrological inheritance fails. But never fear, affinities to the rescue. One child has a Sagittarius Ascendant, the other is a Sagittarius Sun. Do you think these family members have domestic squabbles over one's rights to maintain one's own philosophies and religious beliefs? By the way, Mom in this family has Jupiter in the 1st House and the ruler of the Ascendant in the 9th.

If one or both of your parents is strong Scorpio, strong Pluto and/or strong 8th House, you are more likely than not to inherit this type of characteristic in some form, especially if it is a dominant part of the parent's horoscope. Look at this family example:

Dad: Pluto conjunct the Sun.
Mom: Scorpio Ascendant and Sun conjunct the 8th House
    cusp.
Daughter: 1st House Pluto and the Moon in the 8th House.
Son: Stellium in the 8th House, ruler of the 8th in the 8th.

This family continues to have domestic problems when any one of them tries to manipulate or control any other family member.

An example using the lives of the rich and famous are the horoscopes of Great Britain's royal family.[6] Queen Elizabeth II has Sun at zero degrees Taurus. Prince Charles, her eldest son and heir to the throne, has his Moon at zero degrees Taurus. Both also have Mars/Jupiter conjunctions. The British royal family is one of the world's most opulent & wealthy (Taurus), highly public (Sun & Moon), acting, ceremonial monarchies (Mars, Jupiter) in the world. Mother and son's Mars/Jupiter conjunctions are different in orb, sign and house: yet like Mother, like Son.

The more one studies this mesh network of astrological affinities the more obvious the pattern of astrological family patterns becomes. This type of inheritance, because of the greatly increased number of variables, is more difficult to study statistically. I am unaware of any statistical study on the propagation of astrological af-

---

6. Chart data from Astro Computing Services Computer Data Base (1-800-888-9983). Queen Elizabeth II, London England, April 21, 1926. 1:40AM BSumT Prince Charles. London, England. November 14, 1948. 9:14PM GMT.

finities into the next generation. Affinities, because of its complexity and great number of variables, is better equipped to transmit information to the next generation. Relying again on my own DNA research I offer the following as a mechanism on how affinities can be transmitted.

ASTRO*GENETICS
A Unified Field Theory

If DNA is impregnated with the astrological signatures at birth then astrological and classically biological/genetic inheritance tendencies are interconnected. Our parents' predisposition toward planet and sign placement, and aspects, gets passed on to us through the DNA in the sperm and the ova of our Moms and Dads. Because of the complexity of the DNA replication system the astrological natal signature is broken down into component pieces. The very nature of conception, the union of half Mother donor and half Father donor, implies that the full signatures of either parent are not likely to remain intact in the children. An Aries Ascendant Mom does not mean an Aries Ascendant child; it means a child with a higher percentage of the component astrological pieces which, put together, is represented by Aries, 1st House and/or Mars.

So how does an Astro*Genetic field theory allow us to improve the quality of our family life, heal wounds from the past, create a healthy future to familial relationships? Let's approach these questions from a different angle.

The average astrologer will tell you that your state of mind regarding a particular transit will in part determine how "good" or "bad" the time of the transit will be. Your will and mentality can help you make more out of a more challenging transit, or keep you from fully capitalizing on a more bountiful transit. In the case of the alcoholic family the children are more likely receive the gene for alcoholism. They are more likely to have a predisposition towards astrological signatures which represent alcoholism. Their childhood environment reinforces the mental and psychological behaviors of alcoholism which often leads to alcoholism.

The Astro*Genetic field theory doesn't leave these children in the gutter. There is a built-in antidoom mechanism. Children who have grown up in an alcohol filled environment can't change their moment of birth but they can change their attitudes and expressions and therefore effect (and alter) their genetic predisposition towards alcoholism. They can change the effect of the imprint of astrological signatures in their physical make-up. They can choose how to express their astrological natal signatures in a way more to their benefit than their detriment.

Some individuals already exercise this level of control in their lives. In astrology we use the term "highly evolved" to denote someone who has become aware of the greater potentials of his/her own natal chart, and strives for those heights rather than being bound by the lower or average delineations of their horoscope. With this concept it becomes easy to see why Norman Cousins could cure himself of Cancer by using the Three Stooges to maintain his state of mind and a Will to be Cancer-free; altering or limiting the expression of "death" aspects in his chart.

Mental illness and personality disorders may prevent complete genetic restructuring in some individuals. All of us, though, are capable of removing the scars of a dysfunctional family and regenerating ourselves to some degree. In addition to our mental/spiritual state we can use the circumstances, drugs, psychotherapy, tai chi or yoga, diet and other tools to speed up the healing process. Remember though, these tools are just that: tools. The active ingredient in healing, whether it is physical or mental/emotional, is the mind/spirit. With the placebo effect the sugar pill will cure the headache just as easily as the new extra improved aspirin. DNA is the vehicle which links the physical reality and the astrological reality, creating the Astro*Genetic field. The mind/will/soul/spirit is the part of us that activates the transformation process.

This chapter provides astrological tools to understand yourself as a product of your family. Having this understanding, you have more ammunition to aim at the problem and begin to effect change. Just think. A 6th House Leo Sun could heal, or minimize, a heart problem and be very content to just be strong willed and prideful in the work place—a showman. (Remember to keep the entire natal chart in context, don't just pull out one planet.)

YOUR PARENTS SURVIVED YOUR BIRTH; DID YOU?

No completely incontrovertible study has yet proven any form of astrological inheritance. Whether or not ALL families on the planet have repeating astrological signs, or planets or aspects in their horoscopes one fact remains: we all have families, they all have horoscopes. Whether we consider "Dad" to be a biological parent, a sperm donor, an adoptive parent, a role model of a grandfather or someone else, this person still has a natal chart and a significant influence on our lives. The same holds true for Mom, children and other relatives. They all have charts. And, we, the astrologically knowledgeable can use the information of our family members' charts to help us understand why we handle the potentials in our chart the way we do. We all receive an astrological legacy in the form of our parents' and family members' horoscopes. This fact remains irrespective of the biological relationship between the family members.

Affinities have already been discussed as a way to track astrological themes through following generations, or back into previous generations. Affinities will often illuminate a side of a relationship which gives you greater perspective, and puts you into a better frame of mind to atone for the sins of the past. While your natal horoscope stands alone—complete—you were not born in a vacuum. You were born to parents, or adopted by parents, who had their own problems to deal with in addition to raising you. At an astrological conference in San Diego, during a seminar on the Moon's Nodes in the horoscope, Michael Lutin summed it up: "You were merely transits to your parents' charts. They got over it—you got stuck with it!" This one funny simple truth can greatly increase your understanding of who you grew up to be. The average synastry book will only teach you how to compare one individual's chart to another. It probably doesn't address the life history of stressed relating which resulted from a child, because of his/her very existence, reminding you of a "bad transit." Your children physically and personally embody a time period of your life and astrological archetypes, and live as a constant reminder; as do you to your parents and siblings.

Here is the chart of Judy Garland (inner chart—natal, cusps—natal; outer—transits).[8] During March 1946 and in the months before and after Judy Garland had changed her ways. Her new interest in the domestic side of life was immense; Neptune conjunct Jupiter and North Node. "Judy stayed away completely from pills, or her 'medication' as she had come to euphemistically call them."[7] She

7. Fitzgerald. Kathleen Whalen. PhD. *Alcoholism the Genetic Inheritance*, 1988. Doubleday: New York; p. 13.
8. Judy Garland's birth data is from the Astro Computing DataBase. Source: Fowler. Liza Minnelli's birth data is from the following reference.

was a woman with a purpose and wasn't about to take a chance on letting drugs effect her: North Node in the 12th opposed Moon in the 6th House. Transiting Mars and Saturn in the 1st House quincunxed natal Mars in the 6th House. She was determined to get her act together. Shortly after this time she experienced severe depression and insecurity about her new responsibilities; Saturn semisextile Sun, in addition to the aspects already discussed. This event, she was certain, would break the Hollywood typecasting of her as a naive teenager; transiting Sun conjunct Midheaven, Mercury square Pluto ruler of her 5th House. These transits represent the natal horoscope of Liza Minnelli.[9] Liza became the embodiment of Judy's experiences. You can now look at these transits using traditional synastry, but look at the crispness of focus you can get by considering the child as transits to the parent, and how this moment of transits (along with her Mother's experiences and attitudes) shaped Liza's life.

"She seemed somehow to know what her mother was going through, those big brown eyes sympathetic and loving"; the empathy of Neptune conjunct Jupiter and North Node.[10] Review the Saturn transits listed above. "Liza would attend fourteen different schools. bear responsibilities far beyond those a girl of her age should have had to face; suffer feelings of loneliness and alienation; make attempts to save Judy from suicide; have fights with schoolmates who ridiculed her mother (observe the Cancer planets); and develop an emotionally protective device. 'Wafting,' as she would later explain it, "is when you pretend that you're not really you. At times, 'wafting' was the only way the young Liza Minnelli would be able to deal with the terrible absurdities of her life."[11]

It has even been said that Liza is more than the personification of her mother, she IS her mother as an incredible stage presence; Sun conjunct Midheaven.

Liza physically reminded Judy of a time when Judy was unable to be a good mother. Instead of correcting this stressful time of depression and insecurity, this relationship continued through Judy's life and effected their relationship. Liza can't change her birth chart, but she can break the chains of depression and self-destruction by identifying her mother's influence on her, and healing any wounds

---

9. Spada, James. *Judy & Liza*, Doubleday & Co., Inc.: Garden City. NY, 1983, p. 39.
10. Ibid.
11. Ibid, p. 91.

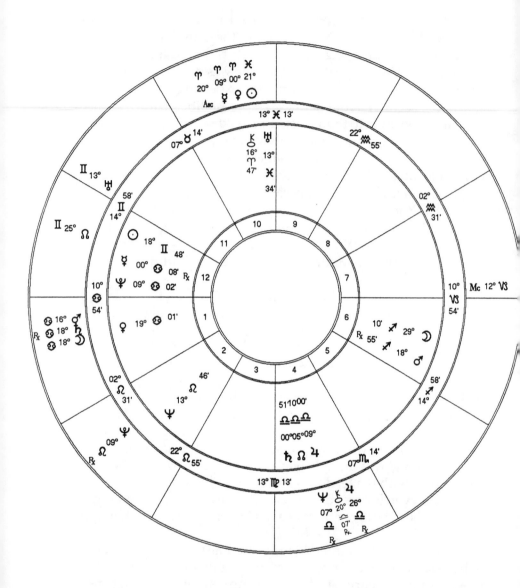

Chart 1
Liza Minnelli
Midpoint Midheaven
Judy Garland
000W00'00"

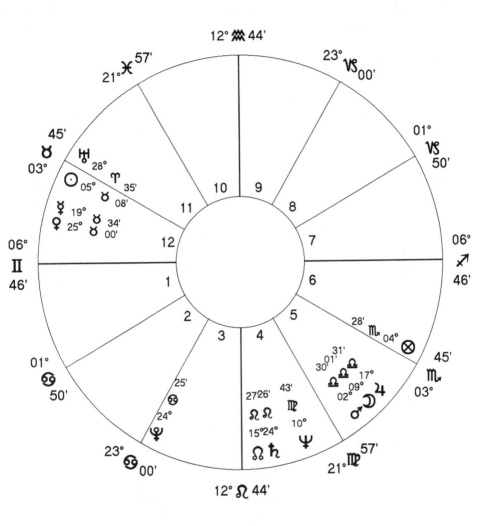

Chart 2
Liza Minnelli
Hollywood, CA
12 Mar, 1946 07:28:00 AM PST

she may still have about her relationship with her mother. Ms. Minnelli will always have Mercury quincunx her mother's Pluto, BUT she DOESN'T have to feel like she is living under the constant pressure of a Pluto aspect. Judy Garland didn't have to continually thrust her daughter into a parental I-need-you-to-care-for-me mode to the point that she did.

This is not to place fault on either the parent or the child. Through the use of the child's chart as transits to the parent's chart you can understand the programming more directly. You may be living day to day with "stuff," programming if you will, that rightfully belongs to a parent. Your kids may be developing "stuff" which will color how they handle the world from your programming. Use your favorite reference on transits as well as your best compatibility book or report to get a fuller picture.

When considering relationship analysis, chart composites and synastry aren't the only options. The author's preference is for the Davison relationship chart, also known as the time/space midpoint chart. Before the proliferation of computer astrology this chart was less than useful since it is extremely difficult to calculate by hand with accuracy. It was introduced by Ronald Davison in his books *The Technique of Prediction* and *Synastry*.[12] This type of chart averages the birth data of two individuals rather than averaging, or finding the midpoint, of two already created natal charts.

At first this chart may seem more abstract than the composite. But, its advantage in that it is REAL ephemeris data. The time/space chart will never have an impossible aspect like Mercury opposed Sun, and can be delineated in any fashion including analysis by progression.

The time/space chart represents the combined forces of two people, whether they are family or not. It will prove especially significant for two relatives with a joint venture: business, financial matters, inheritances, house purchase, any cooperative effort. Rather than using the timing of one or the other of the natal charts, use the timing presented in the time/space chart for the venture. Judy Garland and Liza Minnelli could have implemented their time/space chart to plan for joint performing engagements as well

---

12. Davison, Ronald. *Synastry*. Aurora Press. 1983, pp 244-245. *The Technique of Prediction*. Essex, England: L. N. Fowler & Co. Ltd., 1955 (reprint 1983).

as using it as a tool to better understand their relationship. The duality in their and parent/child role reversal shows up as a Gemini Ascendant and Saturn in Aquarius in the 10th House. They were perfectionistic in staging their shows—Moon in Virgo in the 5th House. Their energy and impact on the audience was mezmerizingly powerful, with Pluto in the 3rd House ruling the 6th of work activities, and Mars conjunct Sun.

TRADITIONAL METHODS OF FAMILIAL SYNASTRY

A more traditional analysis of parents in the horoscope uses the Moon to represent the Mother and the Sun or Saturn as symbolic of the Father. For most of us our mothers were lunar "mothering," yin, the nurturing influence in our early lives, but this won't be true for everyone. Especially now: this is a time when single parent families are common. Dad can just as easily play this role. The converse is true with the "fathering," yang, authority role. The validity of the Moon to Mom, Sun or Saturn to Dad correlations in humans is more of an archetype rather than a practical rulership guide in the horoscope. In some families this will work better than others.

In the families where traditional archetypes fail I refer you again to the work of Richard Roess on parental archetypes. His approach, combined with Jungian analysis and the groundwork of Greene and Sasportas, examines a archetype reversal with Mom represented by Saturn and the archetype of Dad represented by the Moon.

A more contemporary way of interpreting the luminaries in ANY person's chart involves using the Sun and the Moon, respectively as the male and female roles one has in relationships. Whether you are a man or a woman you still simultaneously possess the masculine and feminine, or yin and yang. Males and females in your childhood environment, whether they were biological parents or others, demonstrated these roles. Your parents and the society you are raised in help determine how well you cope with these natal energies. Keep in mind that in our more open contemporary society your children may be learning masculine behaviors from a woman and vice versa.

OUT ON A LIMB
AN ASTROLOGICAL FAMILY TREE

My 5th House Saturn has given me an extra special appreciation for developing family roots. That, an overexposure to Kunta

Kinte instead of disco, and a case of the genealogy bug. Becoming an astrologer allowed me to study long since dead characters in great detail, as well as knowing the living and listening to their stories of the deceased. I worked with birth dates only, since times weren't available, nor were they as meticulously noted a hundred years ago as they are with today's newborns. For unknown birth times I used Noon solar charts.

In the interest of simplicity and a small enough data base to manage effectively I chose to work only with planetary conjunctions of four degrees or less. Some lunar conjunctions are speculatively noted in parentheses. I did count aspects to the angles only for those charts where the birth times were certain; for this same reason I did not consider any arabic parts. Any partial analysis technique will only give a partial picture. But, conjunctions represent a blending of planetary energies—the energies between the two people. These conjunctions are meant to be a quick window into families ties. No bias is intended against any other aspects. Some of my best friends are non conjunction aspects.

The most amazing part of this research was not that parents and their children have relationship issues evident in their synastries. Everyone who has a parent or a child has family relationship issues. The amazing part was comparing the similarities between grandparents and parents, and then these parents to their children, and so on. This progression of astrological patterns—from generation to generation to generation shows a history of development that simple two person synastry couldn't describe.

Observe the conjunctions between this mother and her son, an unplanned pregnancy and an only child (listed as Gramma & Dad respectively in the table). While there was great love between man, woman and child, this family was off to a quicker than expected start with a shotgun wedding. But, there is no such thing as accidents or coincidences; the nodal conjunction alone demonstrates a strongly karmic relationship. The Saturn/Jupiter, a real push-me-pull-you difference in perspectives compounded by a clash of strong wills. Saturn/Jupiter, Node/Node.

His early examples of relationships as demonstrated by his mother were confusing to him (Venus/Neptune). While the Dad was still a toddler Gramma's mother died in childbirth, leaving an entire litter of children. As the oldest child she felt compelled to raise her siblings along with her son. Her son felt neglected and pushed

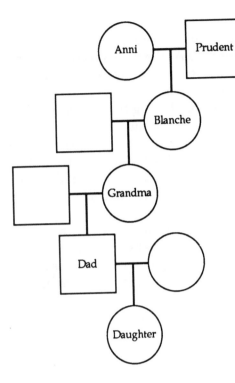

SIMPLIFIED FAMILY TREE
Simplified Family Tree

A = Ascendant (1st House cusp)
D = Descendant (7th House cusp)
⚉ = Bacchus (Transpluto)
⚷ = Chiron

Conjunctions: of 4 or less

Dad – G'ma

☊ ☌ ☊
☊ ☌ ☊
♀ ☌ ♆
⚉ ☌ ♆
♄ ☌ ♃

Dghtr – Dad

A ☌ ☊
D ☌ ☊
⚷ ☌ ☊
⚇ ☌ ♆
⚉ ☌ ☿

Dghtr – G'ma

♂ ☌ ⚉
☊ ☌ ⚷
A ☌ ☊
D ☌ ☊
☉ ☌ ♂
♆ ☌ ☿

Dad – Albert
(his G'pa)

⚷ ☌ ⚇
⚷ ☌ ♆
⚉ ☌ ☊
♀ ☌ ☊
♀ ☌ ♄
(☿ ☌ ☽)
A ☌ ♅

G'ma – Blanche
(her mom)

☊ ☌ ☿
⚇ ☌ ♄
⚷ ☌ ☉

G'ma – Albert
(her dad)

☉ ☌ ♃
♆ ☌ ☊
⚉ ☌ ⚇
♀ ☌ ⚷
♄ ☌ ⚷
♆ ☌ ♄

Blanche – Prudent
(dad)

⚉ ☌ ☊
♆ ☌ ⚉
♀ ☌ ⚉
☉ ☌ ♆
♅ ☌ ♃

Blanche – Anni
(mom)

(♃ ☌ ☽)
♆ ☌ ⚉
⚇ ☌ ☉
♂ ☌ ☊
(☽ ☌ ♀)
⚉ ☌ ♆
⚉ ☌ ⚇

off to the side as he watched his mother care for all of these "intruders." (Venus and Bacchus/Neptune.) At the time, shortly after the Great Depression family resources became extremely limited because of the needs of these extra children.

The son has spent most of his life feeling hurt by his perceptions of his mother's actions, and his relationships for 50+ years suffered accordingly (Venus ruling Libra and relating in general). So far this is a fairly standard type of analysis. But now, when this (hurt) boy grows up he brings these lessons, feelings and events with him. The way he learned how to be a human being will effect the young souls he raises.

The fateful day comes when he is the father with a new baby daughter in his arms. This daughter has been planned for and the Dad-to-be put in his order to have a girl child just like his Mom. This she is. Even in his confusion about his turbulent relationship with his mother he names his daughter after her. As his daughter grows she continues to look like Gramma, talking and acting like Gramma.

The daughter now embodies the strong nodal relationship tie between her Dad and her Gramma; her Ascendant axis is opposed/conjunct both of their nodal axes. She is automatically caught up in 30 years of relationship trouble that has nothing to do with her. Daughter and Gramma have the same strong fiery personality, Mars/Bacchus, Sun/Mars. Over time Dad projects his image of Gramma onto his daughter (which was easy to do since they were so much alike in the first place). He begins to relate to his daughter in the same manner which he related to his mother.

When Dad interacts with his daughter, she never seems to cut him any slack; her Bacchus conjuncts his Mercury. By the time she is an adult their relationship is at an end with all ties broken and civil communication almost impossible. Where the boy/father felt neglected and deceived by his mother, Venus and Bacchus conjunct Neptune, he now uses his powers of communication to take away the daughter's self-control and personal power (Mercury/ Bacchus and Neptune/Pluto). In this family the term for this was "Daddy lectures," sometimes irrelevant, mostly ranting and always a very long litany on personal conduct. She reacts as strongly to this manipulation as her Gramma did when Dad was a boy having a temper tantrum.

One can argue that the Pluto/Neptune conjunction is generational and not at all personally relevant. Yes, that's true. But, the Gramma/Dad Neptune/Venus creates a history of Neptune contacts that prefaces the father-daughter Neptune/Pluto. Even as far back as Gramma's grandparents there was a Neptune, Pluto and Bacchus conjunction. Just because there are other families in the world with the same outer planet synastry pattern does not make these contacts any less important in the personal lives of the individuals who have them.

In this family everyone has experienced a great deal of healing. Dad has come to acknowledge his inner hurt with his mother and has become conscious of how his projection of his mother onto his daughter has affected their relationship. Daughter has come to understand more of the history of her Dad and her Gramma, and also consciously rejected the merry-go-round of their verbal and emotional abuse and stopped participating. Father and daughter can now openly express their love and have long since stopped perceiving each other's actions and words as personally confronting and insulting. Now they can experience aspects in a positive manner; instead of fighting and verbal abuse they can have the greatest of theoretical discussions and debates, Bacchus/Mercury.

This father and daughter broke the chain of family ties which was binding and suffocating their relationship. Looking back a generation or two we see where some of these problems had their roots. Gramma had parents too. She was the first of many children and probably an unplanned pregnancy (she repeated the pattern with the birth of her son). Her mother died giving birth to her youngest brother. Her Dad was generous to a fault and as a result neglected his family in favor of being generous in the pub and at the gaming tables. Gramma loved her mother. There were practical open communications, Mercury/Saturn and Node/Mercury and Gramma had a healing effect on her mother Blanche, Chiron/Sun.

Gramma hated her father, Albert. Her planetary conjunctions with him show the power struggles: Bacchus/Mercury, Pluto/Bacchus, and Neptune/Saturn. With this man as a male role model she unconsciously projected onto her son (Dad). The Pluto and Neptune conjunctions Gramma had with Albert, Albert has with his grandson. In addition we can see the influence of Chiron between Dad and Albert; Gramma healed some of her negative feelings toward father, Albert, with her son at his expense. Gramma has Bacchus/Mercury with Albert; her son has Bacchus/Mercury with his daughter. Same song, different generation.

Not much is known about Gramma's early life, therefore describing her relationship with her parents, Anni and Prudent is questionable. Anni and Prudent have conjunctions with Blanche which shows in her relationship with Gramma. That cycle breaks as subsequent generations don't have Sun conjunctions.

This family is spiritually awake and is currently becoming increasingly aware of the next generation and the past of previous generations. They are effectively breaking the patterns of abuse and manipulation that their parents and grandparents, and their parents before them perpetuated (consciously or unconsciously).

Of course, this was not a quantitative study, but a qualitative one. In the limited number of family trees I have examined I have found exciting results. Quantitative studies would be necessary to establish whether these results would be true for the human population at large.

With the family described above there was a very strong nodal contact consistent in all generations, even though only a few branches of the family tree were described. Since the Nodes represent our relationships with other people it makes sense that synastry with family members would have a consistent nodal emphasis. This emphasis is also an indicator of the karmic ties that most family members have. Remember, you are stuck with your family members, so you have to work out your karmic ties with them whether you like them or not. When the birth times were known conjunctions to the angles were always present.

In some of the families I have studied there were characteristics or events and behaviors that seemed to skip every other generation. The history of the episode or behavior two generations back seemed to be perpetuated through the intervening generation where it was not expressed. In these cases a study of horoscopic family trees was especially useful in giving the younger generation more ammunition to break an obsession or dysfunctional habit.

In examining planetary conjunctions I found that namesake family members have a greater number of conjunctions to the angles; the angles representing one's identity. In one case of a father and son, the son having the father's first, middle and surnames, the conjunctions included: Midheaven/Ascendant, Moon/Ascendant, Mars/Venus, Mercury/Ascendant and three other Mercury conjunctions (Mercury rules communication). Namesakes with only the first or middle name of a relative had a less extensive list of conjunctions.

Often a child would have only one or two conjunctions with one parent, yet have a great number with the other parent. The easier relationship was with the parent with fewer conjunctions. People with few conjunctions sometimes got out of touch with each other or had little contact, but the contact they did have was more harmonious. The most frustrating, aggravating relationships were represented by family members with the greatest number of conjunctions. These were the ones who represented the biggest life crises. These were also the ones who tended to stay in closer contact. The following table represents the total number of times each parent and child's planet was involved in a conjunction. Note the low numbers represented by the angles and the Moon. Remember that for most of these ancestors birth times were unknown, making conjunctions to the Moon and the angles impossible to determine in most cases.

Summary Parent/Child Conjunctions

No. of ☌			Parent's ——	Child's	
9			none	♀	Total no. of:
8			☿ ♆	⚷	conjunctions: 69
7			☉	☊	Parent/Child: 13
6			☊☋	☋☊	Ave. no. of ☌ per
5			⚷ A	D ♄ ♆	parent/child: 5.3
4			♀ ♄	♀	
3	D ♂	♃ ⚷		A M I ♂ ⚷	
2	M ☊☋	♅ ♀		☿ ☉	
1	I ☽			♃	
0			none	☽ ⚷	

A= Ascendant (1st House cusp)
D= Descendant (7th House cusp)
M= Midheaven (10th House cusp)
I=IC (4th House cusp)

In this particular family the children's planets contacted their parents Mercury and Neptune with the greatest frequency. According to this family, they feel certain that psychic intuition has been inherited. This family also readily acknowledges that each generation of children independently do as they please, usually in total defiance of their parent's wishes; children's Pluto and Bacchus conjunct planets in their parent's charts more than any other planet. At the time of this writing no statistics are available on what the average number of conjunctions between a parent and a child are. An average of 5.3 represents just one family. In theory, a family that is personally more interconnected would have a higher number of aspects. A family where members peacefully go their separate ways, leaving no unfinished (karmic) ties may have a very low average number of aspects. These statistics involve five generations of births from 1852 through 1962. A larger number of generations in the sample size will also effect the statistics.

Look at your own family. Listen to the stories your parents tell about your grandparents. If you have living grandparents listen to their side of the stories. Listen to the stories they tell of their youth, and their parents and grandparents. When you cross reference this mass of information with your experiences of your relatives and their horoscopes (use a solar chart if you don't have the birth times) you will begin to see a matrix of astrologically interconnecting charts. Your net of astrological ancestry can emphasize aspects of your idiosyncracies; a way of delineating your natal horoscope in a context of your experiences. Don't complain about the awful aspects of your family members. Learn from them. Not only will you benefit, but your extra insights may facilitate a change in attitude in your relatives, too. When they see the changes in you they may become more aware of the changes they need to make in themselves. Examine your life and see how your children are perceiving you. This is not about blame, it is not what your parents did to you. It is about understanding literally "where your parents are coming from" and breaking the chain of dysfunctionality in whatever form it may be present in your own particular family tree. Cutting out the dead wood of your family tree means being able to stand back far enough to see the whole tree at one time and looking at its growth pattern. In tree trimming lingo this is called "lacing." Like lace, it is a delicate process which considers each branch of the tree as special, and carefully examines each one individually as to whether it needs to be cut out completely or just trimmed and if so, how much it is to be trimmed. Lace your own family tree armed with an astrological measuring and cutting tool. Here's to the health of your tree.

Maria Kay Simms

Maria Kay Simms, who has been professionally active as an artist since 1962, and as an astrologer since 1975, has two major areas of interest in her work. Her technical specialty is Uranian Astrology, and she is the author of the lavishly illustrated introduction to Uranian and the 90° dial, *Dial Detective*. Her interest in exploring the metaphysical/philosophical/religious aspects of astrology led to her first book, *Twelve Wings of the Eagle*, and to the booklet (co-authored with her late husband, Neil F. Michelsen), *Search for the Christmas Star*. In recent years she has further developed the "Goddess emerging" subtheme of *Twelve Wings* through numerous lectures, articles, and most currently, through the development of astrological symbolism in sacred ritual. She is also the designer/illustrator of each of her books, as well as the cover designer of many others. Previously a painter in oils, she now most often "paints" with a Mac II computer.

Maria resides in San Diego, where she is the president of Astro Communications Services, Inc. (new corporate name for the recently merged Astro Computing Services and ACS Publications). She is also the Director of Publications for National Council for Geocosmic Research, Inc. (NCGR) and editor of *NCGR Journal*. She is certified as a professional consulting astrologer by NCGR and by American Federation of Astrologers. Originally from Illinois, she holds the BFA degree from Illinois Wesleyan University. She is the mother of three daughters, and is soon to become a grandmother.

THE IMPORTANCE OF ELEMENTS
IN RELATIONSHIPS

I. Elements in Personality—common idiom
II. How to Determine elements in a horoscope
    A. Quadruplicities—signs
        1. planets in signs
        2. planets houses
    B. Chart "breakdown"
        1. emphasis
        2. lack
III. Visualization exercise
IV. Elements within self
V. The attraction of opposites
VI. Balance within self
VII. Balance within relationships
VIII. The true relationship—within self
    A. projection
    B. mirroring
IX. Conclusion

"What a fiery temper he has!"
"She fairly burns with intensity."
"Her? Nothing but an air-head!"
"He has such a breezy style of speaking."
"What a stick-in-the-mud you are!"
"Now she's what I call a real down-to-earth-person."
"He's drowning in self-pity."
"What a deep well of feeling she expresses."
"Now, theirs is a fiery relationship."
"She always has a way of dowsing his plans with cold water."
"He just smothers her!"
"Did she ever light a fire under him!"
"He's like a breath of fresh air in her life."
"She's a real clinging vine—strangling him."

Fire, Earth, Air and **Water**—the four elements of the ancients are such a familiar part of our idiom that they are taken for granted and understood by all, even by those who would never think to connect them with astrology. At the roots of these idiomatic expressions are ancient symbolic systems the associated the elements with aspects of humanity. Fire is energy, or Spirit. Earth is matter, or Body. Air is the intellect—Mind. Water is emotion, feeling, or Soul.

An important way to categorize the signs of the zodiac is by four "family" groups known as the **quadruplicities**, an astrological term that refers to the four elements. Aries, Leo and Sagittarius are known as Fire signs; Taurus, Virgo and Capricorn are called Earth signs; Gemini, Libra and Aquarius are designated as Air signs; and Cancer, Scorpio and Pisces are Water signs. So, if for example. you were born when the Sun was in Aries, Leo or Sagittarius, you might be expected to have a fiery personality. If you have Sun in Taurus, Virgo or Capricorn, you're likely to be "down-to-earth," and so on.

One of the questions astrologers are most frequently asked is, "What sign am I most compatible with?" The popular, standard answer groups the signs according to the elements, with the theory that people are more likely to get along well with other people of the same element. Sun sign literature often expands that stock answer by saying that Earth signs blend well with Water, and Fire signs do well with Air signs, etc.

But wait—you are much more than just a Sun sign! And if you have a major planetary emphasis in your horoscope in a different element than your Sun, the element of your Sun sign just might not seem to fit. And further, that new person to whom you are attracted might be just right for you, even though his/her Sun sign is in an element that is said to be "incompatible" with your own. If we are going to seriously talk about the compatibility or incompatibility of people according to the elements, we must first look beyond the Sun sign to see what the most important element is for each individual. Then we must take a much closer look at how the elements nourish, squelch or balance each other, both within each individual, and when one individual meets another.

In order to determine your dominant elemental characteristic we need to consider the **whole** chart, not just the Sun. We need to determine in what element or elements the majority of your planets are found. This is called a "chart breakdown" by element. The simplest way to do this is just to count how many planets are in each element. You would have a total of 10 points, one each for Sun, Moon, Mercury, Venus, Mars, Jupiter, Saturn, Uranus, Neptune and Pluto. Many astrologers (including me) also count the Ascendant and Midheaven,[1] and "weight" the count by giving an extra point each to the Sun, Moon, Ascendant and Midheaven.[2]

To take an example, a breakdown of a chart with the Sun in Taurus and Moon in Leo would mean 2 points for Earth (Taurus) and 2 points for Fire (Leo). A Pisces Ascendant would indicate 2 points for Water, Mars in Gemini would be only 1 point for Air, and so on. Suppose the final tally is:

Fire: Midheaven (Sagittarius), Moon (Leo), Mercury (Aries), Saturn (Aries) = 6

Air: Venus (Gemini), Mars (Gemini), Jupiter (Aquarius) = 3

Earth: Sun (Taurus), Uranus (Taurus), Neptune (Virgo) = 4

Water: Ascendant (Pisces), Pluto (Cancer) = 3

Here we have a person whose Sun sign is earthy Taurus, but whose dominant element *by sign* is Fire. Now we also need to do a chart breakdown *by house*.

Since, in the natural zodiac, each sign corresponds to a house (see illustration 1) we also attribute elemental characteristics to planetary emphasis in the houses of individual horoscopes. Planets in houses seem to take on some of the characteristics of the sign that is "naturally" associated with that house, even though a different sign may actually be on the cusp.[3]

In our example sign breakdown, the Sun is in Taurus, but with a Pisces Ascendant, the Sun and Taurus may well occupy the 3rd House, "natural" home of Gemini. Therefore, in a house breakdown, the Sun would be counted as Air. Since the Ascendant and

---

1. The Ascendant is the degree on the cusp of the 1st House and the Midheaven is the degree on the cusp of the 10th House. These degrees which are found by calculating the time and location of birth are considered to be very important "personal points" in an individual's personality. Since these degrees change about every four minutes, even identical twins will often have different Ascendant and Midheaven degrees from each other.

2. Some also count other bodies like the Moon's Node or asteroids but for simplicity's sake, we will not consider them. Personally I think if you do add other bodies than the 10 "traditional" planets, you should "weight" them at 1/2 point.

3. For example: Aries is the 1st House of the natural zodiac. A person who is born with the Sun in Aries would have the Sun in the 1st House if s/he was born just before sunrise. But if s/he was born an hour after sunrise, the Sun would be in the 12th House, and it is likely that the cusp of the 1st House would be Taurus, the 2nd House Gemini and so on. Think of the chart like a clock (see illustration).

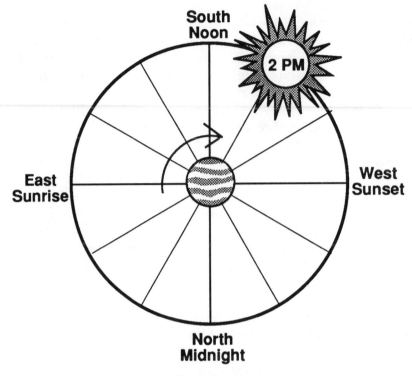

Illustration 1

Midheaven determine the houses, they are not counted as individual factors in the house breakdown. If a planet falls at an earlier degree in a sign than the degree on a house cusp, it will be in the house before. A complete house breakdown of this chart (illustration 2) would be as follows:

> **Fire:** Moon, Uranus, Pluto = 4
> **Air:** Sun, Neptune = 3
> **Earth:** Mercury, Saturn = 2
> **Water:** Venus, Mars, Jupiter = 3

Again we have slightly more strength in the Fire element. This Taurus Sun, whom the standard Sun sign literature would tell to avoid Fire signs as incompatible, might get along very well, indeed, with a partner who has the Sun in Sagittarius (and other factors also emphasizing Fire), for example—and might even find a relationship with a partner whose chart emphasizes Virgo (a sign that the simplistic "stay-in-your-own-element" theory would recommend as compatible with Taurus) to be much too confining.

I trust that I've sufficiently emphasized the necessity to consider the chart as a whole in this, or any other system, of relationship analysis. Let's consider the importance of the elements in personality. Visualizing the "real" elements can aid our understanding of how the elemental personality types can either complement or conflict with each other. Keep in mind these few, basic key words for each element:

Fire—energy, vitality, passion, adventure, impulse, spirit, romance
Earth—solid, stable, practical, strong, sensual, physical, dense
Air—circulating, free, changeable, conscious thought, rational, logical
Water—deep, mysterious, emotional, intense, intuitive/subconscious thought

Now allow my words to create pictures in your thoughts, and let the interaction of the elements of the physical world suggest to you how the symbolic elements might also interact with each other.

VISUALIZE FIRE AND EARTH

You are camped at the edge of a meadow. All around the earth is green, warmed by the Sun. **This is balance.** But now imagine that the Sun shines bright and hot, day after day, and the grass and the flowers begin to wilt, tired from the relentless energy that gives no rest. Yet at night it is cool and as you sit by the meadow you decide to start a small fire. You watch the bright flames crackle and glow and your spirit begins to soar, dreaming your dreams. Soon a spark flies and ignites a patch of dried grass nearby and begins to spread, unnoticed by you in your reverie. **Too much fire!** The heat builds and finally shocks you back to reality. You grab a shovel and pile earth on the fire, putting it out. **Too much earth!** Let's try again. You still really want to have a fire, glowing and sparkling and full of life. But it can't be allowed to burn out of control. What to do? You decide to build a hearth of stones to contain the fire safely. **This is balance**—energy and form. spirit and matter, dreams and reality, enthusiasm and pragmatism—working together!

VISUALIZE FIRE AND AIR

Imagine you are holding a lighted candle. The air is fairly still; the flame burns brightly upward. Now blow a strong breath of air at the flame. Out it goes! **Too much air.** Light the candle again. and then put a glass over it. Soon it's out again. **Not enough air.** Once more, let there be light! This time, just try blowing gently at the flame. Aha! The fire burns even more brightly. But now it has direction. **Balance!** The flow of air can influence the direction and the intensity of the fire and can stimulate its growth or put it out. Fiery vitality needs the conscious direction of intellect to provide focus, but too much abstract logic can be stifling.

Now, imagine sitting in a cold room, trying to concentrate on some paperwork that you need to do. Feel the chilly air on your face, your arms, all over your body, so cold you can barely think. You wish you could just huddle under a blanket and go to sleep. Not enough fire. Build a fire in the fireplace. As you watch the bright, cheerful flames, notice how the air around you begins to feel much warmer and soon you feel much better—are stimulated to get to work again. Balance! But, lost in your thoughts you forget about the fire. A spark is thrown outside the fireplace igniting a pile of your papers. The flames burn out of control, quickly consuming both the "air" of your thoughts and the air within the room, making it difficult to breath ... too much fire. Pure intellect is "cold"—it needs fire's adventuring spirit to stimulate its purpose. But fire's impulse out of control can rattle anyone's ability to think or reason.

VISUALIZE FIRE AND WATER

Let's go back to our campfire now safely contained on its hearth of stone, and put on a pan of water for a nice cup of tea. Soon the water simmers. **This is balance.** But your attention wanders—more of your fiery, romantic spirit's dreams perhaps, or the energetic rush to do six other things while you wait. Your water continues to heat, to boil, to steam and then is gone—and the smell of your scorched pan brings you running with a little surge of fear coupled with anger at yourself for doing such a dumb thing. **Too much fire** for your frazzled, watery feelings! In your upset you overreact and dump a big pail of water on the fire. It sizzles and dies. No more cheery flames and warmth. No tea. **Too much water!** Emotions out of control. Stress can do that to you. But does that mean you should give up your dreams and sit and wallow in a stagnant puddle? Calm down and let's do an instant replay, back to the smell of the scorched pan. This time pour a cup of water in—slowly. A little sizzle and steam, but soon a gentle simmer again. Now pour your cup of tea and relax a bit, renewing your energy. **This is balance!**

VISUALIZE EARTH AND AIR

Remember the three little pigs and the big, bad wolf? If you build the structures of your life with flimsy materials like the first little pig's straw house, the first big gust of the winds of change are sure to blow it down. The "big, bad wolf" could be no more than a new thought—an idea that makes your current reality seem invalid or illogical. Whoosh! There it goes. But now where do you live? **Too much air!** Now build a nice, solid structure like the third little pig's brick house. Imagine yourself in that brick house, so concerned about your safety and security that you've barricaded the door and boarded up the windows. And there you sit. Kind of stuffy, isn't it? Not a breeze anywhere. Soon the air turns stale. and because you've so carefully caulked up every crack against any possible intrusion by the big, bad wolf, eventually the air is all gone and you're finding it increasingly difficult to breathe at all. **Too much earth!** What to do? Let's pry the boards off those windows and install storm windows that will lock when necessary, but with screens that can let in the air. Let's install a screen door, too and put in a skylight and a ceiling fan. Much better. Just a few new ideas can help you change your structure without destroying it. **This is balance!**

VISUALIZE EARTH AND WATER

Let's return to our dried up meadow, turn the soil and plant some new grass seed. This new growth in your life needs only a bit of tender, loving care to flourish and be strong. Imagine a beautiful, nurturing rain that begins to turn it green again. **This is balance.** But now imagine that the rain goes on for days and days raising the level of the water in the nearby stream bed, overflowing its banks. Soft top soil begins to wash into the stream clogging its path. Trails of water are sent off in several different directions cutting grooves in the soil and washing away the sprouting seeds. What a muddy mess! You try to rake things into place again and your shoes get stuck. That's what happens with **too much earth and too much water!** Stuck in the mud.

Now visualize standing on a sandy beach watching the waves come in. Soon the water laps about your feet and it feels good. But now a bigger wave comes and as it flows outward again, you feel the sand go out from under your feet and you nearly lose your balance. So may the structures you have built in your life be as the sand, when the currents of emotion take over. **Too much water.** Now climb over the rocks, away from the beach and stand on a cliff where you can see with a different perspective. Notice how the rocks contain the waters of emotion, of soul. Yet notice how those waters flow around the rocks, into every nook and cranny, reaching out for the soil, nurturing the land, the body of the Mother. The waters must be contained by earth. even as a protective border of stones might have saved your new grass seed from that heavy rain. **Too much earth?** Perhaps... too much containment, too much suppression can hold back the soul for a time. Yet eventually the water will wear away even the solid rocks and new forms and structures will be created. Such is the relationship of body and soul.

VISUALIZE AIR AND WATER

Think about a fresh, gentle breeze blowing over the waves. Smell that sea air. Feel the serenity of the scene. **This is balance!** Now the winds change and increase, blowing the waves into a frenzy, causing them to crash into the land destructively. **Too much air.** The angry waves flow over creatures and plants of earth that live near the water and deprived of air, some die. **Too much water.** Breathe deeply now... relax. Let all the thoughts and images provoked here return to balance and serenity.

Air and water both symbolize ways of thinking. Air is conscious thought, left-brain, logical. Water is intuitive, right-brain thought—often referred to as subconscious or unconscious. Interesting how even our choice of words has devalued the aspect of thinking associated with water. Think about that....

And so we have experienced how we may blend with constructive balance or destructive imbalance the down-to-earth practical realities of life with the logic of air, with the mysteries of emotion and with the inspiration of fire. It is very important to realize that this blend of the elements and the balance or imbalance, is not just a factor in our interactions with other people who emphasize the same or different elements than we do. The most important relationship we have among the elements is the one that exists within ourselves! If we are in balance we are likely to be at peace with ourselves and therefore able to appreciate others just as they are without "buying into" interactions where we allow ourselves to be "burned up," "dowsed," "buried," "blown away" or any number of other terms we could use to express being "thrown off balance."

PROJECTION

So what happens when one is out of balance—and how do you tell if you are out-of-balance? Easy! Look at your primary relationships. If one of the elements is suppressed or neglected within your own personality, the all important special someone in your life is probably expressing that element quite strongly. In fact, he or she is likely to be overdoing it, and you are experiencing varying degrees of upset because of that! This is known as projection.

It's an old adage that opposites attract. Why? I think it is because we all have an instinctive need for wholeness—for balance of all the elements within. But most of us are not clearly aware of that need. We find the traits associated with one or more of the elements—usually those indicated by our chart breakdown—to be "natural" and easy. This is the way we are. The traits associated with another element feel uncomfortable somehow and we suppress them. Then we go out and find or attract someone else to be that suppressed element for us! We project our own need for that element onto the other person.

All this could be OK, except that all too often, we become very uncomfortable or even upset with the other person's behavior! The charts of Myra and Cal provide a good example of two people who each projected onto the other the personality needs that were undeveloped in themselves.

MYRA AND CAL

Myra's chart breaks down to Earth and Water. Her Ascendant is in Air but only one planet is in Fire (Pluto, a slow-moving planet that is in Leo for everyone in her age group). Yet aspects in her chart focus on planets in Fire houses, particularly the 5th House of creative self-expression, which holds the Moon, with Venus, the ruler of the 5th conjunct Mars in the 1st.

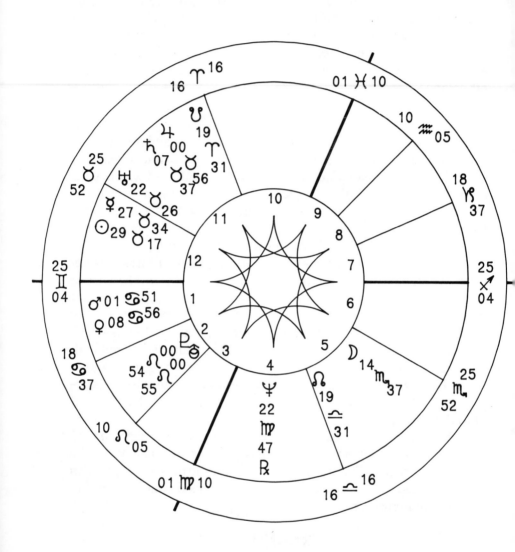

Natal Chart
Myra
20 May 1940 7h20m 0s EDT
Trenton, NJ
Koch 40N14 74W46

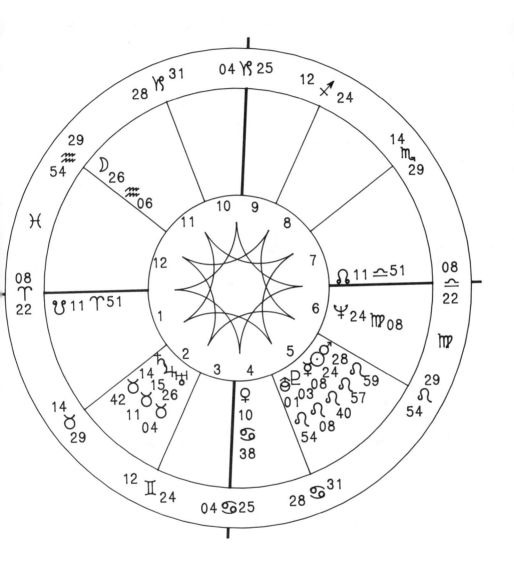

Natal Chart
Cal
17 Aug 1940 21h30m 0s EDT
New York, NY
Koch 40N45 73W57

Signs: Fire—Pluto = 1
           Earth—Sun, Mercury, Jupiter, Saturn, Uranus, Neptune = 7
           Air—Ascendant = 2
           Water—Moon, Venus, Mars, Midheaven = 6
Houses:Fire—Venus, Mars, Moon = 4
           Earth—Pluto = 1
           Air—Jupiter, Saturn, Uranus = 3
           Water—Sun, Mercury, Neptune = 4
Totals: Fire—5, Earth—8, Air—5, Water—10

Myra was raised in a very stable home where practical values were emphasized and she was a dutiful daughter who always did the "right thing" and got good grades in school. As a young girl Myra always fantasized about being in the limelight—perhaps a pop singer with a glamorous lifestyle and lots of travel. She was attractive and had a good voice, but she was fearful of taking a risk on such an impractical goal; so she went away to college and majored in English literature, planning to become a teacher. In her senior year she met Cal.

Cal is Fire personified. He has a stellium in Leo, with Aries rising and only Uranus and Neptune in Earth (both slow-moving planets that are in Taurus and Virgo respectively for everyone in his age group) and Capricorn is on his Midheaven, which according to count gives him quite a bit of Earth. But Uranus squares his Leo Sun which is conjunct Mars, a Fire planet, adding even more energy to his dramatic flair. It's not surprising that Fire strongly dominates his personality.

Signs: Fire—Sun, Mars, Mercury, Pluto, Ascendant = 7
           Earth—Midheaven, Jupiter, Saturn, Uranus, Neptune = 6
           Air—Moon = 2
           Water—Venus = 1
Houses:Fire—Sun, Mars, Mercury, Pluto = 5
           Earth—Jupiter, Saturn, Uranus, Neptune = 4
           Air—Moon = 2
           Water—Venus = 1
Totals: Fire—12, Earth—10, Air—4, Water—2

Cal was a music major who had a part time job playing and singing in a popular band. He too had been raised in a stable home by very down-to-earth parents who enjoyed and encouraged his musical talent, but made no secret of the fact that they would have preferred that he major in business administration. They often had to "bail Cal out" of the adventurous exploits that got him in trouble with the university administration, or when impulsive spending left him broke when bills were due. Cal's concession to his practical parents was an agreement to fulfil the necessary requirements to get his teaching certificate so that he would at least have a job to fall back on if his hopes for a musical career were not fulfilled.

Myra and Cal met in their senior year when they were assigned to the same school as student teachers. They were instantly attracted to each other. Cal represented everything that Myra secretly wanted to be and Myra's warmth and quiet strength seemed like a safe anchor for Cal—she seemed to fit right in with his mother and sister. They were engaged before the year was over, and married shortly after graduation to the delight of both of their families.

For a while the marriage succeeded wonderfully. Both taught school at first, but Cal continued to play and sing on the side, looking for the opportunity that would make him a full time performer. In this he was fully encouraged by Myra who constantly cheered him on, certain he would become a star. Finally Cal got his "break" and he quit his job in the middle of a semester to become the lead singer with a new group. The job didn't pay much, but it was his big chance. Myra was thrilled for him and readily agreed to keep teaching so that they would have a stable income. Whenever she could she went to see him perform and loved every minute of it. Cal required a lot of encouragement and ego boosting, and Myra was good at providing it.

Then Cal's band got the opportunity to go on tour. As his career expanded Cal was gone more and more. Myra continued to teach, but greatly missed being part of Cal's glamorous lifestyle, since she seldom was able to attend his performances. Cal was making more money now, but he was also spending it. Back home Myra received the credit card bills and became increasingly irritated at Cal's extravagance and resentful that she had to be the practical one. She had to keep her teaching job so they would have such necessary benefits as health insurance that Cal's freelance music couldn't provide. And she had to see that the rent got paid on time, because he seemed to always be broke when the big bills were due. He got paid when he performed and when there was no gig, there was no pay and he never seemed to be able to save anything for the off times.

Cal loved his new adventurous lifestyle—he was in his element. But he also loved coming home to Myra and knowing she was there. She was his security. When he came home for a short while between gigs he welcomed the quiet time and seemed, then, a stick-in-the-mud to Myra, who was starved for the glamour that Cal no longer provided for her. Resentful and out of touch with his current performance style, Myra no longer provided the ego-boosting feedback Cal had previously depended on her for. When he was on the road he began to seek that hero-worship and "mothering" from other women. Myra felt betrayed by the relationship. And Cal increasingly began to feel trapped. Finally, they divorced.

Cal was the Fire that Myra wouldn't allow herself to express, while Myra was the down-to-earth security that Cal's romantic, fiery spirit needed to keep him from burning out of control. She took over where his parents left off, building him up and covering for him when his impulses got him into trouble. It worked for a while, but it seldom works forever to have someone else do for you what you really need to do for yourself.

In the years following their breakup, Myra returned to school part-time to begin work on an advanced degree. She met an astrologer who encouraged her to seek out expression for the creative talents indicated by her chart. A tentative beginning in a course in theater arts led eventually to her leadership of the Drama Club at her school and to her own involvement with community theater, where she proved to be a versatile and popular actress, as well as a real asset in backstage organizational projects. Myra had learned to express her own Fire comfortably within the context of her more dominant earthy qualities.

She was later a bit amused to hear that Cal was learning with a bit more difficulty to manage the practical, Earth matters of his life after he married a young performer in his group who was an "airhead" and even more impractical than he. With no one to do it for him for the first time in his life, Cal had to learn to take responsibility and eventually he even took considerable pride in his ability to financially manage his increasingly successful career.

Does this mean that the relationship of Cal and Myra, Fire and Earth, was doomed from the start and couldn't work? Of course not! Any combination of elements and planets-in-signs can work. Some, admittedly, are easier to harmonize than others. But it should never be forgotten that if a relationship is not working, the first person to whom you must look for change is yourself.

SHERRY

In the beginning of this article I said that a stock answer to the question, "What sign am I most compatible with?" is often the "same element as your sign." If true, "Sherry Sagittarius" should be enthusiastic about Aries, Leo or another Sagittarius. Right? Wrong. (I said it wasn't that easy!)

Although Sherry has the Sun, Venus and Midheaven in Fire, her chart is actually stronger in Earth:

Signs: Fire—Sun, Venus, Midheaven = 5
   Earth—Moon, Saturn, Pluto, Mercury = 5
   Air—Uranus = 1
   Water—Jupiter, Ascendant, Mar, Neptune = 5
Houses:Fire—Neptune = 1
   Earth—Sun, Venus, Saturn = 4
   Air—Mercury, Moon, Uranus, Pluto = 5
   Water—Jupiter, Mars = 2
Total: Fire—6, Earth—9, Air—6, Water—7

That looks fairly well-balanced, doesn't it? Actually she is—and probably will be even more so as she matures. Right now, she is still barely into her 20s and she has a bit of a dilemma sorting out her needs for freedom and adventure (Fire) and her needs for security and stability (Earth). Regardless of the exact count, I consider that with a Fire Sun sign and Earth Moon sign, Fire and Earth are fairly evenly matched in her personality.

When two elements that are naturally difficult to reconcile strongly co-exist within the same personality, often one will operate in the open and the other one in the shadows, until the day that the shadowed element suddenly comes out and takes over, often unexpectedly. This seems to be happening to Sherry in her relationships.

Sherry falls in love as one would expect of a Fire sign—quickly and enthusiastically—this for sure is THE ONE! For a while; and then he isn't. It is interesting that her first quite serious relationship that lasted for a year and a half and included talk of marriage after

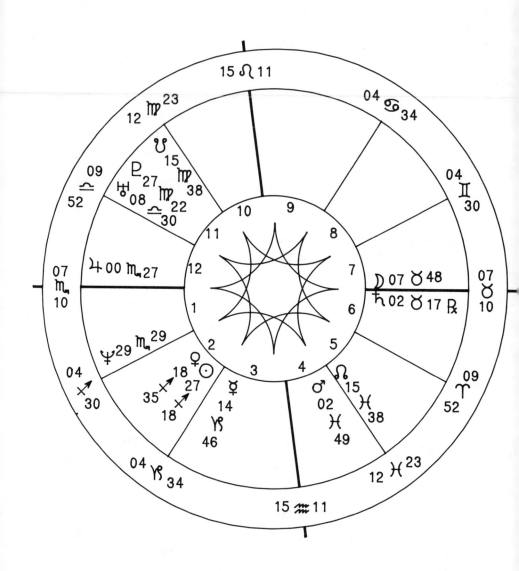

Natal Chart
Sherry
19 Dec 1969 3h10m 0s CST
Chicago, IL
Koch 41N52 87W39

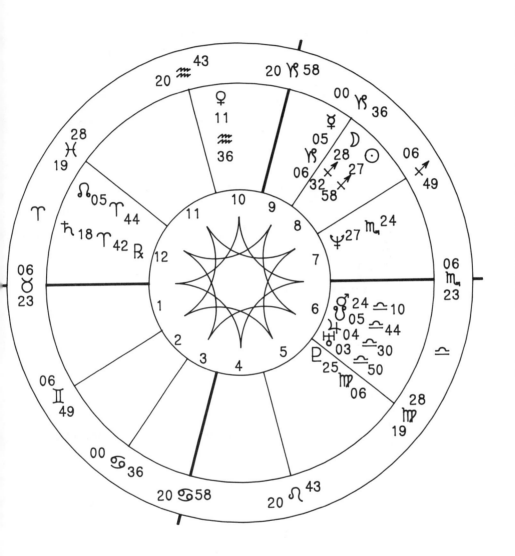

Natal Chart
Shaun
19 Dec 1968 14h15m 0s EST
Cincinnati, OH
Koch 9N06 84W31

college, was with a young man who also had Sun in Sagittarius and Taurus rising.

Shaun has a similar breakdown to Sherry's, with good potential balance in the elements, but he has Sun and Moon in Fire with a larger count in Earth:

```
Signs:   Fire—Sun, Moon, Saturn = 5
         Earth—Mercury, Ascendant, Midheaven, Pluto = 6
         Air—Uranus, Jupiter, Mars, Venus = 4
         Water—Neptune = 1
Houses:Fire—Mercury, Pluto = 2
         Earth—Uranus, Jupiter, Mars, Venus = 4
         Air—Neptune = 1
         Water—Saturn, Sun, Moon = 5
Total:   Fire—7, Earth—10, Air—5, Water—6
```

The trouble with Sherry and Shaun is that they were not able to stay on the same timetable in regard to when they wanted Fire/freedom needs met and when they wanted Earth/security needs met. When one was feeling possessive, the other felt smothered, and the one who was filling either role at any given time could switch without warning. Things worked best while they were at the same school and friends could help talk them out of their temporary jealousies or feelings of being trapped. But when they went to different colleges it was the beginning of the end.

Actually it was Shaun who remained stable in the relationship during that first and last semester of their continued relationship. He was working his way through school and therefore had limited social times, so when he could get away, he visited Sherry's school (about a two hour drive) and he expected her to be available. She was making new friends at school and became resentful of being asked to drop her plans with them whenever Shaun decided to visit. This all took place during the approach in early 1988 of the transiting Saturn/Uranus conjunction in Sagittarius. Saturn and Uranus represent energies that can be in conflict: Saturn—limitation and Uranus—freedom. If one is concentrating on disciplined, creative work, for example, a Saturn/Uranus conjunction could work just fine. But if one is involved in a relationship where freedom and security needs are an issue, well ... you can imagine what happened when that Saturn/Uranus stationed at 27 degrees Sagittarius.

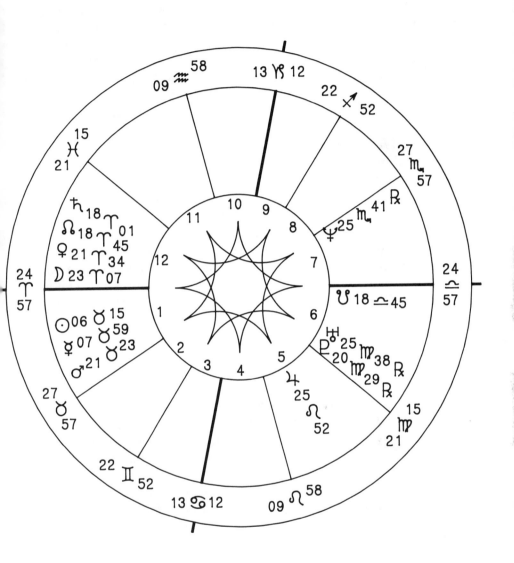

Natal Chart
Bob
26 Apr 1968 4h30m 0s CST
Chicago, IL
Koch 41N52 87W39

Sherry's next big love was Bob, a student at her own college. This time she chose a Sun sign from her other major affinity. Bob's Sun is in Taurus, closely conjunct Sherry's Moon. Interestingly Bob is also Fire/Earth—in fact he is almost all Fire and Earth:

```
Signs:  Fire—Moon, Venus, Saturn, Ascendant, Jupiter = 7
        Earth—Sun, Mercury, Mars, Pluto, Uranus, MC = 8
        Air—nothing = 0
        Water—Neptune = 1
Houses:Fire—Sun, Mercury, Mars, Jupiter = 5
        Earth—Pluto, Uranus = 2
        Air—Neptune = 1
        Water—Moon, Venus, Saturn = 4
Total:  Fire—12, Earth—10, Air—1, Water—5
```

Bob is very hard-driving and ambitious in his work—a take-charge person who is a campus leader and determined to let nothing stand in his way of getting ahead. He and Sherry were the "golden couple" for a while, until they began to play the same freedom vs. possessiveness games that she had played in her previous relationship. As the Saturn/Uranus transit continued through its retrograde and final passes, this relationship endured a number of stormy scenes. Deeply involved in her own work, Sherry at this time preferred the comfort of a steady relationship and wanted more commitment than Bob was willing to give. He alternated between being very attentive—and then impulsively deciding to take out other girls behind Sherry's back. And when she found out she was very hurt. Finally, at the end of the Saturn/Uranus transit, Sherry called off the relationship. Bob still calls occasionally, but she refuses his dates.

Sherry has come to a fairly clear realization, in part through astrology, of her own inner conflicts between a strong need to be secure and be taken care of and an equally strong need to be independent, self-sufficient and free. There have been other boyfriends since Bob, but she has kept these relationships in better perspective, realizing that she will not be happy in the long run unless she first develops her own career before she thinks of marriage. In her first year out of school, she has her own apartment, car and new job. Where in the past she had relied upon her boyfriend to provide the "taking care of" (and then sometimes resenting his consequent possessiveness) she now takes a great deal of satisfaction in managing her life herself.

MARGE AND JACK

Lest the predominant Air and Water people think I am neglecting them, I provide a final example. Here are the charts of Marge and Jack. Marge has the Sun in Leo but her chart has a predominance of Air; and Jack who with the Sun in Scorpio, Moon in Pisces and Pisces rising is in deep Water.

Marge
Signs: Fire—Sun, Pluto, Midheaven = 5
         Earth—Mercury, Mars, Neptune = 4
         Air—Moon, Ascendant, Saturn, Uranus = 6
         Water—Venus, Jupiter = 2
Houses: Fire—Jupiter = 1
         Earth—Venus, Pluto = 2
         Air—Uranus, Sun, Mercury, Mars, Neptune = 6
         Water—Saturn, Moon = 3
Total: Fire—6, Earth—5, Air—12, Water—5

Jack
Signs: Fire—Pluto, Midheaven = 3
         Earth—Jupiter, Uranus, Neptune = 3
         Air—Mars = 1
         Water—Sun, Moon, Ascendant, Mercury, Venus,
             Saturn = 9
Houses: Fire—Saturn, Pluto, Mercury = 3
         Earth—Uranus = 1
         Air—Neptune, Mars, Jupiter = 3
         Water—Sun, Venus, Moon = 5
Total: Fire—6, Earth—4, Air—4, Water—14

Air is supposed to be associated with the intellect, with the function of thinking. Marge is a smart lady in many ways. She runs her own secretarial service, is well thought of by her clients and has no trouble getting all the work she wants. Unfortunately, as sometimes happens with strong airy people, the capacity to think gets distorted into rationalizations in situations where the emotions and romantic inclinations are involved. Water is supposed to be the

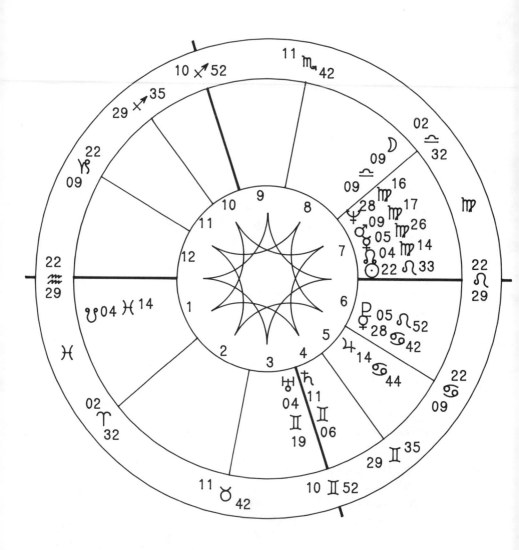

Natal Chart
Marge
15 Aug 1942 20h15m 0s CWT
Minneapolis, MN
Koch 44N59 93W16

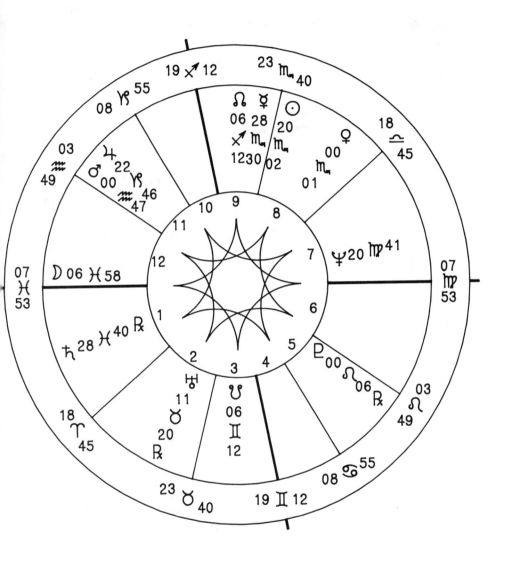

Natal Chart
Jack
12 Nov 1937 14h00m 0s CST
Minneapolis, MN
Koch 44n59 93W16

emotional element, but in my observations if someone is being "carried away" by emotions, it is more likely an Air sign or Air-dominant person in action. Emotion is the natural element for Water—water generally can handle emotions without "losing it." But Air, so logical and rational, can lose all sense of reason when an emotional issue takes over.

At the time Marge turned to astrology for advice on the future prospects of her relationship with Jack, she was contemplating marrying him—again!

This relationship had a long history that started back in high school when Jack had been Marge's first major crush as well as her first affair, and then her first major heartbreak when he turned to another girl.

Marge went off to secretarial school and eventually married and had two children. Her husband was never as exciting to her as Jack, but he was a good father and provider. Marge, in her own words, "had every advantage and comfort" for the 18 years of their marriage—until Jack came back into her life.

Marge returned to her home town for her high school reunion. Jack was also there, fresh from his second divorce. To Marge he seemed even more glamorous than she remembered. He poured on the charm and within a few months he had persuaded her to leave her husband and children and come live with him. A year later, following her divorce, Marge and Jack married, despite the fact that she had discovered that he had a "little problem with drinking." She rationalized that even though his drinking had "gotten a little out of hand" when his previous marriage went sour, now with her loving attention, he would change.

There were other problems: Marge missed her children. Both teenagers, they preferred to remain with their father, in their familiar environment with their friends. When they did come to visit Marge and Jack, he treated them indifferently at best, rudely at other times, while when his own children visited, he was very indulgent.

Additionally, Marge was bothered by Jack's attitude toward business. He was quite willing to, shall we say, bend ethical standards a bit to make a profit. Honesty is very important to her and she would rather do without money than break rules.

Jack functioned well during business hours, but after work came happy hour, so he often arrived home either sullen or overly mellow, depending on his mood and the extent of his drinking.

Sometimes happy hour was spent in the company of other women which made Marge extremely jealous. Yet where Jack was concerned Marge's capacity for reason was gone.

Marge's description of the endless, mostly one-sided conversations she carried on with Jack sound like classic examples of what one might expect from strong Air talking to strong Water. Marge would repeatedly try to elicit Jack to talk to her about what was wrong, what did he think and what she should do to make things better. More often than not this would only drive Jack to withdraw into brooding silence. At other times when happy hour had left Jack in a better mood, he would dodge Marge's questions with alcoholically mellowed attempts at romantic humor.

In their seven years of marriage Marge and Jack divorced, remarried and divorced again. Now Marge was trying to give herself all the reasons why she should try it one more time, and she was apparently hoping to find a counselor who would agree with her.

For each suggested alternative possibility she had a reason or an excuse why it couldn't work. Marge is perfectly capable of supporting herself, however she said she couldn't deal with being in the same town with Jack and not be with him. He is coming around again, trying to persuade her to come back. She wants to get away but she is unable to sell her business; she can't afford to give it up; she doesn't want to work for someone else, and so on and so on. a major underlying issue is quite likely a very strong need to have a relationship (Moon in Libra, Sun and stellium in the 7th House) and a fear that at her age she might not find another husband—although she would not acknowledge any truth in this.

It was no great surprise to me that neither short-term nor long-term astrological factors suggested "happily ever after" but this is not what Marge wanted to hear. I referred her to Al-anon and to an area support group for women in addictive relationships. I haven't heard whether or not she went back to Jack, although I suspect she may have. It would be interesting to know what happens during the Pluto transits to their charts.

In any case, here we have an extreme example of the futility of trying to change someone else's behavior.

LOOKING IN THE MIRROR

Rather than thinking about what you would like to change in the other person, instead look at him or her as a mirror in which a part of yourself is revealed—a hidden part, perhaps, that you may be avoiding. You have attracted that person into your life because s/he represents something you need to learn about yourself. You certainly can't expect to change the other person, or the relationship, unless you are willing to change yourself. If you become more balanced, you will no longer need to project your imbalances. As you become more whole and complete within yourself, the people in your life will also become more whole—or if they choose not to, they will most likely cease to become a major part of your life.

Am I saying that in being whole, you need to be all elements in equal balance? No, not at all. You will always relate to one or two with more ease than the others. I am only saying that all are part of you somewhere, even if unrecognized, and other people can reflect that most unpleasantly when you are out of balance and out of touch with your own needs. The main lesson is that it does little good for you to blame someone else for your discomfort. The only person you can actively seek to change is yourself.

IT'S GREAT THAT PEOPLE ARE DIFFERENT!

Now that you have yourself in better balance, think of how great it is that we are not all alike—that people have varieties of interests, skill, talents, elements! Would you want to be on a committee where everyone was of the same dominant element? You might get along with each other quite well, but what would you accomplish? You need the Fire people to take the initiative, the Earth people to follow through, the Air people to examine the logic, the Water people to provide the intuitive aspect... and so on, and on.

People come together in all kinds of relationships because they have something to contribute to each other—because they have something to learn from each other. Don't ever feel that you should avoid a relationship with someone because you've read or been told that their "sign" is not compatible with yours, or because you are of elements that are not supposed to harmonize well. Astrology does not dictate a list of absolute rules. Instead it shows us a variety of options and choices. If you are attracted to that person it is undoubtedly for a good reason! The important thing is for you to be aware of what is going on. To be unaware of aspects within yourself and project them onto others is to invite problems. To be aware of elements that are weak within yourself and to invite others into your life who are strong in those elements can be stimulating and strengthening.

There are no hard and fast answers as to who is the "right" person for you. Fresh breezes, whirling storms, brisk winds of change, smoldering embers, streaked lightning, flaming passion...deep pools, tides that ebb and flow, rainstorms...solid ground, quicksand, rock of strength...the joys and the sorrows, the responsibility is yours!

The Sun "moves" into another house approximately every two hours as it rises in the east, culminates overhead at midday and sinks below the western horizon...but it is the Earth that is making that daily circuit. The Sun's "motion" through the signs of the zodiac (determined by the Earth's yearly orbit) is approximately one degree a day. So—our example Sun in Aries has now risen above the horizon into the 12th House. The next sign after Aries is Taurus. Depending upon whether the Sun is in the early, middle or late degrees of Aries, and also depending upon the location of birth, as some point during the two hours after sunrise, Taurus will become the cusp of the 1st House—the Rising Sign or Ascendant. The next sign, Gemini would become the cusp of the 2nd House and so in.

Diana Chambers

Diana is a native and current resident of Eugene, Oregon. With a Sagittarius Sun and Ascendant and Virgo Moon, she has merged her astrology and tarot practice with her employment as a legislative aide in the Oregon Legislature. She has four sons and one daughter and is the proud grandmother of nine.

After her husband's death in 1980 and the sale of the family farm, Diana attended an astrology lecture given by Johanna Mitchell and decided on the spot that she had found her direction. She has studied with Virgo dedication since that day and teaches classes when her schedule permits and lectures to local groups.

Diana says, "I credit my astrological proficiency to my mentor, Johanna Mitchell; my idol, Joan McEvers; and my hero, Robert (Buzz) Myers. Their enlightening educational tapes, books and lectures have been steady sources of knowledge and inspiration to me. I am grateful for their patience and encouragement."

FRIENDSHIPS

There are hermit souls that I've withdrawn
In the place of their self-content;
There are souls like stars, that dwell apart,
In a fellowless firmament;
There are pioneer souls that blaze their paths
Where highways never ran—
But let me live by the side of the road
And be a friend to man.

Let me live in my house by the side of the road,
It's here the race of men go by—
They are good, they are bad, they are weak
They are strong. Wise, foolish—so am I;
Then why sould I sit in the scorner's seat,
Or hurl the cynic's ban?
Let me live in a house by the side of the road
And be a friend to man.

—Sam Walter Foss

Everybody needs somebody sometime. Everybody needs someone to care. The "somebody" may change, the "sometime" may change but the need for friendship never changes. Different generations form friendships based upon the social, economic and political conditions of their time. Astrologically, the positions of the personal planets (Sun, Moon, Mercury, Venus, and Mars) in a chart indicate the way in which an individual forms close bonds. The outer planets' (Jupiter, Saturn, Uranus, Neptune and Pluto) positions represent generational themes.

In this chapter about the essence of friendships, we will consider Venus as the initial desire for friends, the 5th/11th House axis as how we give and receive love, chart synastry to show commonality and compatibility, and we'll view the Sun in determining the character and ego needs.

We begin experiencing friendships as part of our early childhood development in the process of learning the art of give and take. It is at the request of our mothers that we learn how and when to be aggressive, by seeing how far we can push before punishment comes. In this formative time, we are already showing friendship tendencies and how we will relate to others. We are docile or persistent, shy or aggressive, quiet or loud. As we grow, these parts of our personalities become set and we begin to define what who, how and when we need friends.

Close friends assure us that we are important. That bond gives us the confidence we need to succeed in life, to feel alive and valuable to the social order in which we live and to share our fears and desires, hopes and dreams, struggles and bitter failures, those inner thoughts and feelings we share only with our intimate friends. We all recognize a difference between acquaintances and friends. That difference is intimacy. When we feel safe, as in the bond of friendship, we can allow ourselves to be vulnerable and share our deepest selves.

VENUS

It's important to our friends to believe we are unreservedly frank with them and important to the friendship that we are not.

—McLaughlin

The placement of Venus in the horoscope through its rulership of the 7th House shows our initial desire for friendship, the way we relate to others, the concepts and expectations we have of love, popularity and social acceptance. The planet Venus indicates what we love; each sign describes a different perspective of love. Far example, Venus in Sagittarius loves honesty and freedom, Venus in Libra loves harmony and graciousness, Venus in Capricorn loves rules and order and Venus in Pisces loves compassion and intuition. The house placement and aspects to Venus describe how these values play out in our individual charts and friendships.

Venus in an Angular house or Cardinal sign is action oriented and has a drive for frequent change to keep the level of excitement high. Those with Angular planets tend to be self-motivating, quick starters and on the selfish side. They can't always be depended on to be there for someone else unless it's their own idea. The exception is Capricorn, who reluctantly steps in to do the right thing. But the basic preference for all Cardinal signs as well as planets in Angular houses is to be forever chasing a new rainbow.

With Venus in a Fixed sign or Succedent house, they are self-reliant and rarely ask for help until it's the last option. They hang on to outdated friendships because they don't care for change; their persistent stubborness can't be matched. They have an emotional need somewhere inside that is intent on doing things themselves in their own way and at their own pace. We think of the Fixed mode as steady and loyal, and they can be but only if we remember to remind them of their value as our friends.

In Mutable signs and Cadent houses, Venus adapts to the needs of others and is most likely to hang back and wait for potential friends to instigate further meetings until a comfort zone has been reached. They are flexible, changeable and open to communication. On the other hand, decisions can be difficult for those who have low aggression tendencies, a typical Mutable characteristic. It's important for people with Venus in Mutable signs to set limits with friends and learn to use communication skills to express their own needs.

The soft aspects (sextiles and trines) to Venus add grace, charm, sociability and popularity to our basic personalities, depending on the other planet involved. The talent for making friends comes naturally and easily. Soft aspects to gentle planets usually go unnoticed and indicate our instinctive reactions. For example, Venus trine the Moon suggests sensitivity and warmth, with a natural flair for finding friends who rush to support our needs. When connected with Mars, Venus is often sensual and magnetic and interactions with the opposite sex are comfortable. Venus trine or sextile Jupiter is outgoing, happy and popular. However, there is a tendency to be extravagant and showy on the social scene, and moderation for this combination is just another word in the dictionary.

Stressful aspects (square, opposition, conjunction and quincunx) to Venus can create a fear of disrupting the harmony of our friendships and may cause us to be superficial, evasive or indifferent. To keep the balance we avoid saying "no" and can become people-pleasers to prevent open confrontation. If we feel our friends do not understand our needs and are unable or unwilling to support us, or if we have no friends at all, we are still, therefore, experiencing the influence of Venus in our charts. If no positive reinforcement is coming from the outer world, we can become self-indulgent in an attempt to fulfill our emotional needs.

An example of the negative side of Venus expressed through self-indulgence to compensate for a lack of emotional support was demonstrated by Susan, a client of mine. This woman in her mid-forties had just ended a long-term relationship, moved to a new area where she had no friends and had sent her only child off to college. These major changes created a huge void in her life. She mentioned that she was buying clothes at a pace that kept her broke and worried. She said she had never been a compulsive shopper before and wanted to know how she could break the pattern. Once she understood that she was suffering from an emotional lack, she was able to curb the spending and begin getting her life back on track.

Susan has Venus in Sagittarius in the 2nd House of money, possessions and feelings of self-worth. It rules the 6th House which has Taurus on the cusp. She had to work extra hours to keep in the black and was critical and down on herself when she impulsively over spent. Venus also rules her 7th House of partnerships. With Uranus in Taurus in the 6th House, she dealt with inner rebellion through compulsive spending binges when she was emotionally needy. She could have chosen overeating or some other form of self-indulgence. It can't be stressed enough that our emotional needs must be met whether it comes through friendship, loved ones or self-gratification. Understanding these emotional needs is the first step to becoming a good friend.

VENUS IN FRIENDSHIPS

Victoria and Jacqueline live in a small town in upstate New York. They met at work and have been friends for about seven years. According to Victoria, "It wasn't an instant friendship because neither of us trust easily, but Jacqueline was going through a crisis and I was there to listen. Later, I went through a crisis and she was there for me. That cemented our friendship."

A glance at their charts tells us why they are close and loyal friends. Both women have Venus in Capricorn, a sign that is resourceful, loyal, shy, sensitive, cautious, patient, reserved and sometimes insecure.

Victoria's Venus is in the 10th House of career, status and reputation. She is popular and respected at work and does more than her share in a responsible, orderly way as she climbs the ladder of

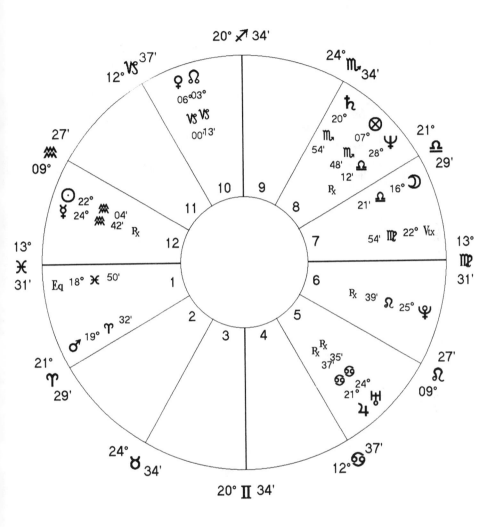

Natal Chart
Victoria
Feb. 11, 1955, 7:50:0 A.M. CST
Paducah, KY
37N05'00" 88W37'00"
Koch Houses

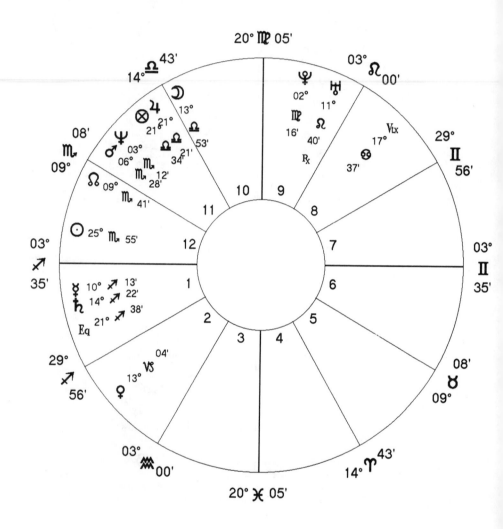

Natal Chart
Jacqueline
Nov. 18, 1957, 7:30:0 A.M. EST
Yonkers, NY
40N56'00" 73W54'00"
Koch Houses

success. Venus is her only planet in an Earth sign. Lack of an element often results in over-compensation and Victoria is an extremely hard worker. Venus rules her 3rd and 8th Houses giving her good communication skills, logical thought patterns and the ability to be deeply analytical as well as a good problem solver. Because her Venus is unaspected, she often appears to be in control and self assured. With Venus strongly connected to professional issues, Victoria must overcome her self-reliance in order to form close bonds and friendships.

Jacqueline's Venus is also in Capricorn in the intercepted 2nd House. Since intercepted planets usually work in an inward way, Jacqueline may have trouble interacting with others comfortably. She appreciates friends who understand her sensitivity and reserve. With Venus in the 2nd House, her own feelings of worthiness and lovability are central issues. The square to her Libra Moon adds tension and a fear of being alone. Uranus quincunx Venus brings unstable and ever changing relationships, a difficult aspect for someone who has so much love and loyalty to give. Venus rules the 6th and 11th Houses so her physical health and feelings of self-worth can be reinforced through interaction with trusted friends. The 6th House quality can also manifest as being critical of friends and co-workers.

Victoria and Jacqueline have a lot in common. They both have Cardinal signs on the friendship houses, the Moon in Libra, the Sun in the 12th House and Venus in Capricorn. Because they view things similarly, Victoria and Jacqueline can always count on help and plenty of advice from each other.

When I asked Victoria why Jacqueline was so special to her, she said, "I get the same loyalty and respect that I give. We laugh, we cry, we share the deepest secrets secure in the fact that they will never be revealed short of physical torture. She is intelligent and backs her statements up with logic. We understand each other without a word being said and we never try to change or 'fix' each other. I can honestly say I would trust her with my life."

Victoria has Cancer on the 5th House cusp, ruled by the Moon in Libra in the 7th House giving her a focus on relationships of all kinds. She has a multitude of acquaintances, as indicated by Jupiter and Uranus in the 5th House, but she shares her deepest trust with only the closest of friends since the 5th House planets trine Saturn in Scorpio in the 8th. The quincunx of Jupiter/Uranus to her Sun/Mercury conjunction in the 12th House has taught her not to trust everyone and has shown her the face of the enemy when she least expects it.

Jacqueline has Aries on the 5th House with Mars in Scorpio in the 11th illustrating a desire to have friends who instigate activities and will take her along for the ride. She wants loyalty and inspiration with a delicate balance of give and take, as evidenced by Venus in Capricorn in the intercepted 2nd House and ruling the 11th of love received. She places strong value on friendships because she feels love relationships have been disastrous for her and loyal friends provide her with a sense of protection from the cruel world of romance. Mars conjunct Neptune often contributes to unrealistic romantic ideals. Her many Scorpio placements suggest she is possessive enough to go down with the ship rather than admit defeat. She frequently stays in romantic as well as friendly relationships that are unrewarding and deflating. Mars square Uranus often discovers unusual excitement in men that "love 'em and leave 'em." When the man of her dreams goes home to the woman with whom he shares his dreams, Jacqueline travels with friends to recuperate and heal before heading back into the abyss of silent desperation (Uranus is in the 9th and rules the 3rd House of travel and freedom).

Jacqueline says of Victoria "The most important aspect of our friendship is that we don't judge each other and, even though we don't always agree, we love each other enough to see both points of view. We give each other space when it is necessary, but we are always there for support."

OPPOSITES ATTRACT

5th/11th House Axis

Never exaggerate your faults. Your friends will attend to to that.
—Edwards

The 5th House depicts the kind of friends we are, how we give love, creative self-expression, the forms of amusement we prefer (big kid's toys) and how important play is in our daily lives. Our unique talents and the ability to be, or not to be, important are products of the 5th House. We all desire to be intimate with a few well-chosen friends who think we are special, who know our faults and shortcomings and love us anyway.

Planets in the 5th House show our need to be social but, as always, we have to consider the whole chart and the placement of the ruler of the 5th House is significant. If the ruler is in the 12th House, our relating ability will probably be more difficult to integrate than it would be with the ruler in one of the more outgoing houses.

The 11th House shows how we receive love and the friends we draw to to initiate us into the fraternity of the group; it also indicates our willingness to share. In the Aquarian 11th House, an intimate party can be several hundred people with an open invitation to another hundred or so. The more the merrier! There is a need through the 11th House to share with the world in an impersonal fashion, so as to keep things from getting sticky or uncomfortable. Another connotation of the 11th House is ambition; "It's not what you know, it's who you know" fits the job description of this house. When Venus is connected to the 11th, friendships may be cultivated for social status.

In friendships, we seek our polar opposites in order to learn about our other sides. Most of us have diverse friends who trigger various parts of our personalities; we seek different friends for changing moods and occasions. Many of us have one or two friends who don't get along with each other, so we mix and match them in much the same way that we pick an outfit for the day.

The flower children of the 1960s (representing 5th House Leo energy) formed communes outside the accepted boundaries of society so they could live together (representing 11th House Aquarian energy). This is a splendid example of how the 5th/11th House axis works in society. Ultimately, the group consciousness of the Western world was changed through the movement to break old rules and establish new ones.

THE FRIENDSHIP AXIS

The following illustrates how each sign polarity operates across the 5th/11th House axis:

Aries/Libra: These Cardinal Fire and Air signs relate well as long as Aries is allowed to instigate, take risks, be competitive and have fun. Libra looks at things with double-vision ability, seeing both sides at the same time and operates with a cool logic that assumes there will be an equal share of give and take.

Aries teaches Libra how to blow his stack and jump into the

next whimsical idea without shifting gears. Aries brings a devil-may-care attitude to the friendship and throws in a healthy dose of breathless excitement to boot.

Libra can tame Aries a bit and show him the art of tactfulness, charm, grace, diplomacy, manners and style. Always maintaining peace and harmony, Libra can get others to do what he wants through subtle manipulation done so cleverly it goes unnoticed. Aries spontaneity and exuberance is appreciated by its opposite sign because Libra enjoys company in all endeavors.

Taurus/Scorpio: Fixed signs are traditionally the most loyal and steady but can be possessive and jealous at times. With the right conditions though, this friendship can last a long time.

Steadfast and enduring, Taurus needs to feel comfortable in all situations and wants friends who will provide emotional support with emphasis on the tangible and touchable. Give Taurus something to put value on and you'll be friends forever.

Scorpio, which I call the all-or-nothing-at-all sign, understands the heights and depths of emotion. Private and secretive, sharing intimate feelings with a select few, it is the most excessive and obsessive of the signs. Scorpio friends will give their all to the friendship.

Taurus can teach Scorpio to be more conscious of personal appearance and creature comforts. Scorpio can teach Taurus about survival and endings. When it's over, it's over and Scorpio never looks back. Either sign can hold grudges for centuries over an unkept confidence or any other form of betrayal. This pair makes good shopping buddies with the money signs in the friendship houses.

Gemini/Sagittarius: These two signs will often talk on the phone daily to share everything that is going on in their lives. This can be a fun-loving friendship because neither sign wants to grow up and take life too seriously. Their differences are mainly communication blocks because both Gemini and Sagittarius crave learning and the sharing of knowledge. But Gemini can be the poorest listener in the zodiac and Fire signs often lack the patience to wait their turn. They argue constantly as each tries, unsuccessfully, to edge the other out. Gemini is curious and restless; Sagittarius is independent and enthusiastic.

Gemini can show Sagittarius how to be a kid again (maybe for the first time); and Sagittarius teaches Gemini how to use information to expand her/his world.

Cancer/Capricorn: Both signs are sensitive, shy and reserved, usually forming friendships for loyalty, protection and a feeling of belonging. They may share the same background where emotional support was meted out in small doses and thus seek friends who can be counted on and trusted.

A Cancer person looks for friends who will love and nurture him to fill an inner need for emotional oneness. Cancer must feel needed and wishes to feel a true sense of security through friendship. Often overly emotional and easily wounded, he cries to release tension he is at the heights of joy or in the depths of despair.

Capricorn has a cautious and conservative disposition and instinctively puts limits and boundaries around everything to create a sense of structure and form. Capricorn wants friends who are steadfast, loyal and are willing to accept complete responsibility for the friendship, quickly developing a sense of duty which includes abundant advice.

Capricorn teaches Cancer about strength, self-control, patience and the joy of solitude, while Cancer points the way for Capricorn to show emotions openly and overcome the fear of intimacy.

Leo/Aquarius: In my opinion, Leo and Aquarius are the most opposite of the signs. Egotistical and self-centered, Leo wants to lead the pack and have the full support of friends. Leo has dramatic flair and an endless supply of charisma, magnetism and playfulness and expects to be loved first and best.

Aquarius is detached, impersonal, remote and cool wanting to share with the group in humanitarian pursuits. He wants to be loved for her/his uniqueness and conceptual intelligence. Far-seeing and futuristic, thinking the present can take care of itself, Aquarians have the ability to love everyone and accept them as they are and can blend into any social experience.

This Fire and Air combination is verbal in a loud and disruptive way and their battles can be heard for blocks, but once the air has cleared and both have made their points, they are best pals until the next outburst. Surprisingly, these two signs often have long friendships that may stem from the need to prove that they aren't quitters; that conflict ultimately strengthens friendships.

Leo teaches Aquarius not to sacrifice love for freedom and Aquarius shows Leo the true meaning of freedom.

Virgo/Pisces: This is the savior/victim axis where we give more than we get in the name of service and loyalty, operating on faith that the other person will see our needs and rush in to fill them.

Pisces people unconsciously set themselves up for disappointment through heightened idealism. There is often a helpless quality that can be extremely draining to friends. When acting in a positive way, Pisces is highly intuitive and spiritual with an endearing ephemeral quality. Negatively it can evidence as martyrdom and self-sacrifice, being too trusting and eager to please.

Virgo tries to help friends to be the best they can be and to operate at their fullest potential, but is often seen as critical because of that deep caring. It is up to the Virgo friend to set limits and boundaries to avoid confusion and a feeling of being exploited.

This axis teaches one to give and the other to take for a healthy relationship to form, grow and blossom into a mutually rewarding friendship with an equal balance between physical (Virgo) and emotional (Pisces). Virgo fears being taken for granted and Pisces fears abandonment. Pisces teaches Virgo how to appreciate chaos and how to use the imagination process to realize dreams. Virgo shows Pisces how to store dreams in precise order to be readily accessible at a later time.

WILL AND DAVID

Will and David are both real estate brokers with widely different natures and lifestyles; complete opposites who are separated by a generation in age. Will arrives at an appointment within seconds of the set time (a fact he points out to anyone who will listen) and David gets there when he gets there. Will is married and David is single. Will is exacting and David is careless. Will carries through on a promise no matter what obstacles he has to overcome and David forgets he made a promise.

They share off-color jokes that are censored for Will's aversion to foul language (the generation gap), a few beers, a few deals and mutual companionship. They are participants in a ritualistic "for men only" morning coffee klatch to catch up on the gossip from the real estate world.

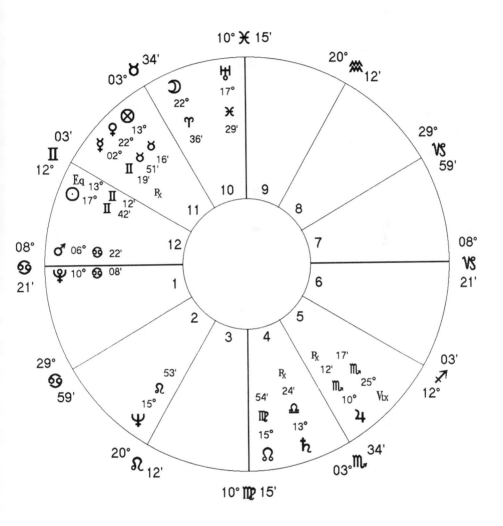

Natal Chart
Will
June 9, 1923, 5:55:0 A.M. PST
Gray's Harbor, WA
46N59'00" 123W53'00"
Koch Houses

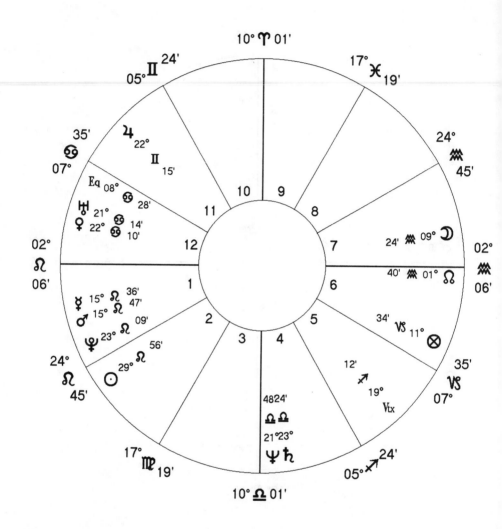

Natal Chart
David
Aug. 23, 1953, 4:00:0 A.M. +5
Winnipeg, MB, Canada
49N53'00" 97W09'00"
Koch Houses

In business, David makes the deals and Will brings them to fruition. David has four planets and his Ascendent in Leo so he is content with fast talk and promises. Once he gets the signature, he leaps forward to the next project. Will, with his Cancer Ascendent straddled by Mars and Pluto square Saturn, is concerned with the welfare of the clients on both sides and is dedicated to organization and thoroughness. Although he sees himself as calm and easy-going, he can wear clients down with calls, letters and reasons why the property is perfect for them in an unrelenting drive to make the sale, a quality that David lacks.

Will has Scorpio and Taurus on the friendship axis, stable and enduring signs that don't take friendships lightly or give them up without good cause. Will says, "Ours is an interesting and sometimes challenging friendship but we've only had one serious problem in 15 years. Usually David jokes his way past my concerns. It works and I have learned from him. At times he is as old as his age, or older, and at times I refer to him as my 36-year-old teenage friend."

With Jupiter retrograde in the 5th House in Scorpio, Will had some difficulty making friends in early life. He knows a multitude of people but claims he doesn't have enough close friends to be pallbearers at his funeral. An apt description of the combination of expansive Jupiter and private Scorpio. Will is generous to his friends but with Jupiter involved in his Grand Water Trine to Mars, Pluto, Ascendent and Uranus, it must be on his terms and in his time frame because that powerful combination cannot be pushed. That close friends will be met in the work environment is indicated by Jupiter's rulership of the 6th House trine Uranus in the 10th. He draws a definite line between work and his home and family.

Venus rules Will's 11th House, the intercepted 4th and Saturn. Venus and Mercury are in the 11th House, both are unaspected and Mercury is also retrograde. Retrograde Mercury can manifest as speech problems and Will had a stuttering problem as a child which he blamed on an insensitive teacher in elementary school. He became a reader rather than a talker and turned into a brilliant student who completed four years of college in three years, graduating magna cum laude. With Venus unaspected in the 11th, Will has always considered himself a loner and felt his mother loved him the least of her four children (another way an unaspected Venus can manifest is feeling no connection with the mother). In the 11th

House and in Taurus, Will's Venus needs could be met by excelling in business and finance, thereby earning respect from his peer group.

Will treats David like one of his children and patiently gives parental advice that usually falls on deaf ears. He says, "David has a large number of acquaintances of all ages. I often wonder why I value him as a friend rather than an acquaintance or associate. Perhaps it can be defined simply by saying I guess I have another son."

David has the Gemini/Sagittarius axis on his friendship houses. He likes to party, play, travel and is usually in hot pursuit of pleasure. Freedom loving Jupiter is in his 11th House and rules the 5th House of creativity, gambling, self-expression and amusement. Needless to say, David has a multitude of friends, one for every occasion, and he finds new ones at every stop with his happy persona and obvious zest for life. Jupiter trines Saturn and Neptune which heightens his intuition, provides a definite gift of gab (Jupiter in Gemini) and the ability to convince people they have made a good choice. The sextile to Pluto increases his charm and magnetism. This combination indicates the super salesman. Because Saturn rules age and Jupiter rules wisdom, David chose an older man for a stable and lasting friendship.

David says, "I met Will about 15 years ago when we were both involved in the same real estate sale. I respect his intellect, wisdom and honesty. He has definitely been one of my mentors. He has a lot of compassion but prefers not to show that quality often. For instance, he has driven miles to help me with a broken down car late at night. It is my hope that some of his high character will rub off on me."

Will adds stability to David's life and doubles as a father figure. It is likely that David has never felt he could live up to his own father's expectations or his mother's dreams, as indicated by the Moon in detached, cool Aquarius opposing his Leo stellium. Venus is in the 12th House conjunct Uranus adding to his cofusion and feelings of not fitting into the family mode. The square to Neptune and Saturn in the 4th House suggests an unstable home life, rules he didn't understand and a feeling of inner guilt because he was unable to please his parents. He says his older brother was the Golden Boy who could do no wrong while he became the one to break all the rules and family traditions. He laughingly describes himself as the black sheep of the family but his friends see him as a free spirit destined to do his own thing.

COMPATABILITY AND COMMONALITY

If you press me to say why I loved him, I can say no more than it
was because he was he and I was I.

—Montaigne

Many similarities between people promote an understanding, easy-going friendship, reinforcing immediate comfort and feelings of compatibility, but there isn't much to learn from each other when people are so much alike.

Aspects between charts provide us with shared avenues of enjoyment and a similar approach to life and friendship. Like aspects, such as one person with Moon square Saturn and the other with Moon opposed Saturn, or having the Moon in Capricorn or the 10th House, is a strong basis for mutual understanding.

DEAN AND LOUIE

These young men are as alike as two peas in a pod! They both have the Virgo rising, Fire sign Suns and Water sign Moons and Venuses. Mercury, ruler of both charts, is in Mutable signs suggesting adaptability and the desire to please.

Virgo rising can be self-critical, analytical, neat, orderly and involved in a perfectionism that can cause them to be their own worst enemy. They believe that they need to be smarter, taller, thinner, friendlier or in some way better because they are riddled with self-doubt. Dean and Louie present the same general attitude to the world and are seen as helpful, kind and easy-going in a quiet, gentle manner. Communication is a key factor in keeping the friendship together. Virgo has a deep caring quality that enables both men to urge each other to success in any undertaking. Since they both have Virgo rising, they don't view each other as critical, but as one who cares and understands.

Dean has Mercury in Pisces indicating a need for time alone to think things through and process ideas. Intuitive and sensitive, he reacts strongly to the moods of others. Mercury closely conjunct Venus adds charm and popularity and helps him make fair judgments and deal with others with tact and diplomacy.

Louie's Mercury is in outspoken Sagittarius in the 3rd House, so he likes to talk. The conjunction to Mars indicates a tendency to jump ahead and speak before thinking. Mentally restless and curious, he loves discussion and debate, is prone to exaggerate and can be fault-finding and exacting since Mercury squares his Ascendant.

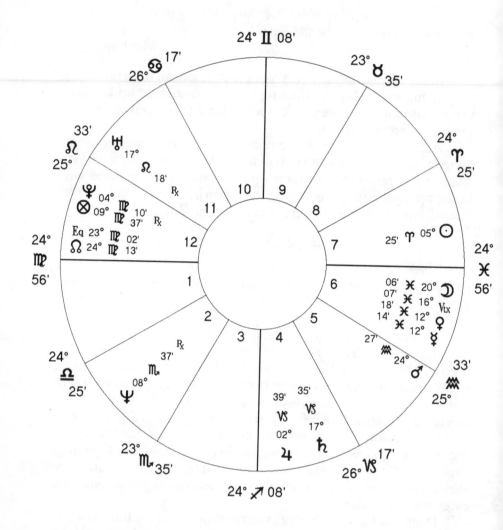

Natal Chart
Dean
Mar. 25, 1960, 5:37:0 P.M. PST
Eureka, CA
40N47'00" 124W09'00"
Koch Houses

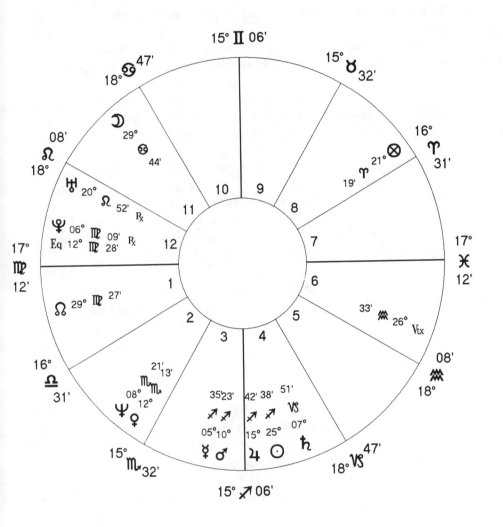

Natal Chart
Louie
Dec. 17, 1959, 11:27:0 P.M. PST
Glendale, CA
40N52'00" 124W05'00"
Koch Houses

With Fire sign Suns, both men share a sense of adventure and daring; they like excitement and competition in their lives. Each can go to the other for inspiration ad a fresh outlook. Louie can calm Dean's hot-tempered actions and help him view events in a wiser way. Dean can help Louie get started and stand up to defend his principles.

Louie has the Moon in moody, sensitive Cancer and looks for reassurance from the outside world that he is loved and needed. With the Moon in the 11th House, he finds approval through his friends. A planet at 0 or 29 degrees is said to have a special purpose in the life: It's caught in a void between one sign and the next because it no longer feels allegiance with the sign it is leaving or comfortable in the one it's becoming. That, coupled with the extremely difficult Moon quincunx Sun aspect, presents a picture of a loving and gentle man who doesn't feel wanted or needed. With the Moon in and ruling the 11th House, the one safe place he can go for support is to compassionate friends.

Dean and Louie met the summer before the first grade at the local ball park where their older brothers were involved in Little League baseball. Louie, the younger of the boys, had just moved from California when his parents traded custody and he came to live with his father and step-mother. Dean is the youngest child in a family of five with three older brothers and a slightly older twin sister. Although he was raised in a stable family, he had big shoes to fill when his turn came on the baseball field and in other sports. He says, "It was difficult to follow so many good athletes and I lacked the basic drive, that killer instinct, to excel in that way. I participated in sports because I felt it was expected of me. It wasn't until I was older that I felt free to myself."

Dean and Louis lived an easy-going, small-town life. They traded hot-wheel cars, rode bikes, went fishing, competed in school sports and graduated from high school before their lives veered off in separate directions; but they still have a close friendship. Any activity that could result in disciplinary action was instigated by Dean's twin sister who was definitely the leader of the pack. With strong Virgo, neither boy wanted to make waves or cause parents any grief; they both tried to be perfect children.

Louie was best man at Dean's wedding and later, as a sheriff's deputy, served him his divorce papers. Louie felt he was the only one who could do it with the right mixture of tact and diplomacy.

Dean and Louie served for several years on the volunteer Fire Department. Louie says, "One of my favorite memories of those years is of Dean, in full fire gear, pedaling his bike and bouncing over the railroad tracks on his way to a fire. He lost it a few times and went down but he was always one of the first firemen to report." The combination of Fire and Water, which creates tremendous mood swings, is also warm and caring. Dean went on to become a nurse and Louie chose police work, fields of service that were first experienced through the shared activities of the Fire Department.

Dean has an unaspected Mars in Aquarius in his 5th House with the dispositor in the 11th. He describes himself as a loner, who spends most of his free time with his daughter as an extremely involved father. After a financially disastrous teenage marriage, he has enjoyed being single and having the freedom to do his own thing (Mars rules his Aries Sun). Uranus in the 11th House indicates friends who are unusual in some way, friendships that are off and on, and the ability to let friends be who they are without judging. The erratic part of this friendship is what actually holds it together because friends who demand too much don't last long in Dean's life.

Louie and Dean have Sun trine Sun, similar likes, temperament and energy; Moon trine Moon, emotional comfort, sympathy and harmony; Venus trine Venus, a love of the same things, ease in the friendship, similar love experiences with women (both are too romantic and idealistic); Ascendants conjunct, having a lot in common, showing the same face to the world, an appreciation of each other; Mars sextile Mars, compatability and friendly competition; Mercury square Mercury, not always seeing eye to eye, some verbal disputes and misunderstandings; and Saturn in Capricorn ruling both 5th Houses and active in keeping this friendship strong. I am including out of orb aspects because even aspects by sign depict the same personality traits and they add to the commonality of these two charts.

Dean has Venus trine Neptune and Louie's Venus is conjunct Neptune. Dean experiences the confusion and fear of abandonment with less stress than Louie. Both have Venus sextile Saturn, an opportunity to help each other overcome feelings of doubt and being able to give encouragement and support.

CHARACTER AND EGO NEEDS

Chance makes our parents but choice makes our friends.
—Jacques Delile

The ego-oriented Sun, the natural ruler of the 5th House, needs recognition and appreciation to feel vitalized. I compare it to a great painting which is nothing without someone to admire it. We radiate through the 5th House in the hope of sharing with the world through society and the 11th House where we find confirmation of our special talents, our personal masterpiece.

The formative years and our familial relationships in that vital time set the stage for friendships, our expectations of others and our ability to socialize. We experience an innate desire to be popular among our peers. Talents can bring the adoration a healthy ego craves. Many young girls envision themselves being crowned the prom queen even while they cast their votes for the most likely candidate. Boys may have an inner desire to be football captain or some other version of Mr. Popularity while being too shy to put themselves forward. Everyone wants to be first or best at something. Imagine the sinking feeling at being the last kid picked in grade school for group games, and the lifelong feelings of rejection that are the natural result of this type of practice.

I believe we find our alter-egos through friends who bring out the dormant side of our own personalities. For instance, if we are shy and don't make friends easily, we pick friends who are outgoing and assertive. People who consider themselves weak find friends who are strong and aggressive. Dominant and pushy types want adaptable friends who do not demand to have their own way. These relationships are formed for mutual pleasure, emotional support and a sense of belonging. Because we are social by nature, we all need interaction with other people to feel complete.

APRIL AND SALLY

April and Sally provide good examples of basic attitudes about life and friendships, and reveal how early experiences influence our behavior as adults. Once we form personality patterns and feelings of self-worth, change is difficult. some people go through their entire lives believing that they are stuck in situations that bring rejection—real or imagined. The following charts are indicative of the positive and negative uses of the same energies.

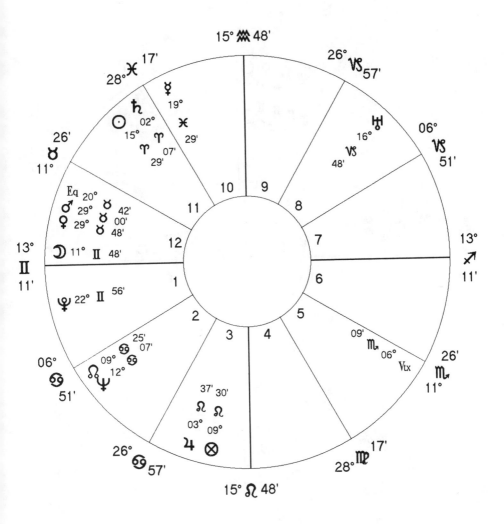

Natal Chart
April
Apr. 5, 1908, 8:30:0 A.M. PST
Walterville, OR
44N04'00" 122W48'00"
Koch Houses

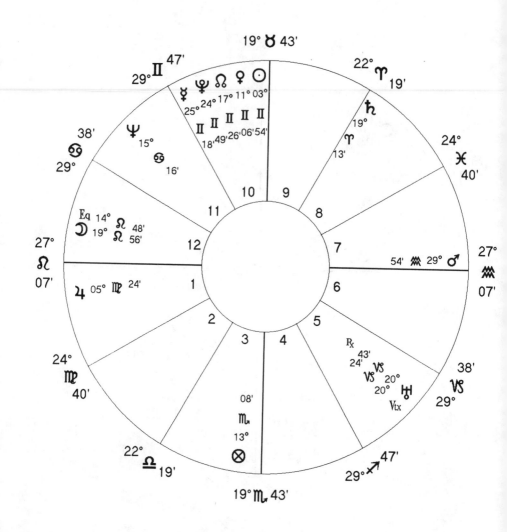

Natal Chart
Sally
May 25, 1909, 11:15:0 A.M. PST
Coos Bay, OR
47N22'00" 124W13'00"
Koch Houses

Sally and April are two women in their eighties who have been friends for over fifty years. They met in a remote logging camp in western Oregon where their husbands were employed. The camp was a typical "company town." The company owned all the buildings, including a central commissary to supply the necessities of everyday life. The women, who rarely left the camp, formed close bonds and cliques within the group of approximately thirty families. When the morning work was done, they gathered for coffee and talk, card games, knitting and other activities. They nursed each other through illness and sorrow, watched each other's kids when the need arose and cooked special treats for every occasion. Their lives were enriched by each other and shared friendships were the only form of social life available. Through the years, although sometimes separated by as many as four states, April and Sally kept in touch and now reside in the same senior citizen apartment complex.

In examining their charts we see many similarities. April is an Aries with Moon in Gemini and Sally is a Gemini with Moon in Aries. Sally's Moon/Saturn is conjunct April's Sun, and both have a T-Square with Neptune and Uranus that involve their Aries planets.

April has Virgo on the 5th House and Pisces on the 11th. The Pisces influence is strong in her chart with Mars, Venus and the Moon in the 12th House, the Sun square Neptune and Mercury, ruler of the Ascendant and 5th House in Pisces. She experiences confusion about what she wants and how to get it. An unwanted second child born less than a year after her brother, April grew up as the family servant and learned early that rewards came only from hard work. Although she had a fairly good relationship with her father, he rarely took her side against a dictatorial mother and eventually, he too learned to rely on April. She was able to lash out (Sun in Aries square Uranus) but only when things had gone too far and she was at the end of her rope.

With that kind of relationship foundation, April was an invaluable friend and couldn't do enough to help when she felt there was a need. In return she got the praise and approval that was lacking in her childhood and increased her feelings of self-worth in the process. The hitch came when she needed some favor in return. She didn't know how to ask in a way that would prove productive, because her wishes had not come true as a child. She did the only thing that came to mind, she used body language or made subtle hints about what she wanted and she usually ended up being disappointed.

The strong Aries Sun is intercepted. It works in an inward fashion and combined with so much Pisces, she relied on others to be as intuitive as she. If a good friend, who owed her so much, could offer assistance at that time, her dilemma would be resolved. If the offer was not forthcoming, she would store the presumed rejection in her mind for later use. When enough rejections added up, the friend was dropped with no explanation.

About Sally, April says, "We met in the logging camp where time hung heavy on our hands and we were compatible enough to stay friends all these years. Sally was always ready for a long visit over coffee when the men were at work and the wash was on the line. Life was hard up there and it would have been intolerable without good friends. Although I never asked for favors except babysitting when I was away from home, Sally was giving and fun-loving. We did silly things together to break the monotony. Sally kept her garbage on the back porch and a neighbor's cow kept getting into it and messing it up, so we poured hot water on it, and as long as we lived in camp, that cow kept a wide berth and never stepped foot on the porch again! She would gaze longingly at it from a distance and go in another direction."

Another time we fixed a rabbit dinner for a neighbor and after it had been eaten, we told her that it was the cat that had been keeping us all awake at night. Things like that kept the whole camp laughing and I have enjoyed her friendship all my adult life. I wish I could look at life the way she does.

"Sally says she had a much easier childhood than April. She has Leo rising and the Sun in the 10th House, in easy-going Gemini. Her father died when she was three (Saturn square Mars) but she had a wonderful step-father (Sun sextile Saturn) and they were a poor, but happy family. She worked away from home to help support her five younger sisters and brothers and would only see her mother on the trail to the boat landing on her way to school. There were no roads in her area in those days. Sally took the mail boat to school all her school years.

Sally has Jupiter, her 5th House ruler, in the 12th and Venus conjunct Neptune, giving her a heightened sense of intuition which has kept this friendship strong for so many years. She has the ability to detach with Uranus in the 5th and when she has had enough, she does just that. Sally never learned to drive, a surprising fact with the

Sun, Mercury and Pluto in Gemini, but April took her wherever she wanted to go.

Sally is involved in everything that happens in the building where they both now live. She knows and likes everyone, the complete opposite of April. The Sun in Gemini in the 10th House rules her Leo Ascendant and, at 82, she still heads most of the organizations. Her nimble fingers fly over her knitting and she turns out an afghan every two or three weeks in spite of all her other activities.

With strong Gemini evident, both women have a need to communicate and they spend many an afternoon reminiscing. Sally is able to get April out of the house for social functions and is adaptable enough to love her in spite of the deep-seated bitterness always present in April's conversations.

Sally says, "I'm cheerful because it is the only way to be. I pass things off. You have to live and learn and go on. I'm not as close to April now because she complains too much, but we have been friends too long for me to let it bother me."

LEO/AQUARIUS

Avoid popularity; it has many snares and no real benefit.
—William Penn

Since I want to cover all the axis combinations and I could find no friendships with the Leo/Aquarius axis that met my criteria, I am including this one as a singleton.

RON

Ron has a 5th House Sun in Pisces. Its ruler, Neptune, is conjunct his Ascendant so Ron doesn't have a clear view of himself; but he has that certain charisma that draws an admiring crowd. Although he was a star athelete and extremely popular in school, he was shy and private when the performance was over. Saturn conjunct his Ascendant indicates a sureness about his personal convictions and the desire to make and live up to his own rules and goals. Saturn is also conjunct his Moon adding caution and reserve to the already deep and brooding Scorpio. Ron enjoyed his popularity as evidenced by the Sun ruling the Midheaven, emphasis on status, honor and reputation, and the 11th House of peer groups, organizations and teamwork.

Aquarius on the 5th House needs independence and space and

may choose unusual or unorthodox friends to bring a quality of daring and excitement into life. Ron says he consistently picked friends who were either too old and experienced for him, or who were dropouts; and there were many battles with his father over these choices. Uranus, ruler of the 5th House, is in the 9th trine the Sun and sextile Jupiter. What he did was done in a big way for freedom and as rebellion to his family, "peasants" as he frequently called them. A heavy emphasis in Pisces often causes us to feel disconnected from the rest of the world.

Venus in Aries conjunct the Descendant and Mars adds to the popularity theme with charm, energy and sex appeal. Opposite Neptune, Ascendant, Saturn and the Moon, the fiery energy is diffused, controlled, quiet. This can signify the "me against them" syndrome.

About friends, Ron says, "I don't really need them. I can live just as well without any. I took a lot of people who were losers under my wing. They attached to me and I let them hang around. I was pretty popular in high school and if someone wanted me to say we were friends, I would. I didn't want anything from them and they shouldn't have wanted anything from me, except loyalty. I was more trusting and loyal than they were and once they took advantage of the friendship, it was finished and I didn't miss them. I had one friend who taught me all I know about drugs and alcohol (Pisces Sun), but he's a loser and I don't need him any more. He borrowed money and never repaid it. I don't need that again. That's just the way I am—kind of a loner. Friends are nice to have but they aren't the only thing. How do you define friendship, anyway? It's like love and you can't define it. If you have friends, loyalty is all that counts and once that is gone, the friendship is over. I'm married now and my wife is my best friend (Mars, ruler of the 7th conjunct Venus). That's all I need."

Understanding the emotional needs and complexities of our friends is essential to long-term friendships (or relationships of any kind). Today, with the high divorce rate and loneliness of single-parent families, coupled with busy careers, we need "someone to care" more than ever. Most married mothers have full time jobs and little free time for the kind of socializing April and Sally enjoyed. It is my hope that the preceeding examples will give you added insights into the world of friendship. With the hectic pace of our modern lifestyles, perhaps we have a greater need than ever to learn how to be, and to have, good friends.

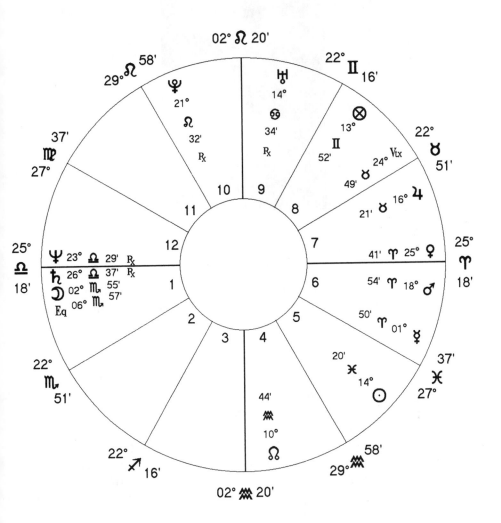

Natal Chart
Ron
Mar. 4, 1953, 9:14:0 P.M. PST
Sandpoint, ID
48N17'00" 116W33'00"
Koch Houses

Bob Mulligan

Bob Mulligan holds two degrees, a B.A. and M.A. in philosophy from Roosevelt University in Chicago. He started his career in astrology while in graduate school.

In 1974 Bob founded his business, ASTROLOGY INFORMATION, and has been a full time professional astrologer since then.

Bob operates a correspondence school with a four year program in training and he has written astrological software programs for computers including a comprehensive chart interpretation program called INDRA.

Traveling continuously, Bob has clients and students around the world. Operating regular local astrology practices in eight cities in the United States, he has written and lectured extensively, and wrote a regular astrology column between 1981 and 1989. He is currently president of NCGR's Prosig.

ASTROLOGY & PAST LIFE RELATIONSHIPS

INTRODUCTION

Astrology can be a way of learning about ourselves. Relationships are another way that we can learn about ourselves. This subject "Astrology and Past Life Relationships" fits into a greater picture of "astrology as a form of therapy," or "astrology as a way of helping us to learn about ourselves." When we use astrology as a tool for self understanding it can speed up the learning process that we go through in relationships.

As astrologers, we are continually deciphering relationships through chart comparisons. I believe that we can be of more help to our clients if we understand the karmic roots of the relationship. In the information presented here are some simple astrological tools for beginning our understanding of past life connections between people, as shown in their horoscopes.

We have a two-fold study before us: 1) the natal chart indicators of past life karma, and 2) interactions between horoscopes, indicating past life karma between these souls.

VERIFICATION

You may ask how we can possibly verify past life information. When we talk about a person's love life, profession, health, location, nationality, etc., we're talking about things in this life, and as such, we can verify our assertions by direct inspection of the facts. Some people have direct knowledge of their past lives, and it is interesting to compare their memories with what shows in their charts. However, most people have no knowledge of their past lives, and so verification is not possible.

And yet astrology as a theoretical discourse, or as a "technology" must refer to something in this life that can be verified, if astrology is to remain relevant to our clients and a growing discipline. We must be able to see an event or characteristic in the horoscope and relate it to an event or trait in the person's life. Otherwise, of what value would it be?

I have taken notes during 16 years of doing case histories with clients and have made attempts to verify the truthfulness of past life information. The material presented here is a simplification and distillation of what I have found to be true and useful in working with my clients; I say true and useful because it is good to keep in mind that the information's usefulness is sometimes more important than its truthfulness.

If indeed astrology is to be considered as therapy, then the information that we as astrologers are giving out to our clients should be of some value to the person. With that in mind, out of maybe 100 clients I work with in any given month, perhaps in only a handful of those sessions would I discuss this type of information. Why? Because the karmic level of appreciation of the chart is hidden, covert, not as open to direct inspection or awareness by the astrologer or the client. When something is hidden it is less open to criticism and correction. For instance, if you argue that I'm doing something now because of something that I am unconscious of, by definition I can't say you are wrong because I'm unconscious of the origin.

This means that the client must take the astrologer's word for something that cannot be verified now, and maybe not even in the future. While the information may be accurate, it lacks motive power in the client's life unless he can come to terms with it. Too much information of this type tends to shift the power dynamic between the astrologer and the client in a way that fosters a negative dependency on the astrologer.

What follows is what I've found that works. I limit my insights to what I can verify. Verification is through direct inspection of my own past lives and the past lives of my clients, as well as through past life regression material given by clients. This material has been further checked by an interactive process in therapy over a period of time.

Specifications:

The following factors are what I have found to be the fundamental indicators of past life relationships in the chart:

1. Any aspect within one degree of exact and on the same degree in the tropical zodiac.

2. Any aspect within one degree of exact regardless of the

placement in the zodiac.

3. Conjunctions.

4. Any aspect within three degree orb.

5. Close oppositions.

6. Aspects to Karmic Points (defined in the theoretical material).

7. Aspects from Personal points (MC, Sun, Moon, Ascendant, Moon's Node, 0 point of Aries) to planets that describe past life connections. (Explained in the theoretical material).

Obviously, several categories of involvement can occur at once, e.g. two planets conjunct within one degree and in close aspect to a karmic point. This is a very strong indicator of past life relationship potential in a natal chart or between two horoscopes.

Here are some working definitions to keep in mind before we examine the theoretical material and look at some practical examples.

DEFINITIONS

Relationships

To live is to relate. Your birth horoscope is really a chart of the first meeting between you and the universe. It shows the way you relate to the cosmos. Your birth chart is the whole universe from your soul's perspective. Consequently, it is possible to read all relationships out of your chart of birth. Therefore we look for past life indicators of relationships in the natal chart before we look at them between charts.

Past Life Relationships

Past life relationships are interactions between two souls or groups of souls, where they have some special bond from the past that requires them to get together in order to reach a karmic balance. Love relationships are generally of this type because love is the most powerful and most pervasive emotion.

Karma

Karma[1] can be divided easily into two different types: regular karma (referred to here as karma) and special karma.

---

1. For a further discussion of karma see: *The Discourse* pp. 301-339; *Beams* pp. 58-68; *Listen Humanity* pp. 93-115. All three books are by Meher Baba.

Regular karma is circumstantial karma; in other words, when you perform an action, and karma, being the law of cause and effect, means you will recieve what you have sent out. You do something nice and somebody in the future will bring that back to you; something nice will have to come back into your life at some point. Or, you do something dastardly to somebody else and get away with it and although the karma isn't instant—it doesn't manifest right away—at some point there has to be a harvest, it has to come back to you. Simply put, everything we do, good or bad, comes back to us. When we create love then love comes back into our life at some point. Someone else brings it back to us.

So, if you murder someone in a lifetime, it doesn't mean that same person will murder you, even though you have the karma to be murdered. Karmic actions seek resolution or balance. This agenda has to be worked out for each soul in a catetory of experience but it does not require the same too souls to be together again in order to achieve this balance. A different soul with similar and matching karma can perform the action for us, now or in another incarnation.

Special Karma

The second type of karma is special karma: every so often, something happens between particular souls that's special and unique. Special karma is similar to something ruled by Venus. Like the planet of love and art, special karma is artistic, beautiful, unique and creative. In this type of karma, the two literal souls get together again to share, create and recreate in some experience. Special karma is our primary interest when we look at charts for the past life relationships manifesting in this life.

Whenever we speak of karma as being the cause of action, inevitably the question of responsibility arises—Do we have a choice? Are we destined to do what we do, to relate to certain people? The question of free will is a very big one, but it really is not a practical issue here. What is important is that when applying astrological information which you, as an astrologer, are honest and have a proper attitude toward your work and your client. No astrologer speaks authoritatively as to what ASTROLOGY can do. All you can say is what you as an astrologer can do. Astrology is much bigger than any astrologer and no astrologer I have ever met really understands it perfectly. Ten years from now the astrology we are so proud of today will be thought of as very simple minded. Consequently, honesty and sanity dictate that when discussing the horoscope, particularly this kind of information, to indicate that these are only tendencies and that in your professional opinion, this is what they indicate.

I use transits, progressions, and solar arc directions as general timing guidelines in a chart, and between two charts, to understand the significance of happenings in relationships. The overall compatibility and expected duration of the relationship should be very obvious in the natal charts alone.

THEORY

A. Houses
B. Signs
C. Planets
D. Karmic Points
E. Aspects

Astrology can be simplified into the four basic building blocks: the signs, houses, planets and aspects. These four ingredients have something to say about our past life karmic patterns with other people.

What is a natal chart but the whole cosmos from one soul's perspective? Consequently, everything in the cosmos is shown in the natal chart, and everyone in the whole universe fits somewhere into everybody else's chart. So when you're assessing relationships between people you should always be able to find that relationship in your own chart, and in the other person's chart, and find it in all of your client's charts.

Houses

One simple system for seeing other people and things in the natal chart is to look at the house that indicates this person, place or thing by its relationship to the person: the 7th House is the first marriage partner, the 9th House is the second marriage partner, the 11th the third, and so on. I have seen this work where people have been married up to seven times. If you follow the houses around, the symbolic indicators of each subsequent marriage partner is shown in each subsequent house.

As you work with the houses you will notice that some have very special significance. The 12th House is the consolidation of

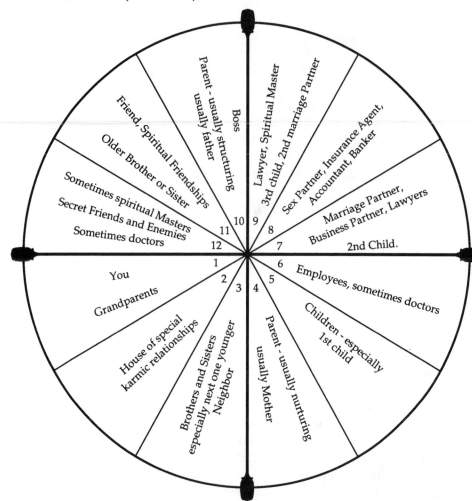

Natal Houses and the people they indicate.
Conjunctions to house cusps can be very important.

what the person brings from the past. If you read astrology books from the last century, the 12th House is the house of secret enemies or things inside of you that get in your way. But as you study astrology more and more you become convinced that this house is a great asset that you can bring forward in this lifetime. In that sense it is the consolidation of everything you have done before.

The 2nd House is extremely important when you're looking at the chart from the karmic level. This house is the memory track. It is the 3rd from the 12th, the 12th House signifying the consolidation of the past. The 2nd House represents the mind of your last life, or the consolidation of your past lives. Special karmic relationships often show up in the 2nd House. Why? This is the house of material resources and self-worth; it shows how we appraise ourselves and is thus extremely important. Relationships that show up here have a great deal to say about what will happen in the course of this lifetime in terms of close critical relationships.

The 3rd House depicts what we are attempting to work out in this lifetime, the residue from our last lifetime or it can be a by-product of a number of lifetimes that follow. In most astrology books the 3rd House is referred to as your early environment and, when as an adult you try to go back you see these areas as transitory and less significant as you get older, and the 4th House gathers strength.

The 4th House is the foundation of the horoscope; it is where we stand, and the pattern that develops in this house affects the overriding karma for the lifetime. So any 4th House relationships become extremely meaningful.

The 9th and 12th Houses denote connections with the spiritual path and a spiritual master. Whenever you speak of karma, cause and effect, and you talk about special relationships it's important to remember that the most significant, the most karmic relationship that anyone ever forms in any lifetime is with a spiritual master. Christians may think of that as a relationship with Jesus, taken as a personal savior. For a Buddhist, it may refer to forming a relationship with Buddha, or if they're part of the general esoteric tradition, to form a relationship with their higher consciousness, the oversoul. In India there is a long tradition of working with a spiritual teacher to advance the soul. That relationship is more primary than the one between husband and wife.

Marriage is the second most potent form of karma. Obviously, when you meet and marry, this person is likely to be someone you have had much involvement with in other lifetimes (not just somebody in another lifetime that you bumped into and liked); this is someone to whom you commit because you feel obligations involving them. Saturn, the Lord of Karma, is exalted in Libra, the sign of partnership. Saturn is the planet that shows consolidation.

Thus even if (or especially if) marriage partners don't get along, if they don't like each other, the fact that they married in this lifetime suggests that some potent karma brought them together.

In using your chart as a tool for your own spiritual development, your unfoldment at that level is different than using your chart as a therapeutic tool. In the New Age there is often confusion between the spiritual and the therapeutic happenings; they exist in entirely different realms even though the vocabulary sounds very similar. Our concerns here are in using the chart as a therapeutic tool. Past life relationships is a special subdivision of astrology as therapy.

The 12th House is most clearly aligned with meditation, the 5th with bhakti, and the 10th House with karma yoga. Most of us have a job which is in the realm of the 10th House of career, but we don't consider it "service," i.e., we don't consider it karma yoga; however, you can use your 10th House that way. Most of us have love relationships, we experience romance, we share 5th House relationships, but we don't often consider the deeper aspect of it as a creative act, as bhakti yoga, as devotion as a higher worship. Many of us spend time in solitude, in prisons or hospitals, but we don't consider it "meditation." We all use our 12th House, we just don't consider it from a spiritual angle. But it's all accessible and this is a possible inclination to consider when you're looking at the houses of the horoscope.

Signs

The signs of the zodiac assume significance in deciphering past life relationships. The Fixed signs are consolidating by nature, they collect energy and are always the repositor of karma. Placements in these signs mirror circumstances that have been a long time in formation. They represent either your greatest assets and strengths or your most toxic areas. So, relationships shown by the Fixed signs often have an added twist. There's a certain spin on those relationships because they tend to be either much deeper and more fulfilling, or to be much more painful than the average relationship.

The Cardinal and Mutable placements in a chart seem to entail a lighter form of karma. These signs have individual karmic significance as do the four element positions in the chart.

Planets

The Moon always represents the past, and points to a consolidation of where you've been in the past. Anything connected with the Moon has to do with a consolidation of your habits from the past, what you have done in the past. Saturn, the Lord of Karma, always represents your obligations. Feelings of separation are created through Saturn, and relationships that form from the Saturnian principle are often the ones with the ability to endure. In Vivian Robson's book, *An Astrology Guide To Your Sex Life*, she commented that many times in the charts of marriage partners you find an aspect of Saturn to either the Sun or the Moon and she had no idea of why that should be the case. If you do a lot of synastry work you often find a strong Saturn in the charts of people who stay together. Saturn is always the glue. Sometimes it may stop people from getting together, acting as a barrier, like a shell that keeps people from recognizing each other; but once they are together, Saturn can be the cement, the special bond of what I refer to as past life responsibilities; and when these bonds are shared in a personal way, they indicate a responsibility to each other.

Pluto often suggests involvement with the public. Pluto rules psychology, the underworld, and has a connection with the symbolic level of our collective consciousness. It reflects the part of us that deals in symbols. These symbolic archetypes get embedded in our general consciousness, and for this reason you will notice between people's charts that Pluto often refers to things that happen on a large scale; happenings that involve millions of people or world events.

You cannot ignore Mars in any of these patterns because Mars is our reason for incarnating (as Alan Leo, the father of modern astrology, told us in his book, *Mars*). Mars is desire. We want something; if we didn't want anything we wouldn't be here. Mars is the propellant that brought us into life and it shows what we are here to do, what our urge is for this lifetime. Mars symbolizes what we want, and by house, sign and aspects, what brought us into this incarnation.

Jupiter is the king of the Gods and spends one year in each sign of the zodiac. Jupiter depicts the grand organizer, the big bureaucrat, the chief administrator. The late Indian astrologer E. Krishnamacharya said of Jupiter, "There is power in the arrangement of objects. It is the synthesizing agent of the whole universe. It keeps the universe in the poise of existence ... The power that is hidden in the arrangement can be compared to the electric current in a cell. No individual part of the cell contains the current. It is the arrangement of the various parts of the cell in the required fashion that produces the current..."[2]

Jupiter is the principle of amassment, of bringing everything together and being able to create something out of it. It is in that spirit Jupiter represents consolidated wisdom from the past. When people discuss the Jupiter principle they tend to think of having a good time doing things to excess, going overboard. But Jupiter isn't just the principle of "big," it's also the principle of administration. And in that spirit, when Jupiter is involved in these past life patterns, productivity is highlighted to bring us out of ourselves, to make us stronger, better, more fulfilled.

Every planet has some significance connected with the past because our whole chart is an imprint of the past. We are how we are, not because of the time that we were born; we were born at the time we were born because we are how we are. This is the prescription, this is the way we came into being. In that spirit, we can look at each of the planets as having some special significance and some special emphasis in past life relationship patterns.

Venus is the planet of alchemy, just as the sextile is the aspect of alchemy. What is alchemy? It is the ability to take something from one level and move it to another level, to see an emerging property. We look at a beautiful work of art, Van Gogh or Rembrandt, and something happens inside as we stare at the painting. We are moved, not by the paint, not by the canvas, but by the image of beauty emerging from it. It's an ineffable quality and that is Venus. In astrology when we consider rulership we often correlate it to "nouns." We attribute the paint and the painting to Venus, when in fact all rulerships are really actions, are really verbs, and when we get deeply involved in what happens behind the surface of objects we are looking purely at the Venus principle. This is why in relationships Venus has the ability to refine, to bring us to some greater sense of inner vision of our lives and what they are about.

Karmic Points

There are some significant karmic points I have found to be helpful in the process of isolating special karma in a chart or between charts. These karmic points are extremely beneficial in regular analysis of the horoscope, but in the context of past life links

---

2. *Spiritual Astrology*, pp. 247-8.

they've really come into their own. Five axes create ten of these points: Ascendant/Descendant, Midheaven/Imum Coeli, East Point/West Point, Vertex/Anti-Vertex, North Node of the Moon/South Node of the Moon. One further karmic point that I have found very effective is the Part of Fortune. These are the primary significators of past life karmic connections operating in this life.

The definition of the Part of Fortune is a point in the chart located by adding the longitude of the Ascendant to the longitude of the Moon and subtracting the longitude of the Sun. The Part of Fortune is always at the same angle to the Ascendant as the Sun and Moon are to each other. It is a point of synthesis and shows how we bring a focus of inner motivation to bear on an issue, project or person. The Part of Fortune shows intensity in a chart or between charts and is a point of karmic emphasis that takes on the coloring of any planets in aspect to it.

The North and South Nodes of the Moon are very intriguing. The North Node of the Moon provides a karmic direction for the individual, so that when you are growing, you're moving toward your North Node. When you move toward the South Node it is toward something that you have done in the past.

It is clear to me that the North Node shows your growth pattern and the South Node represents something you struggle against most of the time. As one famous astrologer who has her South Node in Leo says, "But if you did it good before, why not do it again!"

Aspects to the Nodal Axis show potential for developing relationships that pull your whole chart along. As one of my favorite astrologers, Ron Davison, has pointed out, the Part of Fortune and the North Node are two points in the horoscope that represent synthesis between the three major factors: the Sun, Moon and the Earth (the point of intersection). They synthesize, they bring together, and they are also points of potential growth.

The Ascendant/Descendant axis has to do with how we form a sense of personal awareness, so inter-chart involvement with the Asc/Desc has to do with a feeling of special connection with someone else. The MC/IC axis signifies how we bond with people through group activity and the special obligations that we feel toward others. I call the Vertex/Anti-Vertex the axis of special interest karma.

If a planet is on either of these points, within a degree or so, that point is electrically charged. At the Vertex you may feel that something is being taken away from you completely, or is totally out of your control.

We often think of the Descendant as a point of contact with the public. The axis of awareness is referred to as the Ascendant/Descendant and the Descendant is where you meet the world. In working with comparison charts, we frequently see the Descendant as a place of projection where we give our qualities of self to someone else. I have found the Vertex to operate similarly, but carried to a higher level exponentially. With a placement closely conjunct the Vertex. the level of projection is so intense and complete that it may seem beyond belief. Planets in aspect to the Vertex often feel fated, out of control.

At the Anti-Vertex, 180 degrees away, on the other hand, rather than just identifying with the Ascendant, it is often the place where we feel things are really in our control. We feel empowered. At the Vertex, we feel that decisions are in another's hands, even if we acknowledge the responsibility, we wonder "Could I have done something different?" Often we feel we don't have a choice. It's just like "Well, that's what I am, that's what I had to do and this is how it happened and I knew it was going to be this way but this is what I did." With the Anti-Vertex there tends to be a more pensive quality, a feeling that this is what I would like, this is how I would have it be.

In my opinion the East Point/West Point, is the Karma of Idealization. Why? Because it has to do with our ability to project as well as receive the projection of an ideal from others. This is most obvious when there is a great difference in degree between the East Point and the Ascendant and there is a planet conjunct or in close aspect to the East point in one chart or between charts. When the East Point differs greatly from the Ascendant, it is as if the person is saying with their Ascendant, "Here's what I am," and what he is saying about the East Point is, "Here's what I'd really like to be, this is what I'd rather have. This is what I am moving toward." The East Point acts as an idealization of the self. The West Point reflects the idealization of the marrige partner or a close one-on-one connection with another.

In the Uranian system the East Point is the Ascendant for the Meridian house system, which is a latitude independent system of houses that you determine by directing the MC by Right Ascension in two hour increments around the wheel. The East Point is your Ascendant at 0 degrees of latitude (on the Equator). Because the houses are independent of latitude they're independent of our environment, of the environmental influence.

The symbolic consequence of the East Point is that you view it as your ideal self. If you could have your preference you would express as your East Point rather than your Ascendant. This is most unique in counseling people who have a planet sandwiched between the Ascendant and East Point. When this happens with the East Point in the 12th House, the person feels the need to project into the 1st House. When the East Point is in the 1st House, and a planet is between the Ascendant and the East Point, there is a need to retreat into the 12th House. This principle works the same way in terms relating to the 7th House and the West Point.

Because the East Point/West Point has to do with the idealization of others and of self and because the Vertex/Anti-Vertex has to do with this highly focused, specialized karma, I recommend putting those points in charts when you're trying to assess past life relationships. Not because you need them, but they help your judgment tremendously if you know how to use them. It isn't so important what you use, but it is helpful to keep your charts as clean as possible so that you are not distracted from seeing the most impactive, intrinsic relationships between stellar bodies.

These axes, the four just discussed, Ascendant/Descendant, MC/IC, Vertex/Anti-Vertex, East Point/West Point, including the Part of Fortune and Nodes, are from my perspective the most important symbols in the chart for working out past life relationship patterns. We all view the world through our own outlook and develop our own techniques and style. Any three astrologers discussing the above information would come up with entirely different techniques and styles. That doesn't mean that one is right and the others wrong. It just indicates that we all see things differently. But, if you follow the concepts given, you will find that these are simple tools for getting to the core of special karmic relationships.

The Uranian system is famous for familiarizing us with the use of the 0 point of Aries as a personal point. It works and can be an amazingly descriptive of special karma between people especially as it relates to the conditions of the culture and the world. This point is actually 8 points; it encompasses all 0 degree Cardinal and 15 degrees of all Fixed signs. Those eight points in the zodiacal system, represent special areas of emphasis that affect the whole globe, the world, and if we're assessing the charts of world leaders or people who activate events, they point out the karma germane to these people and events.

Table of Aspects				
Major Aspects		Degree of Separation	Orb of Influence	**Like the Nature of**
♂	conjunction	0°	5°-10°	☉
☍	opposition	180°	5°-10°	♄
□	square	90°	5°-10°	♂
△	trine	120°	5°- 8°	♃
✳	sextile	60°	5°- 7°	♀
Minor Aspects				
⊻	semi-sextile	30°	2°- 3°	☽
⊼	quincunx	150°	5°- 8°	♆
<	semi-square	45°	3°	☿
⊡	sesquequadrate	135°	5°	♅
P	or parallel or			
#	contra-parallel	0° of declination 1°		☋

Figure 2

Aspects

Aspects have significance in issues carried over from the past, both the aspects in each natal chart as well as those between the two charts. I have been talking primarily about the natal chart because we can gather a lot of information about past lives from the natal chart. Before you put charts together you must assess each one individually.

The aspect orbs given in the "Table of Aspects" (figure 2) are applicable both in natal charts and between charts; however, in discussing the highly specialized karma showing active past life relationships, it is wise to narrow orbs to almost nothing. In speaking of highly personalized karma the most telling features are planets on the same degree. Almost as important are aspects within a degree of exact. For this purpose, I rarely use more than a three degree orb. You may want to consider a little wider orb for conjunctions, but most factors show up best with very tight orbs.

Some astrologers feel that aspects show only quantity, not quality i.e, conjunctions are stronger than squares, but not inherently different in quality, just in strength. Many modern schools of astrological thought, including the Uranian and Cosmobiological schools, ignore this type of aspect and concentrate entirely on the nature of the planets involved in the aspect. It is possible to work consistently along these lines and get positive results, but you will be unnecessarily handicapped in past life relationship work. The nature of the aspect contributes so much information to the description of the relationship.

In looking at Figure 2, the "Table of Aspects," you will notice that each aspect is correlated to the nature of a planet. There is a long astrological history of assigning planetary energies to the aspects and these correlations have special significance in past life work by providing further clues to the nature of connections between people. There is a quality to each relatioship shown by the aspect type.

There are three current theories of aspect correlation to planetary natures: 1) A reasoning process based on the zodiac and looking at the meaning of the signs involved starting from 0 degrees Aries. (See *Astrology, the Divine Science* by Marcia Moore and Mark Douglas pp. 413-595, and *Perceptions in Astrology* by Bil Tierney, pp. 1-43 for familiarity with this approach.) 2) Giving rulership of each aspect to a planet. (The germ of this idea is presented in *The Astrological Dictionary* by L. Edward Johndro, pp. 26-41 and *Johndro's Theory of Planetary Rulerships of Aspects Per Se* by Al H. Morrison.) 3) Reasoning by analogous energies. This third type of meaning is the way I ascribe planetary natures to aspects. These systems overlap and there are many derivations of these theories, reflecting the different styles of many different astrologers. (See *The Technique of Prediction* by Ron Davison pp. 38-40.) The correlations used here have borne out through many years of formal observation and are the traditional choices in the ancient wisdom systems. (The clearest exposition on this subject is *Cosmic Astrology* by June Wakefield, pp. 141-142.)

Conjunctions are always the most important, the most striking. Conjunctions are like the Sun, they are both energy points. In a natal chart, you can always start with the conjunction as a point of impact. The house where a conjunction falls shows some past life relationship karma. The houses ruled by the planets in conjunction show circumstances of the past life relationships. So do mutual receptions between these planets. This assessment provides a blueprint when you start comparing charts to know where to begin.

Oppositions are second in significance and often indicate works in progress from the past. The opposition is similar to a Saturn aspect; both relate to our sense of obligation. Both pertain to awareness of self and of others, that that division, that sense of separateness. Oppositions are worked out through relationships with others.

Saturn is in its exaltation in Libra which is the sign of balance; it is opposite Aries, the beginning sign of the zodiac. Cancer is the sign relating to coming into creation. (See Alice A. Bailey *Esoteric Astrology* p. 102, p. 312.) Saturn rules Capricorn, Cancer's opposite sign. Traditional yoga texts tell us Saturn rules the Mooladhara or root Chakra at the base of the spine. This is the resting place of the kundalini, the force that created the galaxies. (Consult any traditional text on yoga. There is a nice diagram in *The Complete Illustrated Book of Yoga* by Swami Vishnudevananda, p. 292.) This Saturn ruled placement is opposite the crown Chakra ruled by the Sun. The Sun is like the nature of the conjunction which is a symbol of union or synthesis.

The alchemical instructions for turning lead (Saturn) into gold (the Sun) is really an allegory for the spiritual path of return from separateness (Saturn) to Union with God (Sun) through the subtle energy wheels of light (the Chakras) located along the spinal column. The inner path starts with facing our outer obligations (Saturn, root Chakra, law of necessity, limitations of time) and continues until reaching union (the Sun, the crown Chakra, self sustainment, infinity).

The opposition works through awareness of others. If you take a piece of string and lay it on the floor, a perfect circle is as large an area as can be inscribed by the string. Two objects on a perfect circle can never be further apart (separate) than when they are in opposition. Opposing planets are separated as far as they can be which implies separateness as a Saturn principle. We fear (Saturn) that which is different (as far away from us as can be, i.e. the opposition) and other than ourselves. (An excellent discussion of this line of reasoning is found in *Symbolism and Astrology* by Alan Leo published by L. N. Fowler.)

Many oppositions in a person's chart generate an energy analogous to Saturn, i.e. frustrating compromises and and motivation by obligation and a sense of limitation. (An interesting discussion of this line of reasoning is found in *The Art of Chart Synthesis* by Tracy Marks, pp. 55-57.)

Squares function like Mars, so they show a desire, an imbalance. The hidden key: all desires unbalance us, all desires move us away from our centers. As anyone who has studied the martial arts can tell us, if we are standing still, balanced, and an angry person attacks us, that person is at an immense disadvantage because the anger unbalances, and moves them off their center. A desire is like that, the square aspect is like that. We want something and we become very aware that we want it. Mars is always Mars: it always represents desire. But the highest manifestation of Mars is bravery or courage, the ability to shore up, to fight for a cause, to be devoted to some ideal.

Both the square and opposition create abrasive energy as opposed to the trine and sextile which create harmonious energy (see *Astrology, Karma and Transformation* by Steven Arroyo, pp. 108-115). The opposition is worked out through dealings with others; the square can show internal frustration and potential for developing a past life relationship that will bring that conflict to the surface. (This idea is graphically expressed by Zipporah Dobyns in *Finding the Person in the Horoscope*, pp. 25-35.)

Trines and sextiles are extremely important in this pattern; the trine often works like Jupiter, suggesting the ability to create new things by assembling ingredients, playing the role of administrator, acting out the management aspect. And like Venus, the alchemical symbol, the ability to transmute, the sextile has this capacity and should not be ignored. When there is really deep karma between people, how is it going to show up? Look for tight conjunctions. If the conjunctions are within one degree of exact, that in itself may be sufficient to detail a relationship that would lasting the whole lifetime.

Duration is one component of assessing whether a relationship is important. You know someone for five minutes, and that person could have such an impact on you that it can change your whole life. Many astrologers have had a client come back ten years later and say "You know, that two hours that we spent together ten years ago changed my life." It happens. Why? Not just because astrology is a potent tool, not just because it is the best form of therapy when it's practiced correctly with integrity, but because when one goes to see an astrologer one is acting out his/her special karma. There is that special karma between you and your client. You will be affected by your clients just as they are affected by you.

EXAMPLES

Now we turn our attention to some specific examples. The following charts are those of clients with whom I have had contact and with whom I have discussed their charts and have received verification from them.

Example 1

In our first example we will compare Meher Baba's chart (#1) to the chart of two of his disciples: Eruch Jessawalla (#2) and Bhau Kalchuri (#3). Eruch Jessawalla's chart shows four major keys that indicate deep karmic past life connections with the chart of Meher Baba.

The Moon at 15 degrees Taurus conjuncts Meher Baba's IC, within a degree. Neptune at 4 degrees Leo conjuncts Baba's Descendant; these are two of the most karmic points being touched off by the Moon and Neptune. Eruch's Mercury conjuncts Meher Baba's Part of Fortune. Again, an incredibly tight conjunction. Finally, his Venus at 6 degrees Virgo, very closely conjuncts Meher Baba's Vertex.

Venus rules Eruch's Sun and Mercury rules the 8th House where his Sun is placed; his Mercury and Venus are in mutual reception and both have very strong rulershlps in his chart. Meher Baha observed a vow of silence for many years and communicated with his disciples and to the world through a unique series of hand gestures. He didn't verbalize at all, yet he wrote voluminously, communicating through hand gestures. Eruch was the primary person who interpreted his hand gestures, which is symbolic of Mercury and with Venus in Virgo Eruch was able to give immense attention to the finest detail; the subtlest movement of Baba's eyebrows could constitute a whole sentence. Neptune on the Descendant could

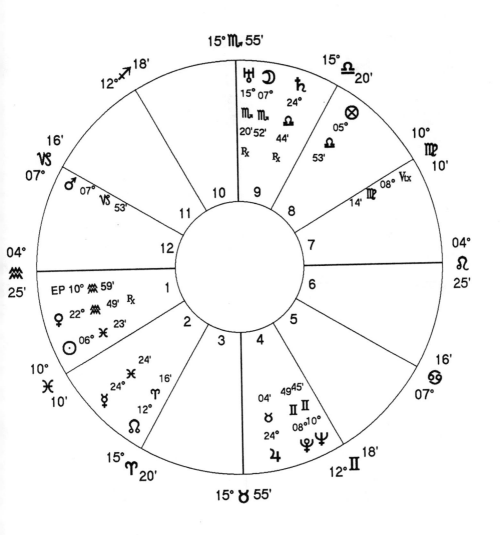

Chart 1
Meher Baba
Feb. 25, 1894, 5:00 A.M. ST
Poona, India
18N32 73E52
Placidus Houses

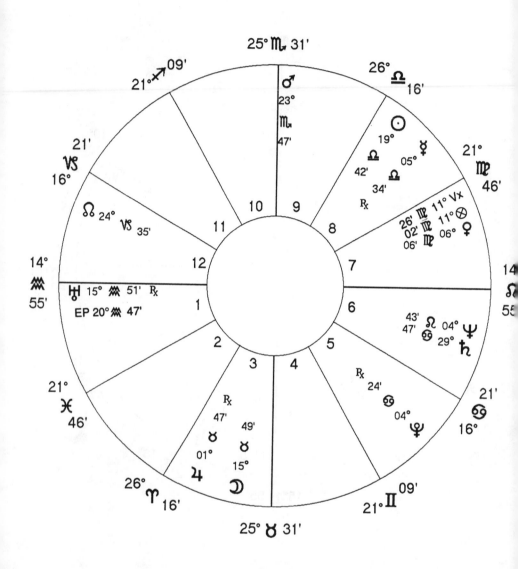

Chart 2
Eruch Jessawalla
Oct. 13, 1916, 2:45 P.M. ST
Bombay, India
18N58 72E50
Placidus Houses

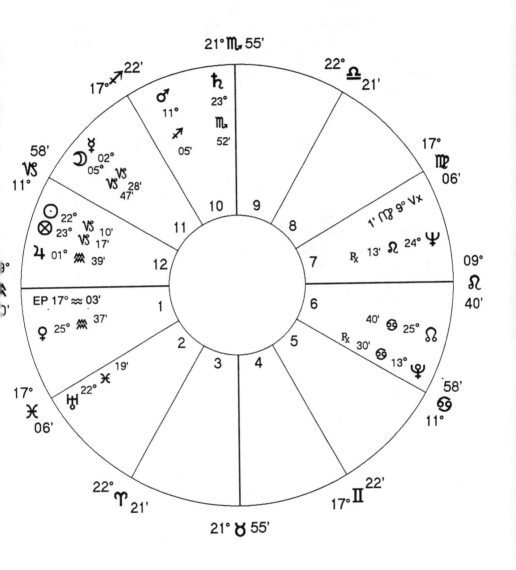

Chart 3
Bhau Kalchuri
Jan. 13, 1926, 8:00 A.M. ST
Balaghat, India
21N48 80E11
Placidus Houses

show a unique type of psychic link, which enabled him to decipher through body language and gestures myriad pieces of information. He took care of Meher Baba's physical body, and was his personal attendant as well. His Moon, conjunct Meher Baba's 4th house cusp suggested a nurturing, mothering contact.

All three (Meher Baba, Eruch, and Bhau) have Aquarius rising and all had highly interesting and unique relationships to each other.

Eruch was still a small child when he first met Meher Baba. His parents were Baba's disciples. The whole family gave up everything to follow him. His parents were the richest people in the town of Nagpur, India and owned the only automobile in the town at the time. They had a gigantic palace and sold everything, gave it away and went and lived a very simple ashram life as happy, free-spirited servants of the Lord for many years. One must assume there was something very deep and bonding going on. Anyone could do something that changed his/her life abruptly, then have second thoughts later; but when someone turns his/her life around and goes in one direction for a long number of years and never looks back, we must assume that there is something at the special karma level going on.

Looking at Bhau Kalchuri's chart (#3) in aspect to Meher Baba's reveals the Ascendant, MC, Vertex and East Point are all conjunct between the two charts. The angles line up closely with each other. The Moon and Mercury in Bhau's chart conjunct Meher Baba's Mars. I enjoy looking at Meher Baba's chart more than anyone else's because it's just perfect in any system you may choose. Mars in Capricorn in the 12th House sextiles both the Sun and the Moon, certainly a very powerful placement, a very focused kind of karma. Mars is right on the cusp of the 12th, strong, potent, very inward, and since it receives a conjunction from Bhau Kalchuri's Moon, it suggests an important, specialized kind of karma, showing something from the past. The 9th House often shows a connection with a spiritual master; both Baba and Kalchuri have Venus ruling the 9th; their Venuses are conjunct each other in the 1st House, in Aquarius, indicating spiritual sympatico between them.

Bhau had been a disciple of Baba's in his last lifetime, died as an old man, incarnated and came back to him as a disciple in this lifetime, so Meher Baba's advent being long, and Bhau, tuning in twice like that, unique placements to say the least, is one of the reasons I thought there would be some good indicators here. Bhau's Jupiter conjuncts Baba's Ascendant, and his Saturn closely trines Mercury in Meher Baba's chart. Mercury is significant in Baba's chart because it's in Pisces (he kept silent for 44 years) sextile Jupiter in Taurus; both Mercury and Jupiter quincunx Saturn in the 9th House; 24 degrees shows up as a repetitive theme between Bhau's and Meher Baba's charts, both having several planets between 21 and 24 degrees in different signs. So Saturn and Mercury closely trine one another tie the two patterns together. Uranus in Bhau's chart is conjunct Mercury in Baba's chart and the Venus's conjunct gives Bhau's chart complete access to this big pattern involving Mercury, Jupiter and Saturn between the charts.

What in Bhau's chart shows that he would incarnate and again become a follower of Baba's? The Sun and the Moon are in a closing angle, a balsamic Moon suggesting that this incarnation is a fulfillment of something that has happened before. The Moon last passed over Mercury. Bhau has done some very important writing on Baba's behalf and has also written a 20 volume biography on Meher Baba's life.

The past incarnation is shown by several other factors. I suggest that the Moon being the symbol of the past, the balsamic cycle implies that he's finishing up something previously begun and Bhau's Moon is such a potent position on Baba's Mars indicates some special karma. The Sun and the Part of Fortune are conjunct right on his South Node suggesting that this life is the consolidation of something he set in motion before. Saturn, the planet of consolidation is in the Fixed sign Scorpio, of mystery, of holding things over; it's in the 10th House, the most elevated planet in his chart. It is the Star of Destiny, ruling the Sun, the Moon, the South Node, and closely trines Baba's Mercury at 24 degrees Pisces, another indication of his ability to interpret Baba's gestures. Bhau's Saturn is widely conjunct his 10th cusp, the house of karma yoga, the ability to put life into motion. Uranus in Bhau's chart conjuncts Meher Baba's Mercury, giving broad scope and universalizing the Baba's message.

Example 2

The second example of a past life relationship carried over into this life is Jo (#4) and Denny (#5). These two people have an interesting relationship. They are both therapists of different types. Jo

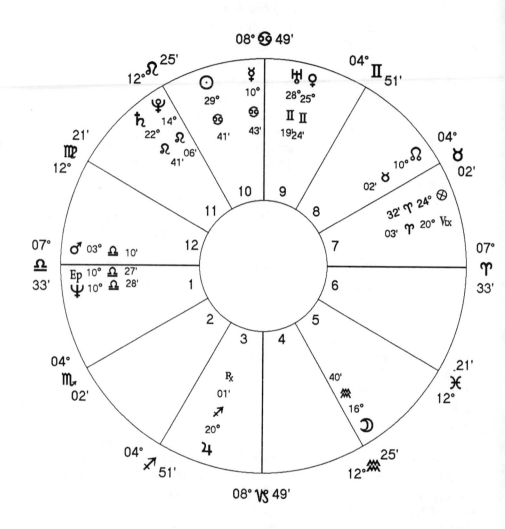

Chart 4
Jo
July 22, 1948, 11:21 A.M. DST
New Bedford, MA
41N38 70W56
Placidus Houses

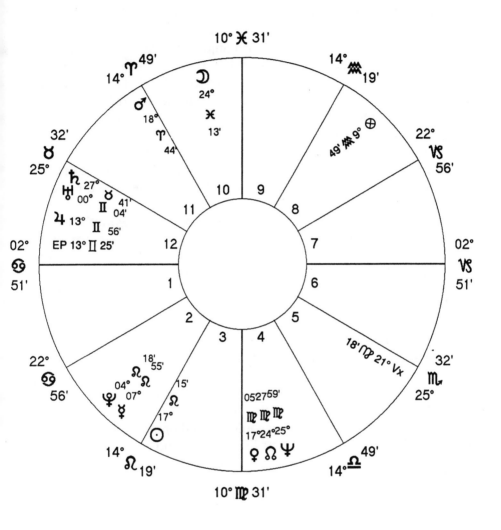

Chart 5
Denny
Aug. 10, 1941, 2:05 A.M. ST
Lancaster, OH
39N43 82W36
Placidus Houses

worked very diligently to get her career on a positive footing and thus did not marry until she was quite mature. Of course, with a 10th House Sun and a strong chart, it was extremely important to secure her career first. With Mars conjunct the Ascendant, Neptune conjunct the East Point, Vertex, and Part of Fortune in the 7th House, we can anticipate that she would have some kind of special karmic relationship in her lifetime. Women with Mars in the 12th House often never marry. Mars so close to the Ascendant, may indicate that she has been cloistered as a Nun or a Monk in a recent incarnation and she has memories of this. I've done some past life work with her. The male imagery in the chart (Sun on the 29th degree of Cancer, Mars in the 12th) indicates she may have some difficulties connecting with an appropriate male in this life.

Denny had been married before, so Jo was Denny's second wife. He has Mars and the Sun closely trine and his Mars conjuncts Jo's Vertex. From the moment they met they were both swept away by the relationship. Jo felt she was off center and Denny sensed something totally inevitable about it. Denny's Mars trines both Jo's Jupiter and Saturn (forming a Grand Trine) and her Saturn conjunct his Sun, sets a very tight pattern of energy involving her Vertex, Saturn and Jupiter with his Mars and Sun (the two masculine symbols). This strong energy pattern brought a sense of closure or completion for both of them. They debated the wisdom of getting married and discussed the possibility of divorce. They proceeded very slowly with the relationship, discussing and debating, but with a sense of fatality all the way, as if they couldn't really make it any different.

Jo's Mercury closely trine Denny's MC indicates to me that the two had been related in the past. Her Saturn conjunct his Sun reflects a sense of obligation between the two of them and this, as it turned out, from past life information, was verified. They had been soldiers together with him as the higher ranked officer and she executing his orders. This past life relationship eventually disintegrated because of her lack of empowerment. They talked a lot and tried to work their way through it. They had gotten off on an unequal footing in the relationship earlier in this lifetime because she was in therapy with him when they met. Any relationship with an unequal power base is difficult and sometimes impossible to balance out in one lifetime.

In speaking of karma, we may ask the question, "Who owes what to whom?" Obligations always flow in both directions. When a karmic obligation must be met it's one person's obligation to give and the other person's obligation to receive. In special karma there has to be some kind of mutual fulfillment for both people. It was not so much that Jo owed something to Denny or that Denny owed something to her, it was that they really owed something to each other. Their path this time around involves learning with her Jupiter and his Sun developing a pattern of growth for both of them. She helps him reorganize his energy. During Viet Nam, he was part of a Rambo-type special forces team and apparently did a good job of coming home and setting his war experiences aside. At age eighteen he was told by the Army that he had a life expectancy of about three months. The Government spent a ton of money training him to do outrageous acts and when the War was over he returned home and had to try to set up some normal kind of life. He became a therapist as a natural by-product of his own evolution. Jo, I believe, really helped him stabilize internally. He had stabilized externally but stabilizing internally was a much deeper, more difficult situation.

Karma is not always quite so simple to work out. I met a woman who had been married for 20 years; there was no great passion between she and her husband; the relationship was pleasant, cordial. He was a noted diplomat in the government and she was very spiritually minded. She gave big dinner parties for him, entertained people from all over the world and was a most charming hostess. The karma was that he had saved her life in another incarnation and she was paying that back; it took 20 years of her life to do so. Jo and Denny's karma is not of that variety. It's not quite so clear-cut. There is give and take in both directions. In a vaster sense, it was Jo repaying karma to Denny for something he had done for her in a past lifetime, but she repressed her feelings in their past relationship.

Each of these people have challenging natal charts, especially in regard to partnership. She, in some sense, held the power in the relationship with Mars ruling her 7th House, but it didn't really feel like that to her. Neither of them felt empowered in the relationship and they spent their whole married life consciously trying to get on target. Jo has Pluto conjunct Denny's 3rd House cusp as well as his Sun highlighting power issues between them. Conjunctions to the House cusps are very important in the Placidus house system.

Example 3

Marti (#6) and Marilyn (#7) are two women living together in a long term committed relationship. When there is special karma between two people of the same gender in a romantic relationship, but certainly not what you'd call a traditional marriage, what do we look for? Marti has never been married, nor has she ever been in a romantic relationship with a woman. She and Marilyn met, fell in love, and have been living together for five years. They seem to have a very wholesome, balanced relationship. Marilyn had been married, has a child and is ten years older than Marti.

Marti has the Moon in the 12th House sandwiched between the East Point and the Ascendant. The Moon in the 12th House acts in an inward way and is quite meditative. With her Gemini Sun, Marti is always attempting to bring out the gregarious side of her nature, and move the soft, sensitive side of the Moon into the 1st House. With the Moon opposing Neptune, there is some confusion about love and need and warmth and givingness; she has worked a lot of it out through her artistic talent. She's an art therapist and does outstanding work. Pluto closely trines her Moon and may be an indicator of some special karma with women. On a more general natal chart level we could explore the relationship with the mother, which is always of extreme foundational importance with any Moon/Pluto contact, but here we are addressing special karmic relationships. When we move from the psychological to the karmic level of interpretation, this aspect generally shows the potential for past life relationships with a woman extending into this incarnation.

The planetary Heliocentric Nodal placements color and emphasize other facets of the horoscope. Marti has the heliocentric South Node of Mars at 20 degrees Taurus on her Ascendant. This is a very potent degree expressing powerful energy, trapped desires and the ability to endure. It also possibly expresses past life karmic issues with men or the masculine form.

Looking at both charts, Marilyn's Venus, Sun and Mercury all closely aligned in Scorpio fall on Marti's Descendant which indicates special closeness. Marti's Venus/Sun conjunction closely opposing Jupiter indicates something to be worked out through someone else. The 2nd House, (desire for sensual pleasure, the material world) and Jupiter in Sagittarius in the 8th may be a desire for control or a feeling wanting to be alone. Marilyn's Jupiter conjuncts her

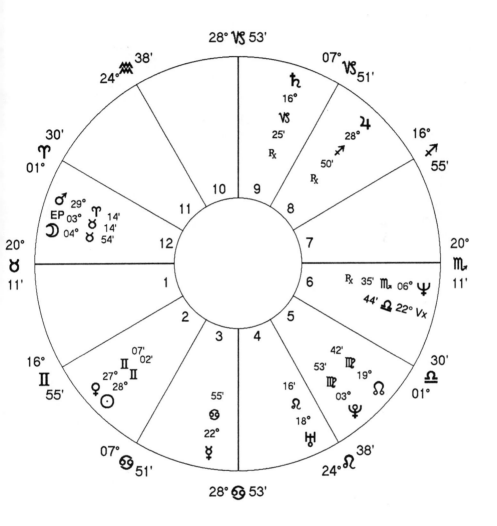

Chart 6
Marti
June 19, 1960, 3:05 A.M. DST
Oak Park, IL
41N53 87W47
Placidus Houses

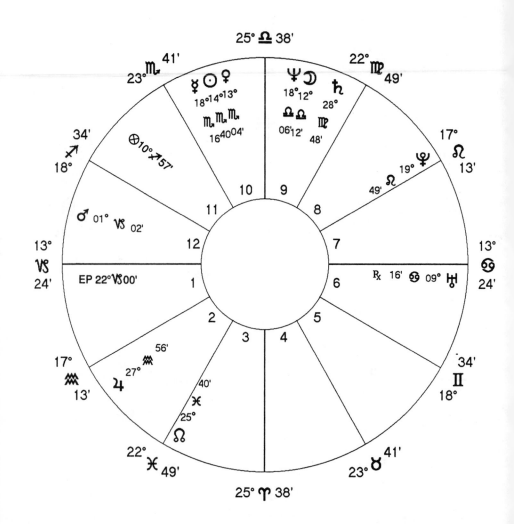

Chart 7
Marilyn
Nov. 7, 1950, 10:35 A.M. ST
Holguin, Cuba
20N53 76W15
Placidus Houses

own Anti-Vertex which can give feelings of deep confidence and the ability to be in control. Jupiter is a hot spot for Marilyn and an indicator of past life relationships carried over. She has a very positive feeling, the capability to access material abundance in the world, the ability to be her own unique person. Jupiter on her Anti-Vertex sextiles Marti's Jupiter within a degree and also trines Marti's Sun/Venus within a degree. This is a very powerful connection between the two charts.

Marti's Mars at 29 degrees Aries is in close trine to Marilyn's 1 degree Capricorn Mars. In past life regression work, Marti generally sees herself in male incarnations, and generally has identified with fulfilling or rounding out a period of more masculine material and with Mercury in the 3rd House square Mars her memories of her own childhood are that she was a spunky kid, pretty violent emotionally, endured upheavals and acted out a lot of things in the family structure. Mars is less in her control in the 12th House, behind the East Point in a different sign. Marilyn's Mars in close trine to Marti's helps amplify her Martian energy to the point that she is able to find a positive expression for it. They both have Mars in the 12th House and this could suggest trouble with, or confusion about men or idealism, or repressed desires, and so on. The important thing here is that the Mars principle is understood and augmented in a positive way for each of them through the relationship.

Marti's Mercury conjuncts Marilyn's West Point (the point opposite the East Point) and also trines Marilyn's North Node; this suggests a very positive series of past life connections. These are just a few basic factors about the past life karma is between these two people.

Marilyn has Saturn conjunct her own South Node, showing some fear of moving out of her set patterns of doing things. She tends to be habit-bound and Marti's Mercury trine/sextile axis from Cancer helps Marilyn have more faith in life and encourages her to reach toward her ideals.

Marilyn's Saturn trine Marti's Midheaven within a degree suggests that the two of them have some past-life obligations to each other in the area of career, the material world and practicality. This has been much of the tone of their relationship. Just because it has been obligatory does not mean that it lacks fun or lightness.

The two of them feel strongly that they chose each other and are glad to be together.

In conclusion, I would caution the reader to not put the cart before the horse. If you are examining two charts with past life indicators between them, don't assume that you have the necessary and sufficient conditions shown for indicating past life relationships. On the contrary, it is very easy to fool yourself in thinking that two people have a very powerful past life connection when they don't really have any relationship at all. However, when two people have a strong, powerful relationship, these past life indicators can be invaluable in deciphering the deep rooted history between the souls.

STAY IN TOUCH

On the following pages you will find listed, with their current prices, some of the books and tapes now available on related subjects. Your book dealer stocks most of these, and will stock new titles in the Llewellyn series as they become available. We urge your patronage.

However, to obtain our full catalog, to keep informed of new titles as they are released and to benefit from informative articles and helpful news, you are invited to write for our bi-monthly news magazine/catalog. A sample copy is free, and it will continue coming to you at no cost as long as you are an active mail customer. Or you may keep it coming for a full year with a donation of just $5.00 in U.S.A. and Canada ($20.00 overseas, first class mail). Many bookstores also have *The Llewellyn New Times* available to their customers. Ask for it.

Stay in touch! In *The Llewellyn New Times'* pages you will find news and reviews of new books, tapes and services, announcements of meetings and seminars, articles helpful to our readers, news of authors, advertising of products and services, special money-making opportunities, and much more.

The Llewellyn New Times
P.O. Box 64383-Dept. 388, St. Paul, MN 55164-0383, U.S.A.
• • •
TO ORDER BOOKS AND TAPES

If your book dealer does not have the books and tapes described on the following pages readily available, you may order them directly from the publisher by sending full price in U.S. funds, plus $1.50 for postage and handling for orders *under* $10.00; $3.00 for orders *over* $10.00. There are no postage and handling charges for orders over $50.00. UPS Delivery: We ship UPS whenever possible. Delivery guaranteed. Provide your street address as UPS does not deliver to P.O. Boxes. UPS to Canada requires a $50.00 minimum order. Allow 4-6 weeks for delivery. Orders outside the U.S.A. and Canada: Airmail—add retail price of book; add $5.00 for each non-book item (tapes, etc.); add $1.00 per item for surface mail.

FOR GROUP STUDY AND PURCHASE

Because there is a great deal of interest in group discussion and study of the subject matter of this book, we feel that we should encourage the adoption and use of this particular book by such groups by offering a special "quantity" price to group leaders or "agents."

Our Special Quantity Price for a minimum order of five copies of *The Web of Relationships* is $44.85 cash-with-order. This price includes postage and handling within the United States. Minnesota residents must add 6.5% sales tax. For additional quantities, please order in multiples of five. For Canadian and foreign orders, add postage and handling charges as above. Credit card (VISA, Master Card, American Express) orders are accepted. Charge card orders only may be phoned free ($15.00 minimum order) within the U.S.A. or Canada by dialing 1-800-THE-MOON. Customer service calls dial 1-612-291-1970. Mail Orders to:

LLEWELLYN PUBLICATIONS
P.O. Box 64383-Dept. 388 / St. Paul, MN 55164-0383, U.S.A.

Prices subject to change without notice.

SPIRITUAL, METAPHYSICAL & NEW TRENDS IN MODERN ASTROLOGY
edited by Joan McEvers

This is the first book in the Llewellyn New World Astrology Series. Edited by well-known astrologer, lecturer and writer Joan McEvers, this book pulls together the latest thoughts by the best astrologers in the field of Spiritual Astrology.

She has put together an outstanding group of informative and exciting topics.

- Gray Keen: Perspective: The Ethereal Conclusion
- Marion D. March: Some Insights into Esoteric Astrology
- Kimberly McSherry: The Feminine Element of Astrology: Reframing the Darkness
- Kathleen Burt: The Spiritual Rulers and Their Practical Role in the Transformation
- Shirley Lyons Meier: The Secrets behind Carl Payne Tobey's Secondary Chart
- Jeff Jawer: Astrodrama
- Donna Van Toen: Alice Bailey Revisited
- Philip Sedgwick: Galactic Studies
- Myrna Lofthus: The Spiritual Programming within a Natal Chart
- Angel Thompson: Transformational Astrology

0-87542-380-9, 288 pgs., 5.25 x 8, softcover **$9.95**

PLANETS: THE ASTROLOGICAL TOOLS
edited by Joan McEvers

This is the second in the astrological anthology series edited by respected astrologer Joan McEvers, who provides a brief factual overview of the planets.
Then take off through the solar system with 10 professional astrologers as they bring their insights to the symbolism and influences of the planets.

- Toni Glover Sedgwick: The Sun as the life force and our ego
- Joanne Wickenburg: The Moon as our emotional signal to change
- Erin Sullivan-Seale: Mercury as the multi-faceted god, followed with an in-depth explanation of its retrogradation
- Robert Glasscock: Venus as your inner value system and relationships
- Johanna Mitchell: Mars as your cooperative, energizing inner warrior
- Don Borkowski: Jupiter as expansion and preservation
- Gina Ceaglio: Saturn as a source of freedom through self-discipline
- Bil Tierney: Uranus as the original, growth-producing planet
- Karma Welch: Neptune as selfless giving and compassionate love
- Joan Negus: Pluto as a powerful personal force

0-87542-381-7, 380 pgs., 5.25 x 8, illus., softcover **$12.95**

Prices subject to change without notice.

FINANCIAL ASTROLOGY
edited by Joan McEvers
Favorably reviewed in the *Wall Street Journal* by financial expert Stanley W. Angrist! This third book in Llewellyn's anthology series edited by well-known astrologer Joan McEvers explores the relatively new field of financial astrology. Nine respected astrologers share their wisdom and good fortune with you.

Learn about the various types of analysis and how astrology fine-tunes these methods. Covered cycles include the Lunar Cycle, the Mars/Vesta Cycle, the 4 1/2-year Martian Cycle, the 500-year Civilization Cycle used by Nostradamus, the Kondratieff Wave and the Elliott Wave. Included topics are:

- Michael Munkasey: A Primer on Market Forecasting
- Pat Esclavon Hardy: Charting the U.S. and the NYSE
- Jeanne Long: New Concepts for Commodities Trading Combining Astrology & Technical Analysis
- Georgia Stathis: The Real Estate Process
- Mary B. Downing: An Investor's Guide to Financial Astrology
- Judy Johns: The Gann Technique
- Carol S. Mull: Predicting the Dow
- Bill Meridian: The Effect of Planetary Stations on U.S. Stock Prices
- Georgia Stathis: Delineating the Corporation
- Robert Cole: The Predictable Economy

0-87542-382-5, 368 pgs., 5.25 x 8, illus., softcover   **$14.95**

THE HOUSES: POWER PLACES OF THE HOROSCOPE
edited by Joan McEvers
This volume combines the talents of 11 renowned astrologers in the fourth book of Llewellyn's anthology series. Besides compiling all this information into a unified whole, Joan McEvers also contributes her viewpoint and knowledge to the delineation of the 12th House.

Each house, an area of activity within the horoscope, is explained with clarity and depth by the following authors:

- Peter Damian: The 1st House and the Rising Sign and Planets
- Ken Negus: The 7th House of Partnership
- Noel Tyl: The 2nd House of Self-Worth and the 8th House of Values and Others
- Spencer Grendahl: The 3rd House of Exploration & Communication
- Dona Shaw: The 9th House of Truth and Abstract Thinking
- Gloria Star: The 4th House of the Subconscious Matrix
- Marwayne Leipzig: The 10th House of the Life's Imprint
- Lina Accurso: The 5th House of Love
- Sara Corbin Looms: The 11th House of Tomorrow
- Michael Munkasey: The 6th House of Attitude and Service
- Joan McEvers: The 12th House of Strength, Peace, Tranquillity

0-87542-383-3, 400 pgs., 5.25 x 8, charts, softcover   **$12.95**

Prices subject to change without notice.

THE ASTROLOGY OF THE MACROCOSM
edited by Joan McEvers

The fifth book in Llewellyn's New World Astrology Series, *The Astrology of the Macrocosm* contains charts and articles from some of the world's top astrologers, explaining various mundane, transpersonal, and worldly events through astrology. It will help you gain insights into the global arenas of politics, social organization, and cultural analysis. It is the perfect introduction to understanding the fate of nations, weather patterns, and other global movements.

Featured are noted astrologers Nick Campion, Carolyn W. Casey, Steve Cozzi, Jimm Erickson, Charles Harvey, Jim Lewis, Richard Nolle, Marc Penfield, Nancy Soller and Judy Johns. Topics include ingress charts, cycles, Astro*Carto*Graphy, cultural and mythological evolution, the chart of England, weather forecasting and more. Charts and diagrams expand and illustrate most of the articles.

0-87542-384-1, 480 pgs., 5.25 x 8, softcover   **$14.95**

ASTROLOGICAL COUNSELING: The Path to Self-Actualization
edited by Joan McEvers

A very prominent, yet rarely discussed astrological topic, is that of the role between the counselor and the counseled. *Astrological Counseling*, the sixth book in Llewellyn's New World Astrology series, explores the challenges for today's counselors, and gives guidance to those interested in seeking a counselor to help them with their own personal challenges. Editor Joan McEvers has enlisted the help of ten top astrologers to discuss this important subject.

Bill Herbst, Donna Cunningham, Gray Keen, Donald L. Weston, Susan Dearborn Jackson, Ginger Chalford, Maritha Pottenger, David Pond, Doris A. Hebel and Eileen Nauman are this volume's featured astrologers. Their articles cover such topics as co-dependency, psychotherapy, reading the body, healing wounded spirits, personal counseling, business counseling, medical counseling, and more.

There are more people consulting with astrologers than there are devoted astrological students. This book helps both groups understand the needs of the modern counseling client.

0-87542-385-X, 368 pgs., 5.25 x 8, softcover   **$16.95**

INTIMATE RELATIONSHIPS
edited by Joan McEvers
Explore the deeper meaning of intimate relationships with the knowledge and expertise of eight renowned astrologers. Dare to look into your own chart and confront your own vulnerabilities. Find the true meaning of love and its place in your life. Gain new insights into the astrology of marriage, dating, affairs and more!

In *Intimate Relationships*, the seventh book in Llewellyn's New World Astrology Series, eight astrologers discuss their views on romance and the horoscope. The roles of Venus and the Moon, as well as the asteroids Sappho, Eros and Amor, are explored in our attitudes and actions toward potential mates. The theory of affinities is also presented wherein we are attracted to someone with similar planetary energies.

Is it a love that will last a lifetime, or mere animal lust that will burn itself out in a few months? The authors of *Intimate Relationships* will help you discover your natal attractions as well as your fatal attractions.
0-87542-386-8, 298 pgs., 6 x 9, softcover $14.95

LOVE SIGNS
by Jeraldine Saunders, foreword by Sydney Omarr
Love Signs is an indispensable, fun-to-read guide that will give you all the basics for creating a better, more meaningful love life. With the aid of astrology, numerology, palmistry and other intimate and mystical knowledge, you will discover everything you need to know about your love prospects with a given individual. As you learn your unique purpose, you will be able to distinguish whether another person's desires are compatible with yours.

Noted author Jeraldine Saunders shows you how to look for love, how to find it, and how to be sure of it. Examine the characteristics of all twelve zodiacal signs. Find out how auric vibrations can affect your seductive charisma. Discover the secrets behind your lover's facial features. Use numbers to learn about that hidden intimate nature. With *Love Signs*, a more meaningful love life is possible for you!
0-87542-706-5, 320 pgs., 6 x 9, softcover $9.95

THE LLEWELLYN ANNUALS

Llewellyn's MOON SIGN BOOK: Approximately 400 pages of valuable information on gardening, fishing, weather, stock market forecasts, personal horoscopes, good planting dates, and general instructions for finding the best date to do just about anything! Article by prominent forecasters and writers in the fields of gardening, astrology, politics, economics and cycles. This special almanac, different from any other, has been published annually since 1906. It's fun, informative and has been a great help to millions in their daily planning. **State year $4.95**

Llewellyn's SUN SIGN BOOK: Your personal horoscope for the entire year! All 12 signs are included in one handy book. Also included are forecasts, special feature articles, and an action guide for each sign. Monthly horoscopes are written by Gloria Star, author of *Optimum Child*, for your personal Sun Sign and there are articles on a variety of subjects written by well-known astrologers from around the country. Much more than just a horoscope guide! Entertaining and fun the year around. **State year $4.95**

Llewellyn's DAILY PLANETARY GUIDE: THE ASTROLOGER'S DATEBOOK: Includes all of the major daily aspects plus their exact times in Eastern and Pacific time zones, lunar phases, signs and voids plus their times, planetary motion, a monthly ephemeris, sunrise and sunset tables, special articles on the planets, signs, aspects, a business guide, planetary hours, rulerships, professional astrologer's directory, and much more. Large 5.25 x 8 format for more writing space, spiral bound to lay flat, address and phone listings, time zone conversion chart and blank horoscope chart. **State year $6.95**

Llewellyn's ASTROLOGICAL CALENDAR: Large wall calendar of 48 pages. Beautiful full color cover and full color inside. Includes special feature articles by famous astrologers, and complete introductory information on astrology. It also contains a Lunar Gardening Guide, celestial phenomena, a blank horoscope chart, and monthly date pages which include aspects, Moon phases, signs and voids, planetary motion, an ephemeris, personal forecasts, lucky dates, planting and fishing dates, and more. 10 x 13 size. Set in Central time, with fold-down conversion table for other time zones worldwide. **State year $9.95**

Llewellyn's Astrological Services

There are many types of charts and many different ways to use astrological information. Llewellyn offers a wide variety of services which can help you with specific needs. Read through the descriptions that follow to help you choose the right service. All of our readings are done by professional astrologers. The computer services are set up on Matrix programs and the interpretations are tailored to your needs. Remember, astrology points out potentials and possibilities; it will serve as your resource guide. Only you can decide what is right. Astrology should help you guide your life, not control it.

If you have never had a chart reading done before, we suggest that you order the Complete Natal or the Detailed Natal Service. We encourage informative letters with your request so that our astrologers can address your needs more specifically. All information is held strictly confidential. Be sure to give accurate and complete birth data: exact time, date, year, place, county and country of birth. Check your birth certificate. *Accuracy of birth data is important.* We will not be responsible for mistakes made by you! An order form follows the descriptions of Llewellyn Astrological Services.

Personalized Astrology Readings

These chart readings are done by professional astrologers and focus on your particular concerns. Include descriptive letter.

APS03-119 Simple Natal: Your chart calculated by computer in whatever house system stated. It has all of the trimmings, including aspects, midpoints, Chiron and a glossary of symbols, plus a free book! We use Tropical/Placidus unless you state otherwise. Include full birth data. . . . $5.00

APS03-101 Complete Natal: Our most thorough reading. It not only gives you the computer chart and detailed reading, but also interpretation of the trends shown in your chart for the coming year. It is activated by transits and focuses on any issue you specify. Include full birth data and a descriptive letter. $125.00

APS03-500 (3 months) APS03-501 (6 months) APS03-502 (1 year) Transit Forecasts: These reports keep you abreast of positive trends and challenging periods. Our reports can be an invaluable aid for timing your actions and decision making. Reports begin the first day of the month you specify. . . . . $15 (3 months), $30 (6 months), $50 (1 year).

APS03-105 Progressed Chart With Transits: Your birth chart is progressed by techniques to determine what it says about you now. Use this reading to understand the evolution of your personal power. Provides interpretation of present and future conditions for a year's time with a special focus as stated by you. Include descriptive letter. $85.00

Prices subject to change without notice.

APS03-102 Detailed Natal: Complete natal chart plus inter-pretation with the focus on one specific question as stated by you. Learn about aspects of your chart and what they mean to you. $65.00

APS03-110 Horary Chart: Gives the answer to any specific question. This is divination at its best, Should you marry? Will you get a new job soon? Give precise time of writing letter. $50.00

APS03-503 Personality Profile Horoscope: Our most popular reading! This ten-part reading gives you a complete look at how the planets affect you. It is an excellent way to become acquainted with astrology and to learn about yourself. Very reasonable price! $20.00

APS03-114 Compatibility Reading: Determines compatibility of two peo-ple in an existing relationship. Give birth data for both. $75.00

Personal Services Order Form

Remember to include all birth data plus your full name for all reports. *When you order the Simple Natal Chart, you'll receive a 25% discount on any one additional computer report, a 35% discount on any second report, and a 50% discount on any additional report.*

Service name and number_____

Full name (1st person)_____

Time_____ ☐ a.m. ☐ p.m. Date _____Year_____

Birthplace (city, county, state, country)_____

_____

Full name (2nd person)_____

Time_____ ☐ a.m. ☐ p.m. Date_____Year____

Birthplace (city, county, state, country)_____

_____

Astrological knowledge: ☐ Novice   ☐ Student   ☐ Advanced

Please include letter describing questions on separate sheet of paper.

Name_____

Address_____

City_____State_____Zip____

Make check or money order payable to Llewellyn Publications.To charge your order use ($15 min.) Visa, MC or Am. Exp. (circle one).

Account Number_____Exp. Date_____

Day Phone_____Signature_____

Mail this form and payment to:
Llewellyn's Personal Services, P.O. Box 55164–388, St. Paul, MN 55164–0383
Allow 4–6 weeks for delivery.

Prices subject to change without notice.